How to FIX IT

Morton J. Schultz

McGRAW-HILL BOOK COMPANY

NEW YORK • ST. LOUIS • SAN FRANCISCO
DUSSELDORF • JOHANNESBURG • KUALA LUMPUR • LONDON
MEXICO • MONTREAL • NEW DELHI • PANAMA
RIO DE JANEIRO • SINGAPORE • SYDNEY • TORONTO

How to FIX IT

Library of Congress Catalog Card Number 72-172666

International Standard Book Number 07-055653-9

*This book was designed by Edward Fox. The editing supervisors
were John Aliano and Judy Duguid. Gerard G. Mayer was
in charge of production.*

SELECTING AN ADHESIVE

ask	Adhesive (in order of preference)
eneral gluing of hardwood and softwood	Plastic resin Casein Polyvinyl
uing particle and chip boards to wood	Plastic resin Casein Contact cement Polyvinyl
uing plywood to decorative plastic laminate	Casein Contact cement Plastic resin
laminate heavy framing members	Casein
r veneering, inlays, cabinet work	Plastic resin Polyvinyl
bond oily woods (teak, pitch pine, yew, osage)	Casein (treat wood with dilute caustic soda solution an hour before gluing)
r end-wood joints, mitered joints, scarf joints	Polyvinyl Casein (heavy mixture)
r doweling	Plastic resin Polyvinyl
uing hardboard to plywood, to wood, or to itself	Plastic resin Casein Polyvinyl Contact cement
uing porous materials (linoleum and canvas, for example) to wood	Plastic resin Casein Contact cement
uing plastic, metal, or foil to wood	Epoxy

USEFUL FORMULAS

rcular measure	Area $= \pi \times r^2$ Circumference $= 2 \times \pi \times r$ π (pi) $= 3.1416$
uare measure	Area $= C^2$ Diagonal $= 1.414 \times C$
ectangular (parallelogram) easure	Area $= a \times b$
iangular easure	Area $= 1/2\, y \times t$

WEIGHT & MEASURES

Avoirdupois weight

27 11/32 grains	= 1 dram (dr.)
16 grams	= 1 ounce (oz.)
16 ounces	= 1 pound (lb.)
2000 pounds	= 1 ton (tn.)

Linear measure

12 inches (in.)	= 1 foot (ft.)
3 feet	= 1 yard (yd.)
5-1/2 yards = 16-1/2 feet	= 1 rod (rd.), pole, or perch
40 rods	= 1 furlong (fur.)
5280 feet = 1760 yards = 8 furlongs	= 1 mile
3 miles	= 1 league

Linear measure — metric equivalents

1 inch (in.)	= 2.54 centimeters (cm)
1 foot (ft.)	= 0.3048 meters (m)
1 yard (yd.)	= 0.9144 meter
1 rod (rd.)	= 5.029 meters
1 furlong (fur.)	= 201.17 meters
1 mile (mi.) = 1.6093 kilometers (km.) =	1609.3 meters
1 league	= 4.83 kilometers

Square (area) measure

144 square inches (sq. in.)	= 1 square foot (sq. ft.)
9 square feet	= 1 square yard (sq. yd.)
30-1/4 square yards	= 1 square rod, square pole or square perch
43,560 square feet = 4840 square yards =	160 square rods = 1 acre

Cubic measure (volume)

1728 cubic inches (cu. in.)	= 1 cubic foot (cu. ft.)
27 cubic feet	= 1 cubic yard (cu. yd.)

Circular measure

60 seconds (″)	= 1 minute (′)
60 minutes	= 1 degree (∘)
90 degrees	= 1 quadrant
4 quadrants = 360 degrees	= 1 circle

Dry measure

2 pints (pt.)	= 1 quart (qt.)
8 quarts	= 1 peck (pk.)
4 pecks	= 1 bushel (bu.)

Liquid measure

1 cup	= 8 fluid ounces (fl. oz.)
16 fluid ounces = 2 cups	= 1 pint (pt.)
2 pints	= 1 quart (qt.)
4 quarts	= 1 gallon (gal.)

How to FIX IT

Introduction

This book is written in response to the many requests for help from readers of my magazine articles and my column in *Popular Mechanics*. These people asked for advice in coping with the myriad repair and maintenance problems that faced them at home, in their cars, and on their boats.

I wasn't able to recommend any of the books available on the subject with any degree of enthusiasm. For one reason or another, each of these volumes fell short of what I thought a repair book ought to be and do. Most were incomplete, omitting such things as elementary car care and repair of simple appliances. Others were difficult to use, were out of date, or did not cover the latest technical and scientific advances in repair equipment and materials, such as new adhesives and paints. Still others were too technical, treating some subjects more in a manner suitable for a graduate engineer or licensed plumber than for the nonprofessional home, car, or boat owner.

I finally decided that the only way to have a book available that would meet the needs of a man or woman who didn't possess special technical skills was to write one myself. This book, then, is a result of the hundreds of questions that home, car, and boat owners have asked me. It solves the problems that you encounter in everyday living. It gets down to the basic care and repair problems that have sent usable equipment to the scrap heap or have put it into the hands of some high-priced mechanic.

How to Fix It covers only essential care and maintenance jobs—those that can be done with ordinary tools found in the home. It does not get into highly esoteric subjects, nor does it get involved with such complex projects as overhauling an automobile engine or replacing the cooling system of the refrigerator.

The philosophy upon which this book is based is that you *can* repair and maintain the equipment you own, even if you are not "handy." *How to Fix It* shows you how by providing detailed repair instructions and by outlining service procedures that will prevent a breakdown of your car or boat, and in your home.

Next time something needs to be repaired or serviced, reach for this book instead of calling a service man. Turn to the appropriate section and go to work. You should have no trouble—and may even find it a heck of a lot of fun!

M. J. S.

Contents

Contents

How to FIX IT

ADHESIVES

Technically, glue and adhesive are not the same, although the two terms are used interchangeably. *Adhesive* describes a synthetic material which is made from plastic or resin. *Glue* describes an organic material that is derived from animal hide, bone, or hoof.

Pure organic glue is hardly ever used anymore, because modern adhesive (or "glue") is vastly superior. It will bond practically anything to anything.

However, adhesives differ in their functions. Some, for example, are designed for specific jobs, while others will do a multitude of things.

The discussion in this section will acquaint you with the several different types of adhesives which you have available to you. Before doing this, however, some points need to be stressed. First, you should always make certain that you are using the right adhesive for the job at hand. The information in this discussion will help you to determine whether you are doing this. But you should also read the manufacturer's recommendations for use that are printed on the package.

Furthermore, directions on the package will explain how to apply the adhesive. If you want to obtain the best possible results, these instructions should be observed.

The following are descriptions, in alphabetical order, of the most widely employed adhesives:

Animal glue is one of the few organic materials still being sold. It is a high strength liquid material that is excellent for general woodworking applications where the object will not be subject to moisture. Use animal glue on wood, leather, and cork. Workpieces should be put under clamping pressure until the glue sets, which takes about one hour. Animal glue tends to thicken as the temperature drops below 70°F.

Casein glue is a powdered wood glue for heavy duty work where strong joints are required. It has to be mixed with water before use. Casein glue can be applied at low temperatures and requires only moderate clamping pressure when put on workpieces. However, the material is not waterproof and may tend to stain some dark or acid woods. It is excellent for use on oily woods that won't take other kinds of glue, such as teak, yew, and lemonwood.

Clear household cement is a general purpose adhesive that dries clear in a short time. It is sold in small ready-to-use tubes and will bond porous and nonporous materials (Fig. 1).

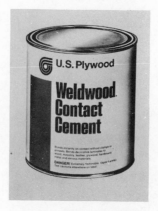

Figure 1. Clear household cement is a general all-purpose adhesive that has several uses.

Figure 2. Contact cement bonds without the need for clamping.

Figure 3. Most modern adhesives are available in small tubes.

Clear household cement should not be used on objects that will be put under stress. Most brands are moderately water resistant, but they all will weaken if the cemented joint is soaked for any length of time. Clamping is not required, but allow the cement to become slightly tacky before pressing the workpieces together. Hold them under hand pressure for a minute or two. Clear household cement should not be used for repairing large size objects.

Contact cement will bond on contact without clamping (Fig. 2). It is used primarily for bonding plastic laminates to counter tops, table tops, and other flat surfaces. However, contact cement will also do an excellent gluing job when applied to leather, linoleum, and thin gauge metal (Fig. 3).

The cement should be applied to both surfaces and allowed to dry for about 30 minutes before the parts are pressed together. Once the parts are brought into contact, they bond instantly and can't be shifted for alignment. However, one way to overcome this drawback is to use slip sheets of wax paper between the parts while aligning them. When parts are lined up, carefully slide the wax paper from between the parts while pressing the surfaces together.

Epoxy resin adhesive is the strongest of all adhesives available to the homeowner and can be used for gluing practically anything. However, it is expensive and impractical to use when other less costly adhesives will do.

Epoxy resin adhesive comes in two separate containers (usually tubes), the contents of which have to be mixed (Fig. 4).

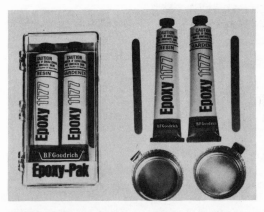

Figure 4. Epoxy adhesive consists of a resin and
a hardener that have to be mixed together.

Figure 5. Fabric
cement is used for
repairing tears in
fabrics.

Once mixed, the adhesive remains in a workable condition for a
brief time. Therefore, try to mix only as much as you need and
use the glue as quickly as possible.

Epoxy adhesive will harden under any condition, even underwater. Use it where an adhesive must withstand extreme
stress. The glue is completely waterproof and is not affected by
extremes of temperature.

Fabric mending adhesive will repair tears in cotton, canvas,
denim, most other fabrics, and leather (Fig. 5). It can be used
with or without a supporting patch to repair canvas awning,
luggage, sportswear, tents, and clothing. The adhesive will with-

Figure 6. Panel adhesive will secure paneling
to wood studs without the need for nailing.

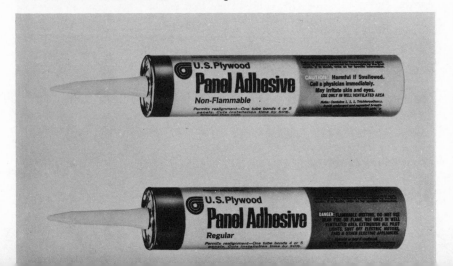

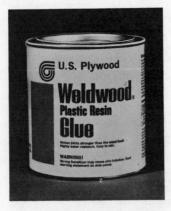

Figure 7. Use plastic mending adhesive to fix plastic items.

Figure 8. Plastic resin is an excellent glue for use in furniture repair and construction.

Figure 9. Polyvinyl white glue is another all-purpose product that adheres to many surfaces.

stand normal washing and ironing. However, some brands will not stand up under dry cleaning fluids.

Panel adhesive comes in cartridges that fit an ordinary caulking gun (Fig. 6). It should be used only to attach panels of gypsum wallboard, hardboard, or plywood to studding or to existing walls. One cartridge will bond a maximum of six 4 × 8 foot panels. Panel adhesive does not bond instantly, thus allowing you time to align a panel. Only a few hinge nails along the top of the panel are required.

Plastic mending adhesive is designed for repairing flexible and rigid plastic objects that are made of such materials as styrene, vinyl, acrylic, and phenolic resin (Fig. 7). It is a clear, flexible adhesive that can be used to mend such things as torn plastic raincoats, plastic toys, and above-ground swimming pools.

Plastic resin glue is a strong, highly water-resistant wood glue that should be used for high grade furniture and cabinet work (Fig. 8). It will not stain acid woods, such as oak and mahogany.

This glue must be used at temperatures of 70°F or above. For maximum strength, joints must be smooth and fitted accurately. Firm clamping pressure must be maintained for at least 10 hours to insure a good bond. Plastic resin glue is resistant to mold and rot and will leave little or no glue line to mar the finished appearance.

Polyvinyl white glue can be used for all types of interior woodworking jobs where waterproof joints are not required. It is

Common Repair Jobs and Their Adhesives

Key:
1 – polyvinyl white glue
2 – animal glue
3 – casein glue
4 – plastic resin glue
5 – resorcinol glue
6 – contact cement
7 – epoxy resin adhesive
8 – clear household cement
9 – plastic mending adhesive
10 – fabric mending adhesive
11 – panel adhesive

Repair Task	1	2	3	4	5	6	7	8	9	10	11
General woodworking, light duty, interior	×	×									
Heavy duty woodworking			×	×	×		×				
Waterproof wood joints				×	×		×				
Laminating plastics to wood or metal		×				×					
Gluing metal to wood						×	×	×			
Repairing and bonding metals							×				
Ceramic and masonry repair							×				
Bonding glass to glass or metal							×				
Bonding plastic to metal, wood, plastic						×	×	×			
Repairing flexible plastic								×	×		
Mending leather, cloth, canvas								×		×	
Leather to wood or metal						×			×		
Rubber to metal, wood, glass						×					
Installing hardboard, plywood, gypsum board panels						×					×
Cloth to wood, plaster, cardboard	×	×				×		×			
Cardboard or paper to itself or to wood	×							×			
Porcelain and china, light duty						×		×	×		
Porcelain and china, heavy duty							×				

also an excellent adhesive for gluing together paper, fabric, cardboard, cork, and leather. Polyvinyl white glue is nonstaining.

Clamping with moderate pressure is required and workpieces should be kept at room temperature. The glue sets in about 30 minutes, with full strength being achieved in about 24 hours. Wood joints formed with polyvinyl white glue will withstand moderate stress.

Resorcinol glue is completely waterproof. It is a two-component adhesive that must be mixed for use. Resorcinol glue will form very strong joints and should be used for outdoor jobs where a high degree of waterproofing is needed, such as in repair of lawn furniture. However, the glue must be applied at temperatures of 70°F or above, and firm clamping is needed for at least 24 hours.

The chart on the previous page outlines some common repair jobs that you encounter around the home and recommends which adhesive to use. In most cases, several types will be adequate. However, consider such factors as the conditions under which the task must be performed and cost of the adhesive before deciding on the exact one to use.

AIR CONDITIONER

When a room air conditioner fails to function or doesn't cool as it should, the trouble will usually lie with the unit's electrical circuit or with the refrigerant system which consists of the compressor, evaporator, condenser, and associated tubing. In any event, if the problem cannot be corrected by using one of the methods described here, it is suggested that you *not* poke inside. Call a professional air conditioner repairman.

Figure 1. A dirt-clogged filter is a major reason why air conditioners don't cool properly.

Figure 2. Vacuum dust from the unit, but do not apply pressure to fragile metal parts.

Suppose the unit starts, but fails to provide ample cooling. How long has it been since you have cleaned or replaced the filter?

The filter traps dust, dirt, and pollen contained in incoming air. A clogged filter will reduce an air conditioner's cooling ability and can cause ice to form on the cooling coils (Fig. 1).

Filters of later model room air conditioners are made of a synthetic material that can be reused after it is cleaned. In some cases, cleaning is done by washing the filter in cool water. In other instances, cleaning is accomplished by brushing the material with a soft-bristle dust brush.

Filters of older units are generally of a fibrous material. These have to be replaced when dirt-clogged.

Incidentally, before doing any work on a room air conditioner, disengage the line cord from the electrical outlet as a safety precaution.

Another reason that a room air conditioner may fail to cool an area is an accumulation of dirt and dust on the louvers and condenser. Remove the cover from the unit and sweep louvers out with a dust brush. Now, gently run the nozzle of a vacuum cleaner over exposed parts (Fig. 2).

Insufficient cooling may not be the fault of the air conditioner but of unsealed areas in a room that allow warm air to enter. Be sure that all windows, for example, are properly caulked.

Open areas that are frequently overlooked are those around the air conditioner itself. These cracks can be caulked from either the inside or the outside. Be sure that a sufficiently wide bead of caulk is applied so that the crack is thoroughly sealed (Fig. 3).

Several things may fail to happen when you turn on an air

Figure 3. Cracks around room cooling units allow hot air to leak in. Seal them with caulk.

Figure 4. Prongs that are misaligned will cause an interruption in electrical service.

conditioner. For example, the compressor and fan motor may fail to start, the fan may run but the compressor may not, or the compressor may start but shut down soon after.

If you turn on the unit and it makes noise, press in on the unit's cover with your hand. The cover may be loose and vibrating. If it is, pressure will stop the noise. Tighten the cover.

If noise does not cease, shut the unit down at once. Prolonged operation may lead to more serious and costly damage. A serviceman should be called.

Before seeking service assistance for other problems, however, there are a few procedures to apply yourself. If the unit fails to start when you turn it on, inspect the fuse or circuit breaker to make sure it is operative.

If the fuse hasn't blown or the circuit breaker hasn't tripped, examine the plug on the end of the unit's line cord. Prongs that are too close together or too far apart will cause an interruption in electricity which is being fed to the unit. Align the prongs and test the unit (Fig. 4).

If the air conditioner's fan operates, but the compressor fails to start (there will be no cooling), be sure that the unit's thermostat isn't set below the setting at which the compressor will automatically switch on.

APPLIANCE SURFACE

A scratched appliance surface (Fig. 1) can be restored to like-new condition by using lacquer coatings that you buy from an appliance dealer or from an automotive supply dealer. You will need primer, finish coat, and blender. All three are available in aerosol spray cans.

It would be ideal if you could obtain the code number of the color now on the appliance from the dealer from whom the appliance was purchased. This will allow you to order the exact

Figure 1. A scratched surface worse than this can be restored if correct lacquers are used.

Figure 2. Sand the damaged area with a piece of wet No. 360 sandpaper until metal is exposed.

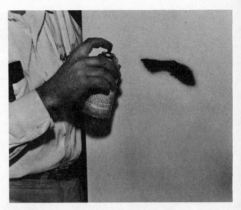

Figure 3. After old paint has been re-moved and the area wiped clean, spray on the primer.

Figure 4. Professional results will be obtained if you apply spray paint prod-ucts with care.

paint. Otherwise, you will have to match color as best you can by eye.

Follow the steps below to restore a marred appliance sur-face:

• *Wash* the entire surface with a hot water and detergent solution to remove dirt and wax. Rinse with clear water.

• *Sand* the marred area. Fit a sanding block with a piece of No. 360 sandpaper. Dip the sandpaper into water and sand, but use a circular arm motion (Fig. 2). Dip the sandpaper into water frequently to avoid putting additional scratches into the sur-face. Stop sanding when old paint has been removed and the bare metal surface is smooth. Wipe the area clean and dry with a cloth (Fig. 3).

• *Mask* surrounding surfaces before painting to keep paint overspray from hitting them. Cover chrome strips with mask-ing tape. You can use newspaper or cardboard to mask broader areas.

• *Apply primer*, but carefully (Fig. 4). Use short bursts and move the aerosol can back and forth with a smooth and fairly rapid motion. Keep the spray nozzle 8 to 10 inches from the sur-face and never start the spray directly on the bare surface. Aim it instead at a piece of scrap cardboard which you should tape alongside the damaged area and bring the spray across the damaged surface with a smooth motion. Apply primer until the area is covered, but do not go to excess. Application of too much primer will cause the paint to sag.

(If the appliance is light in color, apply a white primer. Use a gray primer if the appliance is dark.)

Figure 5. This picture shows the restored surface. Compare it with that seen in Fig. 1.

• *Sand* the area lightly after allowing the primer to dry for at least 10 minutes. Use No. 360 sandpaper, which should be dipped into water before and during this sanding step.

• *Apply the finish coat.* Make *one* pass only with the spray — that is, one sweep across the surface and one sweep back. When the paint is dry to the touch, make one more pass. Let that dry. You may have to make 4 or 5 passes before the job is done, that is, when the new color appears to match the surrounding color and the finish coat dries to a gloss.

• *The blending coat* is needed to get a more precise match of color. Spray the blender over the area with a straight-across motion, extending the coverage out about 4 inches to each side of the area. Let this coating dry for about 30 minutes.

• *Compound* the surface with rubbing compound to remove lint. Use a gentle, circular rubbing motion (Fig. 5). Finally, wipe the compound off with a clean cloth.

ATTIC FAN

An attic fan is driven by a belt which extends between a pulley on an electric motor and a pulley on the fan. Attic fans can fail in two ways: (1) they can fail to operate when switched on; (2) they can fail to provide adequate cooling. The conditions that cause these problems are bad shaft bearings, a bad fan belt, and shutters that bind (Fig. 1).

If an attic fan fails to operate when it is turned on, first make sure that the fuse hasn't blown or the circuit breaker hasn't tripped. If fuses insist on failing or the circuit breaker trips after it has been reset, there is a malfunction in the electrical circuit. Do not attempt to operate the fan. Call an electrician.

An attic fan may fail to operate if shaft bearings have fro-

Figure 1. Attic fans fail because of (a) bad bearings; (b) bad belt; (c) stuck shutter.

Figure 2. Turn the blade by hand to check for bad bearings. It should spin freely.

zen. To check for bad bearings, be sure that the fan's switch is off and rotate the blade by hand (Fig. 2). The blade should revolve freely, without binding and without making noise. If blades bind or there is noise, bearings have failed. The unit should be overhauled by a professional repairman.

Caution: Although a fan may continue to operate with damaged bearings, do not allow it to do so. The motor can overheat and burn out, which will lead to a more costly repair, or the motor will create enough heat to start a fire.

If an attic fan doesn't provide sufficient cooling, the fan belt may be damaged or may be too loose. Inspect the backside of the belt for glazed, cracked, and frayed areas. A damaged fan belt should be replaced with one of the same size. Replacement belts can be purchased at an appliance store or at a hardware store.

In most cases, replacing the fan belt is done by loosening the bolts which hold the electric motor. This reduces the tension on the belt and allows it to be removed from the pulleys. The new belt is placed on the pulleys and the motor is retightened.

To determine if the fan belt is too loose, press in on it at a point which is midway between the pulleys (Fig. 3). The belt should "give" about ½ inch. If belt "play" is more than this, tighten the belt by loosening the bolts holding the motor and force the motor against the belt. Now, retighten the bolts.

Insufficient cooling may also be caused by failure of shutters to open when the fan is turned on. Pivot points may have rusted.

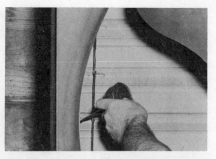

Figure 3. A properly adjusted fan belt has about ¹/₂ inch of free play. Look for damage.

Figure 4. Cure binding shutters by lubricating each pivot point with a drop of SAE 20 oil.

To repair this, free the shutters by working them by hand. Now, lubricate each pivot point with a drop of SAE 20 motor oil (Fig. 4). After oil has been applied, wiggle the shutters a few times to allow oil to penetrate.

AUTOMOTIVE, BATTERY

A weak battery that will keep a car from starting is one that can frequently be restored to usable service. Furthermore, periodic maintenance as described here will extend expected battery life by as much as 100 percent.

Figure 1. A booster battery is one of the best ways of getting a lifeless engine going again.

Figure 2. A battery hydrometer is a valuable tool to have in your automotive tool inventory.

(The procedures described here apply as well to other equipment, such as boats, which use lead acid storage batteries.)

If a car fails to start because of a dead battery, you can employ a booster battery and a set of jumper cables to get the engine to start (Fig. 1). Be sure that the car's ignition switch is turned off. Connect the positive post of the booster to the positive post of the car's battery and the negative post to the negative post. Be sure connections are correct before making them. With the booster connected, start the car in the normal manner. Disconnect the booster when the engine starts.

Once a battery fails for the first time, you should determine its state of charge to establish whether it still possesses useful life. This is done with a battery hydrometer, which can be purchased at an automotive supply store for about $3. The hydrometer is used to determine specific gravity, which is a measure of a battery's state of charge.

To check specific gravity, draw electrolyte from the first cell into the hydrometer and record the reading (Fig. 2). It is not necessary to fill the hydrometer tube. Just be sure that enough electrolyte is drawn in so that the bulb in the hydrometer is riding free.

After taking the reading, return electrolyte to the cell from which it came. Proceed to the next cell until readings from all cells have been taken.

Compensation must be made for the temperature of the electrolyte. Most hydrometers have built-in thermometers that allow direct conversion of the specific gravity reading (Fig. 3). If yours doesn't, insert an ordinary thermometer into one of the battery's cells and take a temperature reading.

Figure 3. When reading a hydrometer, hold it at eye level. Pinch the tube to avoid fluid loss.

Figure 4. Frequent charging of your car's battery will assure that it will be forever ready.

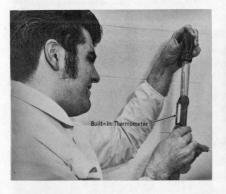

For each 10 degrees above 80°F that the thermometer shows, add 0.004 specific gravity points to the reading. For each 10 degrees below 80°F, subtract 0.004 points. For example, if the reading is 1.250 and the electrolyte temperature is 20°F, subtract 0.024 points from the reading to give a correct specific gravity of 1.226.

Incidentally, when reading a hydrometer, hold the rubber nozzle closed so that electrolyte doesn't drip. Take readings with the tool held at eye level as seen in Fig. 3.

Compare the specific gravity reading of each cell with that of the other cells. If it is 0.050 points (or more) less than the others, the cell is dead. Discard the battery.

Now, add all of the readings and average them. The following will explain what your result means:

Average Specific Gravity	Battery Condition
1.260 to 1.280	Fully charged
1.230 to 1.250	75% charged
1.200 to 1.220	50% charged
1.170 to 1.190	25% charged
1.140 to 1.160	In trouble
1.110 to 1.130	Discharged

If a battery shows a charge of 50 percent or less, recharge it with a trickle battery charger, which you can buy in an automotive supply store for as little as $10 (Fig. 4). If you prefer, have a service station charge the battery for you. Twelve to twenty-four hours are needed for a rundown battery to obtain full charge. The exact time depends upon its state of charge to begin with.

If your battery charger does not possess an automatic shut-off that reduces output when the battery approaches full charge, check specific gravity frequently while the battery is charging. A battery will be damaged if overcharged. Remove the charger when specific gravity shows the battery to be at or near full charge.

Remove battery caps before charging the battery so that pressure inside the battery will readily dissipate. Make certain that no open flame or spark is brought near the battery, which will be giving off an explosive mixture of hydrogen and oxygen as it is charging.

It is particularly important to keep a battery as fully charged as possible during cold weather. An undercharged bat-

Figure 5. Wash all sides of the battery, including the bottom, with the baking soda solution.

Figure 6. Placing tape over vent caps will prevent baking soda from neutralizing battery acid.

tery will freeze and keep a car's engine from starting. It will also be severely damaged.

A battery that is 50 percent charged, for example, will freeze at −12°F. One that is 25 percent charged will freeze at 3°F. Conversely, a fully charged battery will not freeze until the temperature is at −70°F.

A battery's specific gravity provides an indication of the way in which the car's generating system is functioning. If the battery does not maintain specific gravity after recharging, there is probably a malfunction in the generating system, which should be isolated and repaired before a serious breakdown occurs.

Batteries should be cleaned once a year to remove electrolytic salts and dirt that form on the case and cause self-discharge. Salts and dirt establish a conductive path over which energy escapes. Using a brush, wash the battery case thoroughly with a mixture of one tablespoon of baking soda to one quart of water to neutralize acid salts (Fig. 5).

Before doing this, however, be sure that the battery caps are tight and apply a small piece of tape to the top of each cap (Fig. 6). Caps have small holes in them that allow venting of internal gas. Baking soda that accidentally seeps into a cell through a cap will neutralize acid in that cell and ruin the battery.

When the baking soda solution stops foaming, rinse the battery thoroughly with water (Fig. 7). Apply another application of baking soda and rinse again. Keep doing this until an application of baking soda fails to foam, which means that acid salts have been completely neutralized.

Figure 7. Allow water to pour over the battery so all traces of baking soda are washed off.

Figure 8. Be very careful not to enlarge the vent holes as you clean dirt from the caps.

After the battery case dries, put the battery into the car and use a piece of thin wire to clear dirt from cap vent holes (Fig. 8). Unimpeded venting is necessary to prevent internal damage.

Clean posts and cable terminals with a small wire brush or a piece of sandpaper to assure uninterrupted current (Fig. 9). Connect terminals *tightly* to posts and apply a thin coating of petroleum jelly (Vaseline) to retard corrosion (Fig. 10).

Be sure that battery acid is up to level. If it isn't, add water.

Check acid level frequently. If you must add water often, the generating system is probably overcharging. Have it checked before serious damage occurs.

Figure 9. Clean battery posts are needed to have an uninterrupted flow of battery voltage.

Figure 10. Only a small amount of petroleum jelly is needed to prevent a buildup of corrosion.

AUTOMOTIVE, BODY CLEANING

Although cleaning the exterior of a car seems like a simple cut-and-dried task, there are several factors to be aware of so that the finish of the car is protected. They are as follows:

• Never wipe dust and dirt off the body with a cloth. Particles will scratch the finish. Be sure that the body is wet and use a chamois, which is a very soft material made of animal skin that is specifically manufactured for this purpose. You can buy a chamois at a hardware store or at an automotive parts supply store.

• The body of a car should be washed often to remove gasoline, tree sap, road tar, excretions from insects and birds, and smoke residue from factory chimneys. Frequent washing is of particular importance in areas where salt comes into contact with the finish, such as in shore areas. Thus, washing is even more vital during the winter than in the summer because of road salt that is thrown on snow-covered highways.

• Always use cold water to wash a car, and never wash it in the direct rays of the hot sun or if the finish is hot. Use a mild detergent or a commercially packaged car wash as the washing agent (Fig. 1). These have proved most suitable for modern car finishes.

• If stains such as road tar and tree sap prove stubborn, get rid of them with a commercially produced remover (Fig. 2). Use as directed on the package. Tar removers are available in gasoline stations and in automotive parts supply stores.

Figure 1. Wash your car with a good quality car wash solution. Follow instructions on the can.

Figure 2. Road tar and hard-to-remove material can be treated with a commercial preparation.

Figure 3. Restore luster to the car's finish with a high quality automobile polish-cleaner.

Figure 4. Bring the finish to a high gloss with a power drill. Keep the bonnet pad fully flat.

• Use a soft brush or sponge to clean wheels and hub caps, but do not use this brush or sponge on the car's finish. The dirt it picks up will scratch the finish.

• A commercially produced automotive polish that is made by a well-known manufacturer is suitable for use on your car's finish (Fig. 3). Keep in mind that polishes and cleaners that do the fastest and easiest job are not necessarily the best ones to use. A polish that contains a large quantity of abrasive will do the job quickly, but it will also scratch paint and could etch or damage bright metal parts.

• Speaking of bright metal, before polishing it wash with lukewarm water and mild soap. Rinse off thoroughly. It is a good idea to avoid the use of metal polishes, because many contain abrasives that are harmful. Use the same mild polish that you use on the body. If road tar and other hard-to-remove spots remain, use a chemical cleaner which specifically states on the package that it is safe for use on acrylic finishes.

• Apply the polish by hand. However, you can use an electric drill that is fitted with a wool polishing bonnet to remove the polish and bring the finish to a high gloss (Fig. 4). Do not press down hard on the drill and keep the full bonnet flat against the finish.

• Convertible tops should be washed frequently with a neutral, noncaustic soap suds solution, lukewarm water, and a soft-bristle brush. Rinse the top with a great quantity of water to assure full removal of soap. After washing a convertible top, be sure that it is thoroughly dry before it is lowered. Lowering the top while it is still wet or damp can cause mildew and wrinkling.

AUTOMOTIVE, BODY NOISE

Many car owners put up with squeaks, groans, and rattles because they don't know how to locate the cause of noise. This section outlines methods that are employed by professional body repairmen that you can use to find the cause of body noise.

Start by driving the car. It is unlikely that you will be able to pinpoint the source of a noise with this road test, because noise travels. However, this is not the purpose of a road test.

The test is important, because it will allow you to distinguish the type of noise which is being created—a rattle, squeak, wind noise, or what have you. Different kinds of noise have different causes. Thus, by knowing the noise, you can check the most likely reasons for it.

For example, the rushing sound that wind makes is distinctive and very different, let's say, from a rattle. If you can describe the noise as wind, you can proceed to check conditions which are known to produce the noise, such as loose molding strips and worn window weather stripping.

A road test also allows you to distinguish between a body noise and a chassis noise. The chassis is that part of the car that supports the body and consists of such areas as the frame, wheels, and other machinery. In other words, those parts of a car that aren't considered the body should be considered the chassis.

It is important for you to keep in mind that noise which occurs as the engine idles and the car sits still is normally caused by the chassis. For instance, a squeak or rattle that you hear when the engine is idling can often be traced to a loose mounting bracket or pulley, a loose or worn motor mount, or a slipping drive belt.

Furthermore, a noise which occurs only at a steady speed range is usually the result of a chassis problem. Unbalanced wheels, for example, will cause the car to vibrate at about 45 miles per hour. This will create rattles at 45 miles per hour.

This section will not concentrate on chassis noise since there are so many variables. It usually takes an experienced professional with his equipment to track down the source of chassis noise (Fig. 1).

Fortunately, most noises that emanate from a car are produced by the body. These are easier to track down than chassis noises. One of the most common (and most elusive) noises of all is a rattle. The best way to find its source is to use a rubber mallet. Start at one end of the car and methodically tap each area

Figure 1. The source of chassis noise is often difficult to find without special equipment.

Figure 2. A rubber mallet that is employed properly makes the most effective noise locator.

Figure 3. Door realignment is done by loosening hinge bolts and moving the door in or out.

Figure 4. Proper adjustment of this striker requires removal of the striker from the pillar.

Figure 5. After the striker has been unscrewed, a striker shim is installed beneath the part.

gently with the hammer (Fig. 2). Rattles can be caused by nuts and bolts that were left in doors during manufacture, misaligned doors, worn window regulators, and loose windows.

If a door rattles when you strike it near the bottom, the noise is no doubt caused by a loose object lying in the door well. The trim panel will have to be removed to extract the object.

While working at the door, grab hold of the handle and shake. If the door rattles or seems loose, it is probably misaligned. To confirm this suspicion, check the width of the gap that is formed between the door and fender and also between the door and pillar. Compare these with the gap widths of the opposite door. If they aren't nearly the same, the door should be realigned by loosening hinge bolts, repositioning the door in or out as necessary, and retightening bolts (Fig. 3).

Check the door striker-plate-to-lock distance to determine if the striker needs to be adjusted. A misadjusted striker will cause the door to rattle.

Clean off the striker and lock and apply a little grease to the striker. Open and close the door a couple of times. This will create a pattern in the grease. If the impression of the lock's jaws in the grease is more than $5/32$ inch away from the striker plate, adjustment is necessary.

Some strikers have to be unscrewed so that shims can be placed beneath them (Figs. 4 and 5). Adjustment of other strikers is made by screwing the striker out or in.

Now, strike the trim panel side of the door with your rubber mallet. If you hear a rattle, window regulator parts are worn and the regulator is loose. The trim panel has to be removed to make repairs.

If a window rattles or vibrates as you tap it gently, weather stripping has worked loose or is worn. In any case, pull the weather stripping away from the window channel and wash the channel and the back side of the weather stripping with kerosene. Apply a liberal coating of rubber cement to both surfaces. When the cement becomes tacky, press the weather stripping firmly into the channel.

If the trunk lid or hood rattles when struck with the mallet, bolts have worked loose. Tighten every one you find.

If you haven't found the cause of a rattle to this point, get beneath the vehicle and tighten all body bolts (Fig. 6).

While you are beneath the car, check other things that can cause noise if they are loose, such as the tailpipe and parking brake cable (Fig. 7).

Wind noise is a big problem for car owners because of the great amount of molding strips used on vehicles. If a piece of

Figure 6. Obviously, loose body bolts will lead to noises. Make sure that all bolts are tight.

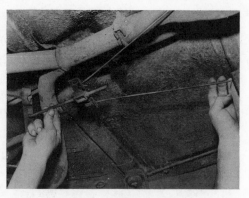

Figure 7. A loose parking brake cable and other loose parts beneath the car will cause noise.

molding is not tight, wind rushes between the body and the strip, creating a "whoosh" sound.

To track down the loose molding, place tape over one strip at a time and road test the car (Fig. 8). When you no longer hear the noise, you have found the noisemaker. Remove the strip and fill its back with automotive caulking compound that you can buy in an automotive parts supply store. Reattach the molding.

If wind noise isn't being caused by loose molding, check each window and door by using the same trick. Tape the cracks around one window or door at a time and road test the car (Fig. 9). When noise ceases, replace or reseal the weather stripping of

Figure 8. Irritating noise is produced when wind rushes beneath a loose strip of molding.

Figure 9. Wind noise from windows is checked for by taping cracks and then road testing.

Figure 10. If weather stripping needs resealing, wash with kerosene and use strong adhesive.

the offending door or window. The procedure for doing this is the same as described above for window channels (Fig. 10).

The radio antenna can also produce wind noise as it slices through the air. To check it out, lower the antenna and determine by road test if the noise is eliminated or reduced.

A groaning or squeaky noise when a car with a unitized body hits a bump can mean that a weld has snapped. A unitized body is welded directly to the frame. There are no body bolts. If a weld has snapped, it should be rewelded.

AUTOMOTIVE, Engine Cleaning

Thorough cleaning of a car requires that the engine as well as the body and upholstery be purged of dirt (see Automotive, Body Cleaning, and Automotive, Upholstery). Engine cleanliness, however, is necessary for reasons other than esthetic ones. Dirt can cause mechanical problems, including overheating, hard starting, poor acceleration, and stalling.

Dirt on battery posts and terminals, for example, can impede electric current and keep the engine from starting. Furthermore, dirt on accelerator and choke linkage causes performance difficulties.

Purging an engine of dirt no longer requires the expenditure of money for steam cleaning. There are several good prod-

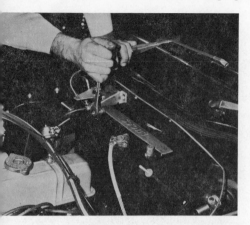

Figure 1. By disconnecting battery cables, you make sure that there will be no short circuit.

Figure 2. A clean battery will provide longer service than one that has accumulations of dirt.

ucts on the market, particularly engine degreaser and cleaner, that do an excellent job.

To begin with, disconnect battery cables and keep them disconnected until cleaning has been completed (Fig. 1). This is a precautionary measure to guard against an accidental short circuit which could damage electrical components and create a spark that will ignite the highly flammable engine cleaner.

With battery cables disconnected, clean dirt and electrolytic salts from cable terminals and from the battery as discussed in the section entitled Automotive, Battery (Fig. 2).

Now, on four-, six-, or eight-clip type clothespins write numbers from 1 to 4, 1 to 6, or 1 to 8, depending upon the number of cylinders in the engine. One clothespin should have the word "coil" written on it.

Remove each spark-plug-to-distributor-cap cable and also the coil-to-distributor-cap cable. Clip the respective clothespin to the cable so that you will be able to match the cable to its spark plug later on (Fig. 3). Clip the clothespin with the word "coil" on it to that cable. Cables must be reinstalled correctly.

To match the cable to its correct place in the distributor cap, cover each hole with a small piece of masking tape on which has been written the number that corresponds to the number on the clothespin (Fig. 4).

As you remove each cable, wipe it clean with a cloth. Now, cover the distributor cap and coil with polyethylene sandwich bags to protect them from water during the degreasing operation (Fig. 5).

*Figure 3. To identify ca-
bles, clip on numbered
clothespins.*

*Figure 4. You should also
identify the cable-dis-
tributor position for easy
installation.*

*Figure 5. Plastic sand-
wich bags provide pro-
tection for coil and
distributor during the
washing.*

The next step in cleaning an engine is to unclip the under-hood insulation pad, if there is one. If it isn't too dirty, wash it with detergent and water. However, if it is filthy, buy a new one or leave it off the car altogether. Degrease the underside of the hood before installing the pad.

Next, remove the carburetor air cleaner. Lay the filter element aside (replace it with a new one if it is dirty) and hose down metal parts. If parts are greasy, give them an application of engine degreaser, but do not get any on the filter element.

Now, with a small scrub brush or an old toothbrush and kerosene or gasoline, clean dirt from the carburetor and all linkage. Be thorough. The carburetor must be cleaned separately from the rest of the engine because, as with the distributor, it will be covered when the engine is being cleaned to keep water from entering it.

To clean carburetor and accelerator linkage and the choke plate and shaft, use choke cleaner (Fig. 6). Choke and engine cleaners are available in spray cans for easy application from automotive supply stores.

Cover the carburetor with household cling-type plastic food wrap. You should now clean debris and bugs from radiator fins with a soft bristle brush.

Before spraying on engine cleaner, inspect the engine for caked-on dirt. Scrape off as much as you can with a putty knife. In other words, try to leave only surface dirt for the engine cleaner.

Spray all parts of the engine and engine compartment, including the radiator, underpart of the hood, fender splash shields, and firewall (Fig. 7). Follow application instructions

Figure 6. Pay special attention to small but important areas, such as throttle linkage pins.

Figure 7. Spray the engine and compartment with the cleaner.

Figure 8. Use plenty of water to purge the engine of grime.

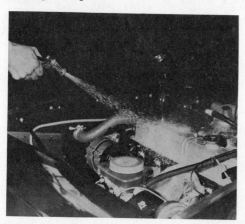

Figure 9. Forceful water pressure should be used to rid fender wells of caked-on material.

printed on the can. Generally, the engine should be warm when cleaner is applied. Thus, you should allow it to idle for several minutes before performing the first step of cleaning, which is to disconnect battery cables.

Allow the degreaser to eat away at dirt for about 15 minutes. Now, wash the entire engine and engine compartment with a forceful stream of water from a hose (Fig. 8). If some dirt and grime remain, apply a second application of engine cleaner.

After cleaning has been completed, reinstall the carburetor air cleaner and reconnect spark plug and battery cables. Be sure cables are firmly attached. Start the engine and allow its heat to evaporate remaining water.

To do a thorough job, lift the car and clean underbody components, including the underside of the engine block, transmission case, differential, exhaust system parts, and suspension components. The most important part to clean to prevent a mechanical problem is the driveshaft. If mud gets on and sticks to the shaft, an unbalanced condition will be created that will cause the shaft to whip. You will feel this as vibration.

Use engine cleaner to clean the driveshaft as well as all other parts beneath the car.

As you might imagine, a buildup of mud and dirt can add a considerable amount of weight to a vehicle. This can affect fuel consumption and handling. Mud builds up in the fender wells in particular.

To clean away this dirt, simply direct a high-pressure stream of water into the well (Fig. 9).

AUTOMOTIVE, ENGINE WON'T START (GENERAL)

This discussion concerns an automobile engine that won't start or is hard to start because of a malfunction within the engine, as opposed to an engine which won't start because of cold weather. Climatic starting problems are discussed in the section that follows.

When an engine doesn't start or is hard to start, the way in which it acts will often lead you to the reason. An engine that doesn't start (or is hard to start) will either not crank at all, will crank sluggishly, or will crank with pep but will not fire.

If an engine doesn't crank at all or cranks sluggishly, the trouble most times is a rundown battery. The quickest way to get started is to connect a booster battery. This is done by connecting a charged battery directly to the battery in your car by means of slave (jumper) cables. The booster may be a battery that is in another vehicle.

When employing a booster battery, remember that every battery has a positive post and a negative post. Slave cables, which you can buy in an auto supply store, are also negative or positive and are color coded to designate which. The positive cable is always red. The negative cable could be black, green, yellow, or any color but red.

Polarity between the booster battery, slave cables, and the battery that is receiving the boost must be correct from the start. This means that the negative post of the booster battery must be connected to the negative post of the battery being boosted by the negative slave cable, and that the positive posts of the two batteries must be connected by the positive slave cable (Fig. 1). If a reversal of connections is made for even a sec-

Figure 1. Be sure connections are correct to prevent serious damage to the car's alternator.

ond or two, the AC generator (alternator) in the car could be burned up.

With the booster connected, try to start the car. If the car starts, disconnect the booster. You should check the battery with a hydrometer and, if it is still in serviceable condition, charge it (see the section on Automotive, Battery).

If a booster battery is not available, you may be able to start the engine by pushing. If your car has a manual transmission, line up the bumpers of the two cars, place the transmission into second gear, and depress the clutch. Be sure that the ignition switch is on.

As the car starts rolling, keep an eye on the speedometer. When it reaches about 10 miles per hour, let out the clutch. If the problem is a weak battery, the engine will start.

Push-starting a Car with Automatic Transmission

Manufacturer	Type of Transmission	Instructions for Push-starting			
		Start With Trans In	Turn On Ignition At (Mph)	Shift To	At (Mph)
American Motors	Flashomatic (1)	Neutral	15–20	L	15–20
Chrysler Corp.	Powerflite	Neutral	0	L	25
	Torqueflite, aluminum (2)	Neutral	0	L	15
	Torqueflite, cast iron	Neutral	0	L	15–20
Ford Motor Co.	Cruisematic, C4 & C6	Cannot be push-started			
	3-speed (3)	Neutral	30	L	30
	2-speed	Neutral	25	L	25
General Motors	Buick Twin Turbine	Neutral	0	L	15
	Corvair Powerglide	Neutral	0	L	20–25
	Dual Coupling Hydra-Matic (4)	Neutral	30–35	D	30–35
	Powerglide, aluminum (1)	Neutral	0	L	25–30
	Powerglide, cast iron	Neutral	0	L	25–30
	Tempestorque, 61–63 (5)	Neutral	0	L	20–25
	Turboglide	Neutral	25	L	25–30
	These cannot be push-started:				
	Buick Dual Path Drive				
	F-85 Hydra-Matic				
	Jetaway Hydra-Matic				
	Roto Hydra-Matic				
	Turbo Hydra-Matic 350				
	Turbo Hydra-Matic 400				
	Super Turbine 300				
	Super Turbine 400				
	Tempestorque, 1964				

(1) Can't push-start after 1966
(2) Can't push-start after 1965
(3) Can't push-start after 1967
(4) Can't push-start after 1958
(5) Can't push-start after 1962

It is more difficult to start a car that is equipped with an automatic transmission by pushing. Some cars with an automatic transmission lack a rear pump that allows the engine to be driven through the transmission. These, therefore, will not start with a push.

Since your chance of push-starting a car that is equipped with an automatic transmission depends on the type of transmission which is in the car, you should determine what type of transmission you have. Every transmission has a model number imprinted on the transmission pan or case. Find this number and take it to the parts department of a dealer who sells that make of car.

The chart on the previous page outlines the information you need to know about push-starting a car with automatic transmission. If the requirements for push-starting are met but the car won't start, the battery is completely dead.

If the battery in the car is okay and the engine won't start, the cause of sluggish starting is probably the starter, which should be tested with an ammeter to determine if it is drawing more amperage than is specified (Fig. 2). For example, if the starter is drawing 400 amperes when it is supposed to draw 125 to 225 amperes, a malfunction exists inside the starter, or battery cables have developed excessive resistance.

Is there corrosion on top of battery posts? If there is, clean off posts with sandpaper as described in the section Automotive, Battery.

In time, battery cables can deteriorate because of high underhood temperature and grease. If the cables in your car haven't been replaced in 30,000 miles and there is excessive amperage draw, replace them now (Fig. 3). If this fails to solve the problem, have a mechanic repair the starter.

An engine which cranks normally but doesn't start usually has a failure in the fuel or ignition system. The first thing to make sure of, though, is that there is gasoline in the tank.

If there is, isolate the trouble area by removing a spark plug cable from a spark plug by grasping the boot and twisting it (Fig. 4). Do not pull the cable.

Insert a screwdriver inside the boot so that it contacts the cable's terminal and hold the screwdriver about ¼ inch from a clean ground, such as a bolt. Have someone crank the engine. Be sure to hold the screwdriver by its handle so you don't get shocked.

If a spark jumps the gap between screwdriver and ground, the cause of the starting problem is either bad spark plugs, a

Figure 2. The starter amperage draw test will reveal a problem with cables or with the starter.

Figure 3. Battery cables will deteriorate as time passes. No-start will eventually result.

Figure 4. To remove spark plug cables, grasp and turn boots. Don't pull on fragile cables.

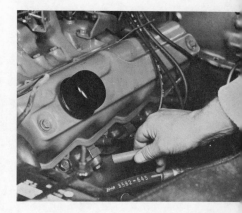

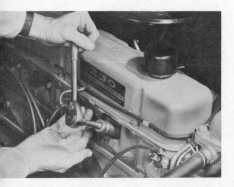

Figure 5. Use a six-point deep socket that fits the spark plug to remove it from the engine.

Figure 6. The choke butterfly can lead to starting problems, if not functioning properly.

Figure 7. A choke plate that is binding because of dirt can be freed by using choke solvent.

Figure 8. A fuel pump pressure test will reveal whether a weak pump is stopping quick starts.

Figure 9. A fuel filter that is clogged is a cause of no-start that is not often considered.

Figure 10. The compression test will make internal engine problems readily apparent to you.

malfunction in the fuel system, or low engine compression. If there is no spark, a problem exists in the engine's ignition system.

Assuming spark, here is what to do:

1. Remove a few spark plugs and examine the electrodes to make sure they aren't fouled (Fig. 5). If spark plugs haven't been replaced in 12,000 miles, they should be serviced or replaced. (See the section Automotive, Spark Plugs for details.)

2. Examine the choke plate which is inside the carburetor throat. Make sure it is moving freely (Fig. 6). If the engine is warm, the choke plate should be open. If the engine is cold, press the accelerator pedal to the floor once and check the choke plate. If should be closed.

A choke plate that is binding is usually clogged by dirt. Use choke cleaner, which you can buy in an auto supply store, to dissolve dirt (Fig. 7). If dirt is not the cause of the choke plate binding, then parts such as the thermostatic spring and choke piston have gone bad. Have the assembly dismantled and repaired.

3. Have the fuel pump tested to make sure it is delivering sufficient gasoline (Fig. 8).

4. If the fuel filter hasn't been replaced in 12,000 miles, it may be clogged with dirt that is preventing gasoline from reaching the carburetor. Replace the filter with a new one, which you can buy in an auto supply store. Be sure that it is the right one for your engine.

Most gasoline filters are connected into the line between the fuel pump and carburetor by means of clamps. Loosen clamps, pull the old filter from place, and attach the new filter (Fig. 9).

5. Check engine compression with a compression gauge. This is done by removing spark plugs and inserting a compression gauge (Fig. 10). Determine the correct compression rating of your engine (it varies from one engine to another) by consulting an automotive manual, such as Motor's *Auto Repair Manual*, which is usually available in a public library.

A reading which is 10 pounds or more *above* that specified for your engine indicates that carbon has built up inside the engine. This will prevent starting when the engine is warm. A reading that is 10 pounds or more *below* normal indicates a bad head gasket, rings, or valves. In any case, professional engine work is indicated.

If the problem hasn't been found to this point, it is probably inside the carburetor with a bad or misadjusted float, damaged needle valve and seat, a faulty accelerator pump, or dirt-clogged passages. The carburetor should be overhauled.

Let's assume that you get no spark when performing the

Figure 11. Sometimes the only way to uncover a cause of no-start is with test equipment.

test described above. This means that the cause of the no-start problem is in the ignition system with either a defective coil, bad condenser, an open circuit, bad distributor points, or an incorrect distributor point setting. To pinpoint the exact trouble, the ignition system should be inspected by a mechanic who possesses modern electronic testing equipment (Fig. 11).

AUTOMOTIVE, ENGINE WON'T START (WINTER)

A battery that has been robbed of its power by cold weather is the main reason that engines refuse to start in the winter. Information on how to deal with this problem has already been detailed in the sections on Automotive, Battery, and on Automotive, Engine Won't Start (General).

This section outlines several suggestions to employ so that starting in cold weather is facilitated. We must assume that the engine has been tuned up so that there is no nonclimatic reason for the engine failing to start [see Automotive, Engine Won't Start (General)].

Other than a weak battery, the number one reason that engines fail to start properly in cold weather is the driver himself. There are many who believe that an engine requires a great deal of gasoline for quick wintertime starts. They pump the gas pedal to excess, which causes the engine to flood,

The right way to start a cold engine in any weather, but especially in winter, is to depress the accelerator pedal to the floor one time only. Hold it one-third to halfway down as you activate the ignition. The engine should start within 15 seconds, even in the coldest weather. If not, stop cranking before you run the battery down.

If you flood the engine by accident, shove the accelerator pedal to the floor and hold it there as you crank. You are allowing air to clear the carburetor and cylinders of gas. Again, if the engine doesn't start within 15 seconds, stop cranking. You don't want to add a rundown battery to your trouble.

The viscosity of the engine oil you use has a great deal to do with the ability of the engine to start in cold weather. Each reduction in oil viscosity lowers the minimum starting temperature by about 15°F. However, you cannot use oil with a viscosity that is too low for the temperature, since oil that is too thin will not provide the engine with suitable lubrication.

Consult the owner's manual for your car to determine what viscosity oil you should use in your area of the country in the winter (Fig. 1). If the manual has been lost, you can safely go by the recommendations that follow.

If the lowest anticipated temperature in your area during the winter is from 0°F to 32°F, use SAE 20W or SAE 20W-40 motor oil. If the anticipated temperature is between 0°F and −10°F, use SAE 10W, SAE 10W-30, or SAE 10W-40 motor oil. If the anticipated winter temperature in your area is −10°F or below, use SAE 5W or SAE 5W-20 motor oil. (*SAE* stands for the *S*ociety of *A*utomotive *E*ngineers motor oil grading system. *W* stands for winter grade.)

One of the best aids that you can use to get an engine started in cold weather is starting fluid, which dries up moisture in

Figure 1. Motor oil must be of the proper viscosity to assure quick starts during the winter.

Figure 2. Engine starting fluid can be bought at an auto parts supply shop or service station.

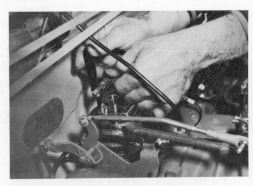

Figure 3. Distributor breaker points must be adjusted to specification for good starting.

Figure 4. Grease will help protect parts, particularly ball joints, from damaging weather.

Figure 5. Tires carry a heavy load. Are they safe? No cuts? Good tread? Correct pressure?

Figure 6. Safe driving in winter demands that you perform a thorough brake examination.

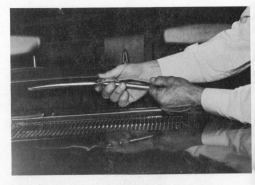

Figure 7. Check windshield wipers. Good visibility is often a problem even with good ones.

the fuel system and dissipates ice. However, starting fluid is essentially an ether compound that is highly volatile. It is very important that you use it properly.

Remove the carburetor air cleaner, be sure that the ignition switch is off, and direct a 5-second spray of the fluid directly into the carburetor throat (Fig. 2). Do not spray for a longer time. Then, try to start the engine. If it doesn't start, do not use the starting fluid again. It will not help.

Be sure that you are in a well-ventilated area when spraying and that there is no open flame or spark. No smoking! When warm weather approaches, store the can of starting fluid in a cool place, such as a basement. Do not leave it in the car's glove compartment. The aerosol spray can may explode if the temperature gets too high.

The best way to avoid starting problems, of course, is to prepare your car to meet cold weather. The following list outlines those service procedures that should be taken before winter strikes:

1. Check the electrical and ignition systems. Clean, adjust, and replace parts as necessary (Fig. 3).
2. Check the fuel system. Clean and service filters and make sure that the carburetor air cleaner is clean.
3. Check for engine compression loss.
4. Drain and flush the cooling system. Use a cleaner to remove rust. Check antifreeze potency at the beginning of and midway through the winter.
5. Check the cooling system for leaks. Replace worn hoses and faulty gaskets. Check fan belt tension and thermostat and car heater operation.
6. Lubricate the chassis and change the oil so that the correct viscosity for your part of the country will be used (Fig. 4).
7. Inspect the exhaust system for leaks.
8. Check tires and mount snow tires (Fig. 5). If you prefer, carry skid chains in the trunk.
9. Check brake linings, hoses, and hydraulic brake fluid level (Fig. 6).
10. Inspect windshield wipers and defrosters (Fig. 7). Add windshield-washer antifreeze to the windshield-washer reservoir.

AUTOMOTIVE, FUEL CONSUMPTION

If your car doesn't provide the degree of fuel mileage that you think it should, you can probably get more by making mechanical adjustments and/or by readjusting your methods of driving. The causes of excessive fuel consumption can be placed into one of two categories: (1) the way in which you drive; (2) mechanical deficiencies that rob the engine of power and add to the normal resistances that the car must overcome.

Whether or not you adopt some or all of the measures recommended here, especially those concerning driving, is a matter for you to decide. Some drivers don't regard the amount of fuel they save by reducing highway driving speed 5 miles per hour as worth the trouble.

Before dealing with corrective measures, we must ask the question, "How do you know that your car is using an excessive amount of gas?"

The method usually employed by drivers to determine this—the odometer–fuel-gauge averaging method—is not accurate. The only accurate method of determining the degree of gasoline consumption is by use of a fuel-per-mile gauge, which is connected into the car's fuel system as the car is driven over a planned test course (Fig. 1).

The test course should involve four different test conditions, with readings from the fuel-per-mile gauge recorded before and after each test. The engine should not be allowed to sit at idle during the test except where traffic conditions, including traffic lights, force unavoidable stops.

The test course should include:

1. A drive on a highway in one direction.

2. A drive over the same highway in the opposite direction, which will equalize the effects of head or tail winds encountered during the first test.

3. A drive through a light-traffic urban area.

4. A drive through a heavy-traffic business area.

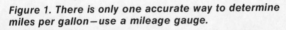

Figure 1. There is only one accurate way to determine miles per gallon—use a mileage gauge.

You should be behind the wheel. Having someone else drive the car will not provide an accurate indication of how much fuel is being used, since each driver has different habits which affect fuel consumption.

You can arrange for a fuel consumption test by contacting the service department of a new car dealer in your area that sells your make of car. The test may reveal that your car is not using as much fuel as you think.

However, if the car is using an abnormal amount of fuel or if you want to try to economize on fuel even more, you should keep two facts in mind. First, the more you hit the accelerator pedal, the more fuel will be wasted. And, second, the more that a car's engine is allowed to idle, the more fuel will be wasted. Thus, stop-and-go city driving will naturally cause more fuel to be consumed than highway driving.

The following are several driving techniques that will add miles to your fuel consumption rate:

1. Avoid needless engine idling. Do not allow your car to sit with the engine running when it can be avoided. Shut off the engine or get rolling. Your engine will burn as much fuel in 3 minutes of idling as it will when driving ½ mile at 30 miles per hour.

2. Use steady foot pressure on the accelerator pedal. When starting from a dead stop, press the accelerator pedal slowly and steadily. Avoid quick, jackrabbit starts. Flooring the accelerator pedal and then backing off on it just burns gasoline — gasoline the car does not need for acceleration.

3. Use proper passing procedure. Never run up on a car ahead, slam on the brakes, and then hit the accelerator pedal to pass. This wastes fuel. Instead, start the pass well in back of the car to permit a smooth swing-out, pass, and swing-in.

4. Drive at moderate speeds. Gas consumption increases as speed increases. Stay within posted speed limits. They are considered moderate as well as safe.

5. Do not use your brake unnecessarily. For example, try to time traffic lights so that you won't have to stop. More gasoline is consumed by stopping and starting than by coasting up to a light and, as it turns green, reapplying a steady pressure to the accelerator pedal while the car is still in motion. Keep in mind that a car uses gas most when it is accelerated from a dead stop.

6. Never fill the gasoline tank to the very top, especially in hot weather. Gas expands as it heats and will overflow the gas tank if it is too near the top. Be sure that the gas station attendant doesn't add any more fuel to the tank after the automatic shutoff nozzle of the gas pump flips off.

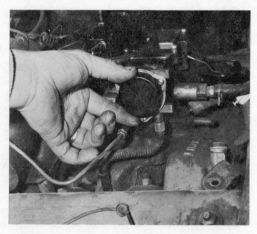

Figure 2. A dirty air cleaner leads to an overly rich fuel mix and unnecessary burning of gas.

Figure 3. A choke adjustment on the carburetor is used on many cars to get a correct setting.

Mechanical deficiencies that rob you of gas are many and are summarized below. Most can be looked for and attended to when the car's engine is being tuned.

Fuel system malfunctions. If the engine sounds as if it is idling faster than normal or if black smoke comes from the exhaust pipe, which indicates that a rich fuel mixture is being burned, have the following investigated:

• High fuel pump pressure
• Dirty air cleaner (Fig. 2)
• Overly rich choke adjustment (Figs. 3 and 4)
• Improper adjustment of the carburetor fast idle, idle mixture, accelerator pump stroke, and/or antistall dashpot (Fig. 5)
• High carburetor float level

Figure 4. In other models, the adjusting mechanism must be removed from a well and then set.

Figure 5. The carburetor must be set properly if you are to expect good fuel consumption.

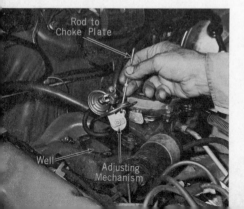

Figure 6. Damaged, dirty carburetors will eat up fuel and cause poor engine performance.

Figure 7. Have the engine timed periodically to assure good operation and full fuel economy.

• Internal carburetor damage, such as worn jets or faulty power valve (Fig. 6)

• Binding of the accelerator linkage

Ignition system malfunctions. You are wasting fuel if there is no spark delivered to a cylinder to burn fuel. Unburned gasoline will be expelled through the exhaust pipe. Look for the following:

• Leaks in high tension cables

• A weak coil

• Worn, dirty, fouled, or incorrectly gapped spark plugs

• Incorrect ignition timing (Fig. 7)

• Incorrectly adjusted or worn distributor breaker points

• An inoperative distributor spark advance unit (Fig. 8)

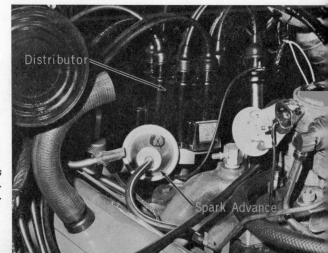

Figure 8. The spark advance is necessary for correct timing. It should be in good condition.

Figure 9. The compression test will reveal if internal damage is causing excessive gas loss.

Figure 10. Consider having the engine's valves adjusted if the car uses more gas than normal.

Engine/power train malfunctions. If engine and power train are damaged, gasoline will be lost. Watch out for:
- Loss of engine compression (Fig. 9)
- Burned or sticking valves
- Improperly adjusted valves (Fig. 10)
- A defective positive crankcase ventilation valve
- A stuck manifold heat control valve (Fig. 11)
- A restricted exhaust system
- An improperly adjusted automatic transmission

Gas leaks. Leaks account for a good deal of gas loss. The most likely areas where they occur are:
- The fuel line where it connects to the carburetor (Fig. 12)
- The fuel line where it connects to the fuel pump
- In the seams of the gas tank filler neck
- At the gas tank cap. Be sure it is tight, especially after the tank is filled
- At the gas tank itself

Figure 11. If it is stuck, the manifold valve won't allow gas to vaporize. More fuel will be used.

Figure 12. Fuel leaks lead to fuel loss. Make sure that all lines are securely tightened.

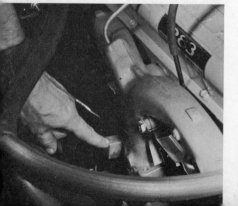

AUTOMOTIVE, LUBRICATION

By setting up an at-home lubrication center for your car, you are able to accomplish two objectives. First, you will be able to give your vehicle frequent and careful grease jobs that help to avert mechanical troubles, such as ball joint failure, and that enhance the riding qualities of the car. Second, you will save money by doing your own grease jobs.

Lubrication equipment can be purchased in an automotive supply store. You will need an all-purpose grease gun of the type seen in Fig. 1. This gun, which develops 10,000 pounds of pressure, accommodates grease cartridges that are placed into the gun in much the same manner as caulking cartridges are placed into a caulking gun.

If the all-purpose gun doesn't come equipped with a flexible extension adapter, buy one. The adapter, which measures about 1 foot, allows you to apply grease in places that cannot be reached with the gun alone, such as upper ball joints.

Another piece of equipment that you will need is a trigger-type oil can, which is used to apply penetrating oil to door and hood hinge pins (Fig. 2).

Finally, you may need a suction gun, but wait to buy it until you do. The gun is used to add lubricant to manual transmissions and to differentials (rear end) (Fig. 3). It is also used to remove the lubricant from these parts if they require flushing.

Lubricants (greases and oils) that will be needed are as follows:

Figure 1. The main tool in an at-home lubrication kit is a grease gun with an extension.

Figure 2. The trigger-type oil can permits the application of lubricant to door hinge pins.

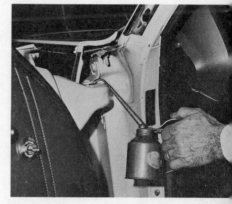

Figure 3. Wait to buy this suction gun until the differential needs replenishing with grease.

Figure 4. The level of grease in the rear end is checked by removing the filler hole plug.

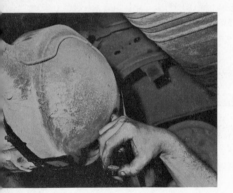

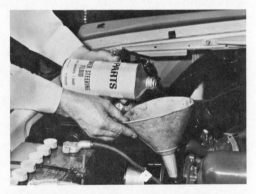

Figure 5. If your little finger does not contact the lubricant, add grease to the differential.

Figure 6. Power steering fluid must be added if an inspection reveals that the level is low.

• Multipurpose chassis grease for lubricating the front suspension and steering linkage.

• Multipurpose gear lubricant to replenish the supply in a standard differential and in a manual transmission. To determine if the differential and transmission need to be relubricated, remove the filler plug and insert your little finger (Figs. 4 and 5). If lubricant cannot be touched, replenish the supply.

If your car is equipped with a positive traction differential, which is an option on most models, be sure that the lubricant you use is specifically designed for this type of differential. Grease for standard differentials should not be used since it will cause the differential to chatter.

• Power steering fluid for replenishing the fluid in a power steering reservoir (Fig. 6).

• Automatic transmission fluid for replenishing the supply in an automatic transmission.

• All-purpose white grease for lubricating metal body points that slide or rub against other body points, such as latches, hinges, and catches (Fig. 7).

• SAE 20 engine oil for lubricating points where penetration is necessary, such as hinge pins.

• Silicone spray lubricant for use on rubberized parts that begin to squeak or bind, such as window channels (Fig. 8).

There is one other item that you cannot do without and that is the lubrication chart for your particular vehicle. It shows you what points have to be lubricated, how often they should be lubricated, and what lubricant to use.

The lubrication chart is contained in your car's service manual. You may be able to purchase this manual for about $5 by writing the technical publications department of your car's manufacturer. Be sure to specify the year and model of your car when ordering.

If the manufacturer declines to sell you a manual, perhaps a dealer in your area who sells your make of car will allow you to borrow the manual so you can have a copy made of the lubrication chart.

As was mentioned above, recommended lubrication intervals vary from car to car. General Motors, for example, recommends that chassis parts on some of its models be lubricated at least once every 6,000 miles of operation. Ford and Chrysler recommend that some of its models be lubricated every 36 months or 36,000 miles.

As long as you have your own lubrication center, you can lubricate your car as often as you like. Keep in mind that you

Figure 7. Use all-purpose white grease on metal-to-metal surfaces such as car hood latches.

Figure 8. Silicone spray lubricant is excellent when used to stop squeaks from rubber parts.

Figure 9. A certain amount of oozing at a ball joint seal is okay. A mass of grease isn't.

Figure 10. Wipe around the ball joint plug so that dirt won't get in and scar the surface.

cannot harm a car by frequent lubrication—you can only increase its serviceable life.

No matter how often you decide to lubricate your car, be sure that you inspect suspension and steering ball joints every 6 months or 6,000 miles of vehicle operation, whichever comes first. This visual examination will guarantee that ball joint seals haven't ruptured, causing ball joints to lose grease. A greaseless ball joint will wear to a dangerous point and can cause a car to go out of control.

To check a ball joint, simply inspect it around its rubber seal to be sure that grease is not leaking from the joint (Fig. 9). A ball joint that shows signs of a ruptured seal should be replaced.

Although ball joints might not show signs of having lost grease, they should be lubricated when you grease the car. If the ball joint has a plug in it, it must be removed. Do this by cleaning dirt from around the plug (Fig. 10). Metal plugs are removed with the appropriate size wrench (Fig. 11). Rubber plugs are simply pried from the joint.

Figure 11. Before a ball joint can be lubricated, remove the plug and insert a zerk fitting.

Now, insert a grease fitting into the joint. You can get the correct size fitting (commonly called a zerk fitting) from a dealer of auto supplies. This fitting accommodates the grease gun. Apply grease until it begins to ooze out from around the rubber seal.

If you wish, you can replace the plugs in ball joints with zerk fittings. If not, you can remove the zerk fitting after greasing and reinstall the plug.

AUTOMOTIVE, Overheating

The time to fix an engine overheating problem is before overheating occurs. In other words, you should check your car's cooling system annually to make sure that those conditions which cause overheating aren't being fostered. This periodic inspection is done similar to the way in which you would look for the problem if the engine were overheating. This procedure follows and is presented in a logical sequence that allows you to perform the service in the quickest and least expensive manner possible:

1. Perform a pressure test to uncover leaks in the cooling system and to determine if the radiator pressure cap is in serviceable condition. To do this, you will need a pressure tester which costs about $15 in an automotive supply store.

However, the service station which you patronize probably has such a tester. Most service station operators will let a customer borrow a tester or will do the test for him, especially for a good customer.

Figure 1. The pressure tester puts the cooling system under a load which uncovers leaks.

Figure 3. *The pressure tester is used to determine if the radiator cap is sealing properly.*

Figure 2. *Quite often a leak from the radiator will be revealed by a corrosive trail.*

Figure 4. *Dirt that is lodged beneath the cap's rubber seal can be eliminated with paper.*

The most common type of pressure tester requires that you test the radiator cap and the cooling system separately. There is another type of tester that attaches to the engine and allows you to check both cap and cooling system at the same time. However, it is not generally available and will not be mentioned again.

To check for leaks in the cooling system, remove the radiator cap and attach the tester to the radiator filler neck (Fig. 1). Pump up the tester until its dial shows the amount of pressure at which the cooling system is rated. This rating may be from 12 to 17 pounds per square inch, depending upon the model of your car. To get the exact rating, examine the top of the radiator cap. The rating is recorded here.

Allow pressure to be maintained for about 10 minutes. At the end of this time, observe the tester's dial. If it indicates a drop in pressure, there is a leak in the cooling system, so examine it carefully. The most common areas of leakage are hoses, thermostat housing (because of a bad gasket), and radiator.

Leaking hoses and thermostat housing are discussed below. If the radiator is leaking, pour a can of radiator stop leak into the radiator as directed on the can (Fig. 2). This product is available at service stations. If leakage is minor, the stop leak will seal it. If not, the radiator will have to be removed from the car and repaired by a professional mechanic or replaced.

The condition of the radiator cap is determined by washing the cap in water to begin with and then attaching it to the pressure tester. Pump up pressure until the dial reads the pounds per square inch recorded on the cap (Fig. 3). Pressure should maintain itself. If the dial shows a drop in pressure, remove the cap from the tester and slide a clean piece of paper or business card beneath the rubber seal around the cap (Fig. 4). Press down on the valve and then pull the paper out. Do this around the entire circumference of the seal to dislodge dirt that may be preventing the cap from sealing properly.

Test the cap again. If pressure still doesn't maintain itself, the cap is damaged and should be replaced.

2. Examine hoses and hose clamps. If a hose shows a leak during the pressure test, it must be replaced. This is true if coolant appears around the hose clamp and tightening the clamp doesn't stop it.

Even if a leak isn't apparent, a hose may still be faulty or approaching the end of its life. To check this, squeeze each hose (Fig. 5). If it feels mushy, replace it. If tiny cracks appear in the hose as you squeeze it, replace it.

All hoses must be examined. This includes the upper and lower radiator hoses, the small bypass hose going from the water pump to the engine block, and heater hoses (Fig. 6).

Incidentally, if your engine suddenly begins to overheat during high speed operation for no apparent reason, the lower radiator hose may be the cause. This hose has a spring inside of

Figure 5. *If a hose feels mushy or small cracks appear as you squeeze it, replace the hose.*

Figure 6. *Keep in mind that the heater is a part of the cooling system. Examine its hoses.*

Figure 7. Note that the clamp is positioned approximately ⅛ inch from the end of the hose.

it that keeps the hose from collapsing during high speed driving. If the spring loses tension, the hose will collapse and restrict the flow of coolant to the engine.

To replace a hose, you must drain the cooling system as described below. Remove the old hose, and clean the connection with a wire brush. Coat the connection with a water-resistant sealing compound, which is available at a service station, and slide the new hose into place. Use new clamps. Position clamps about ⅛ inch from the end of the hose. Make sure that the clamp is not seated at the end of the hose (Fig. 7).

3. Check and adjust engine drive belts. These belts are frequently overlooked as a cause of overheating. Yet a loose or damaged belt prevents the water pump from delivering the amount of coolant which the engine needs.

Examine the inner circumference of belts for cracks and glazed marks. If damage is apparent, replace the belt. Have your service station attendant check belt tension with a drive belt tension gauge (Fig. 8). Tension specifications vary from car model to car model, but the service station should have specifications at hand. If drive belts are too loose, have the service station attendant tighten them (Fig. 9).

Figure 8. Proper belt tension is important. The only true way to get it is with a dial gauge.

Figure 9. A loose fan belt will cause overheating and erratic operation of air conditioning.

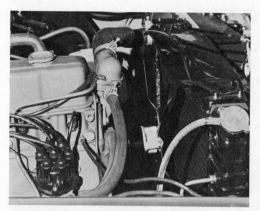

Figure 10. The arrow points to the thermostat housing. Remove it to replace a leaking gasket.

Figure 11. When the temperature reaches opening range, you may feel water surge in the hose.

4. Check the thermostat. The purpose of the thermostat is to allow the engine to warm up quickly. This part stays closed when the engine is cold, which restricts the flow of coolant. As the engine reaches operating temperature, the thermostat is supposed to open and allow coolant to flow.

If a thermostat is damaged so that it doesn't open properly, overheating will result because no coolant will be flowing. Conversely, if the thermostat is damaged so that it stays open all the time, the engine won't heat up properly. This will be reflected most significantly in the winter time by a lack of warm air from the heater.

Begin a check of the thermostat by observing to see if coolant leaks from around the thermostat housing during the pressure test. If it does, the thermostat housing gasket is ruptured. Drain the cooling system as described below and remove the housing, which is normally held by two bolts (Fig. 10). Scrape off the old gasket, apply water-resistant sealing compound to the gasket seating surface, and install a new gasket which you can buy in an automotive supply store.

If the engine overheats or doesn't reach normal operating temperature, first determine the temperature at which the thermostat in your car is supposed to open by consulting an automobile manual, such as Motor's *Auto Repair Manual*, which is available in most public libraries. Or call a dealer that sells your make of car and ask him.

Be sure that the engine is cool and insert a thermometer that is calibrated to at least 200°F into the radiator filler neck (Fig. 11). Start the engine and allow it to get warm. The coolant should heat up to the approximate rating of the thermostat, and this temperature reading should maintain itself. If temperature soars past this rating or if it doesn't reach it, the thermostat is damaged and should be replaced by draining the cooling system, removing the thermostat housing, and lifting the thermostat from place. Whenever the thermostat housing is removed, be sure that a new gasket is installed.

5. Drain coolant and flush the cooling system (Fig. 12). Open the drain cock at the bottom of the radiator and remove the threaded drain plug(s) from the engine (Fig. 13). Six-cylinder engines have one engine block drain plug, while eight-cylinder engines normally have two, one on each bank. Be sure to open (turn on) the car's heater as draining is done, so that all coolant will drain from the system.

When draining is completed, flush the cooling system by first closing the radiator drain cock and replacing the engine block drain plug(s) tightly. Fill the system with plain water (Fig. 14).

Start the motor and allow the engine to run until it reaches normal operating temperature. As this is taking place, occasionally increase acceleration by depressing the gas pedal gradually to a good rate of speed and holding it there for a few seconds. This allows forceful circulation of water and will help to dislodge rust and scale.

When engine temperature reaches the normal operating range, drain the system. If the water comes out colorless, the system is clean. If not, repeat the flushing procedure, but first allow the engine to cool before adding fresh water.

If the water is very dirty as it drains from the system, use a

Figure 12. Brown sludge around the filler neck is a sure sign that the system needs flushing.

Figure 13. To insure complete drainage of the system, engine drain cocks should be removed.

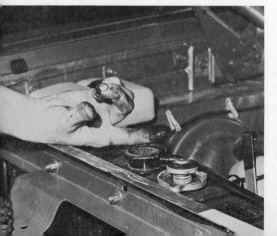

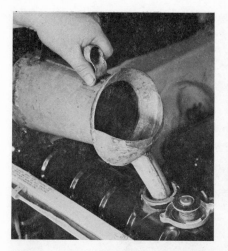

Figure 14. If you should fill the system with the motor warm, be sure the motor is running.

Figure 15. Check antifreeze before and during the winter to guard against engine freezeup.

cooling system cleaning compound during the flushing process. This can be purchased at a gasoline station. Add the compound to the system as directed on the can.

You should always use a good quality ethylene glycol antifreeze in your cooling system all year round. This product contains the chemicals which are needed to protect the cooling system from corrosion. Thus, it should be used even though the climate in your area is not one that will threaten the engine with freezing.

To provide your cooling system with maximum protection against corrosion (and to provide protection against freezing to −34°F), use a 50 percent concentration of ethylene glycol, that is, 50 percent antifreeze to 50 percent water. If you do not drain antifreeze from the cooling system each year, be sure to check its freeze protection with a hydrometer before cold weather sets in (Fig. 15). This can be done for you by a service station operator.

AUTOMOTIVE, ROUGH IDLE

There are about 20 different reasons why an automobile engine will idle rough. Obviously, plunging ahead indiscriminately without first considering all the facts at your disposal is a time-consuming and expensive way of repairing the malfunction. Rough idle is not always caused by a mechanical problem.

Figure 1. Waterproof compounds are available that protect ignition parts from wet weather.

How can you pinpoint the cause of the problem? To start with, ask yourself, "Does the condition occur when I first start the engine, but disappear when the engine warms up?"

Temporary rough idle of this nature is most often caused by rain, snow, or excessive humidity in the air which dampens wires, distributor cap, spark plugs, and other ignition parts. If the condition is particularly annoying to you, spray ignition parts with a waterproof ignition compound which is sold in aerosol spray cans at automotive supply stores (Fig. 1). Use as directed on the can.

Another question to ask yourself is whether rough idle occurs only when the air conditioner is turned on. If this is so, the carburetor idle speed is not properly set. The correct way to set idle speed varies from engine to engine. Thus, if you wish to do the job yourself, you will have to consult the car's service manual or an automotive repair book, such as Motor's *Repair Manual* or Chilton's *Repair Manual*. These repair books are available in most public libraries.

If rough idle is a continuous problem that occurs under all operational conditions, the cause is either in the fuel or ignition system or inside the engine. How can you tell?

Start by asking whether rough idle is the only operational problem the engine is experiencing or whether another condition prevails as well. In most cases, the malfunctions that cause rough idle will also cause another problem, and the combination of the two can assist you in finding the malfunction.

For instance, does noise come from the engine at idle and during acceleration? If it does, the reason for both rough idle and the noise is probably a broken valve spring, worn camshaft lobes, or a bad valve lifter. The engine needs to be disassembled and repaired.

Rough idle accompanied by engine noise and lack of power on acceleration when the engine is hot are conditions which indicate that valves are burned, warped, pitted, or sticking. Again, engine repair is indicated.

Fortunately, however, rough idle is not usually caused by anything as serious as bad valves or a worn camshaft. Most times the cause of the malfunction is to be found in the ignition or fuel system. But where? You can again use other operational conditions, if they exist, to help you find out.

Suppose, for example, that in addition to idling rough the engine is hard to start, perhaps it stalls, and maybe it misses at other speeds as well. A combination of any of these with rough idle indicates an ignition failure—specifically, incorrectly gapped or worn spark plugs, incorrectly gapped or damaged distributor contact points, or a weak coil.

Check the conditon of spark plugs first (see the section dealing with Automotive, Spark Plugs). Follow this with an inspection of distributor contact points. If points are badly burned or pitted, replace them. Make sure points are gapped to the specification provided in the car's service manual (Fig. 2).

Figure 2. Distributor breaker points must be properly gapped, if rough idle is to be avoided.

If spark plugs and distributor contact points are okay, check for a weak ignition coil by pulling the high tension cable from the center socket of the distributor cap and holding it ¼ inch from a clean ground on the engine, such as a bolt. Have someone crank the engine. If the coil is in good condition, a blue spark will jump from the cable terminal to ground.

If rough idle is accompanied by lack of engine power on acceleration, focus your attention on the spark advance mechanism. Check it by pulling the vacuum hose from the engine vacuum port and drawing in on it as you would on a straw. If you can draw in—that is, if there is no vacuum—the diaphragm in the spark advance mechanism is ruptured, and the part should be replaced.

If the vacuum advance checks out okay, then the reason for rough idle and lack of power on acceleration is inside the engine with a blown head gasket or uneven or low compression. Perform a compression test. The engine will undoubtedly need work.

If the cause of rough idle hasn't been uncovered to now, consider the fuel system. Logic will again help you to determine if the malfunction is here.

For instance, one of the main reasons for rough idle is an engine that is operating on an excessively rich fuel mixture. Other operational conditions that will accompany rough idle if over-richness exists are an engine which is hard to start and/or an odor of gasoline.

The problem can be caused by an over-rich idle adjustment, an automatic choke that is set too high, a float level that is set too high, a dirty carburetor air cleaner, or a dirt-clogged carburetor (Fig. 3).

Figure 3. If the carburetor has not been cleaned in many miles, it may cause rough engine idle.

Figure 4. You will locate the PCV valve in one of the valve covers. Pull it from its seat.

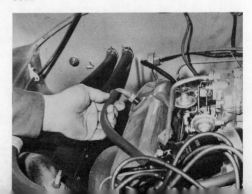

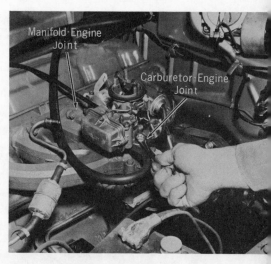

Figure 5. If the valve has to be replaced, just pull it from its place in the vacuum hose.

Figure 6. Air leaks which produce rough idle occur at these spots. Be sure bolts are tight.

Another reason for rough idle is a clogged positive crankcase ventilation system. Pull the PCV valve from its seat in the valve cover and hold your finger over its tip as the engine runs (Fig. 4). You should feel a strong vacuum. If not, replace the PCV valve with a new one (Fig. 5).

Incidentally, if the PCV system is badly clogged, rough idle will be accompanied by an increase in oil consumption. In fact, oil will be thrown out the filler tube by pressure and over the engine block or into the carburetor air cleaner.

That leaves two conditions that will cause rough idle: an air leak around the intake manifold and carburetor, or faulty ignition wiring. These will not cause any other operational problem other than rough idle.

To check for an air leak around the intake manifold and carburetor base, mix some light engine oil with a little kerosene and apply the mixture around the carburetor-manifold joint and manifold-engine joint. Start the engine. If an air leak exists because of a bad head gasket or loose mounting bolts, engine speed will increase and you will see the oil mixture being drawn in through the leaking area.

Tighten mounting bolts and conduct the test again. (Fig. 6). If the condition isn't repaired, check the manifold and carburetor castings for warp and/or replace the gasket, which is probably ruptured.

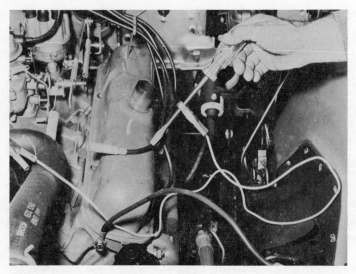

Figure 7. If an ignition wire is leaking, a spark will jump from the wire to screwdriver.

The last major cause of rough idle is faulty ignition wiring. To check on this, use a screwdriver and a length of wire that has an alligator clip attached to each end. Hook one of the alligator clips to the shank of the screwdriver and the other to ground. Start the engine and remove a cable from a spark plug. Probe around the cable and spark plug boot with the screwdriver (Fig. 7).

If sparks jump from the cable, that cable is leaking and should be replaced. Reconnect the cable and proceed to the others in turn, until all are checked.

AUTOMOTIVE, SPARK PLUGS

Spark plugs are one of the most important parts of a car. They produce sparks that ignite the fuel mixture in the engine's cylinders. In fact, a spark plug in an eight-cylinder engine produces approximately 20 sparks per second and is subjected to temperatures of 3000°F at its electrode end.

Spark plugs also provide the car owner with a means of analyzing engine malfunctions. This is explained later in this section.

First, however, it is important to discuss spark plugs and their relationship to engine performance. This relationship can be presented in the form of three questions:

1. Are the plugs in your engine the proper ones for driving conditions?

2. Are plugs in a useful state, or should they be serviced or replaced?

3. Is the ignition system providing full output, so that plugs can do their job properly?

The spark plug recommended by the manufacturer of your car is designed to meet an almost equal amount of idling, slow speed, and fast driving operation. However, it might not be the one that will allow your engine to work without malfunctioning.

The correct spark plug for an engine is the one that meets the thermal conditions that are present most often inside the engine (Fig. 1). If the spark plug cannot dissipate engine heat fast enough, it will begin to glow and cause preignition, which refers to igniting of the fuel mixture before the spark occurs. Preignition can cause serious damage to an engine.

Conversely, if a spark plug stays relatively cool, it cannot burn away deposits that form on the tip of its insulator. These deposits can eventually bridge the electrode gap and cause a short circuit (Fig. 2). No spark will occur, and the engine is said to be misfiring.

Thus, in selecting spark plugs for your car, heat range, as it is called, becomes a major factor. Heat range is determined by the length of a spark plug's lower insulator (Fig. 3). The longer this insulator, the hotter the temperature at which the plug will operate; the shorter the insulator, the cooler the temperature at which the plug will operate.

Each size spark plug is manufactured in a number of ranges from "cold" to "hot." A cold plug rids itself of heat rapidly and won't overheat and cause preignition when temperature in the cylinder is relatively high. You would use a cold plug

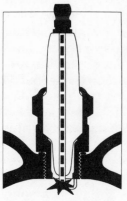

Figure 1. When spark occurs at the proper instant across the plug gap, ignition is normal.

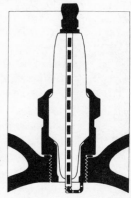

Figure 2. When deposits bridge the electrode gap, a short occurs and the plug won't fire.

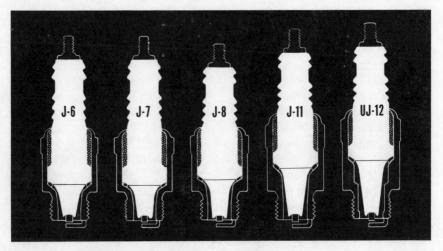

Figure 3. Every plug falls into a specific heat range from the coldest (left) to the hottest.

when the engine is operated primarily under heavy load conditions, such as in predominately high speed operation or when the car is pulling a trailer.

A hot spark plug rids itself of heat slowly and is used to discourage plug fouling when cylinder temperature is relatively low as it would be, for instance, under predominately idle and stop-and-go city driving conditions.

Since each size of spark plug is manufactured in a number of heat ranges (as you can see by Fig. 3, as many as five may be offered), how does one determine exactly which spark plug is best suited for his engine? Begin with the spark plug that is recommended by the manufacturer of your car. You can determine which by consulting the owner's manual to your car or by checking with a dealer who sells that make.

Operate the car for a week or two with the recommended plug. Then, remove a few from the engine and examine the tips. If they are gray or light tan and are coated with a light chalky deposit, continue using this spark plug. However, if tips are sooty or oily, the engine needs a hotter plug. If tips are ghostly white, a colder plug should be used.

In switching to a hotter or colder spark plug, move to the one that is next on the heat range scale. Test it as you did the plug which is recommended by the manufacturer.

In finding out what plug the manufacturer recommends, you have determined what size spark plug your engine takes. The correct size is the one whose thread and reach will fit the dimen-

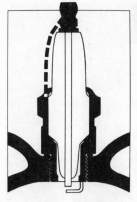

Figure 4. Flashover is caused by dirt and grease on the plug insulator and by worn out boots.

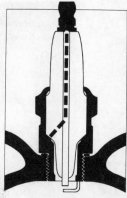

Figure 5. A cracked insulator, which allows voltage to leak to ground, causes engine misfire.

sional requirements of the engine. Size is given in code, but this is unimportant.

For example, if the spark plug recommended for your engine is a J-8, it means that your engine requires a spark plug that has a 14-millimeter thread and ³/₈-inch reach. However, all you have to tell the auto supply dealer from whom you buy parts is that you need the next colder (or hotter) plug from J-8. He has size, reach, and heat range charts which will tell him what plug that is.

Spark plugs should be serviced after every 5,000 miles of use. You will need a small ignition file and a spark plug feeler gauge, which can be purchased from a dealer of auto supplies. You will also need an old hacksaw blade which has been ground to a ⅛-inch taper at one end.

Remove plugs from the engine with a 6-point deep socket. A socket that is ¹³/₁₆ inch will fit most plugs. Loosen each plug, but before taking it from the engine blow foreign particles from around the plug with an ear syringe that you can buy in a drug store. If particles accidentally drop into the cylinder as a plug is being removed, they can damage the cylinder.

As you remove each plug, wipe its porcelain clean with a rag and examine it closely for visible damage. If dirt and grease are allowed to accumulate on the plug insulator, a condition called flashover may result which causes misfire (Fig. 4). Furthermore, a cracked insulator will divert high voltage to ground. This will keep the plug from firing and will cause engine misfire (Fig. 5). Discard damaged plugs.

Incidentally, as you remove each plug from the engine and after wiping it clean, mark from what cylinder it came. A plug should always be reinstalled in the same cylinder. This can be done by writing the cylinder number on the plug with a grease

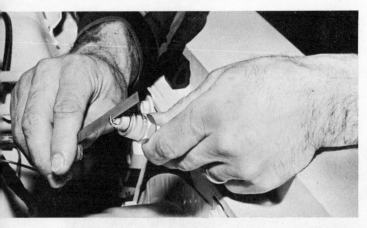

Figure 6. Use an ignition file to square a plug's electrodes. Filing also removes deposits.

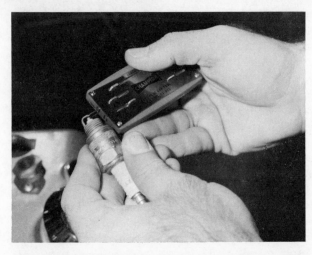

Figure 7. Be sure to purchase a spark plug feeler tool. There are others that can't be used.

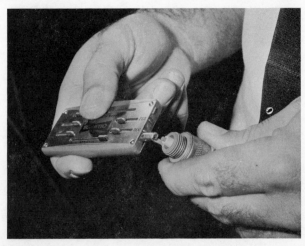

Figure 8. Use no other tool to bend the side electrode but the bending bar of the feeler tool.

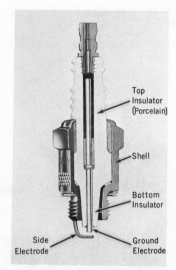

Top
Insulator
(Porcelain)

Shell

Bottom
Insulator

Side
Electrode

Ground
Electrode

Figure 9. This cross-sectional view of a spark plug will help you identify important parts.

pencil, but be sure to wipe this off before reinstalling the plug. If you think that you will be confused when it comes to matching spark plug cables with their respective plugs, also mark the cylinder number on the cable. This can be done by writing numbers on clip-type clothespins and clipping each clothespin to the respective cable.

To service spark plugs, first clean the electrode end by scraping deposits from the insulator with the hacksaw blade. Scrape hard. You won't hurt the plug.

Now, file the electrodes with the ignition file until sharp, bright, and square edges are obtained (Fig. 6). Finally, reset electrode gap to specification with the feeler gauge.

Insert the proper size feeler between electrodes (Fig. 7). The electrodes are properly gapped if you can pull the feeler from between electrodes, but there is slight resistance.

Spark plugs are usually set for a gap of 0.035 inch. However, there are exceptions, so be sure to check the owner's manual for your car or with a dealer.

If gap has to be adjusted, bend the plug's side electrode with the small bending bar, which your spark plug feeler gauge should have (Fig. 8). Do not bend the center (ground) electrode (Fig. 9). You will damage the plug beyond repair. Furthermore, do not use any other tool except the bending bar for the bending operation. Bending an electrode with pliers, for example, will ruin the plug.

It is important that electrode gap be checked even if you install a set of new spark plugs. Plugs are not set at the factory.

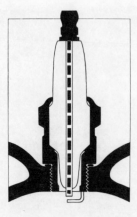

Figure 10. When plug electrode gap becomes too wide, voltage won't be able to jump the gap.

If the gap is allowed to become too wide or too badly worn, the engine will misfire (Fig. 10). Naturally, if spark plug electrodes are so badly worn that they can't be gapped, replace the plugs.

To reinstall spark plugs, start each plug into its seat in the engine slowly and carefully so that threads aren't crossed. Tighten them as much as you can by hand.

If plugs are equipped with gaskets, give them one-half turn with the socket to assure a gastight seal (Fig. 11). If plugs don't have gaskets, they are of the taper seat design (Fig. 12). Use the socket to seat them firmly, but this does not mean that you should ram them down as much as possible.

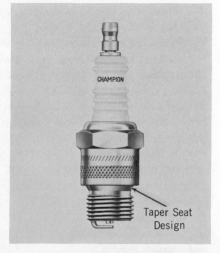

Figure 11. Some spark plugs use gaskets. Replace them whenever plugs are serviced for reuse.

Figure 12. Other plugs have a taper seat that seals gases effectively if snugly installed.

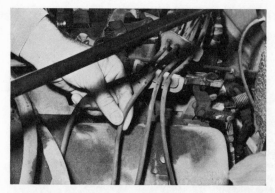

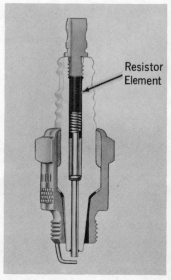

Resistor Element

Figure 13. Worn spark plug cables will leak current, resulting in no spark and misfiring.

Figure 14. Some engines use resistor spark plugs rather than resistance-type plug cables.

By the way, if the plugs you use need gaskets, always use new gaskets when reinstalling plugs. Once a gasket has been compressed and then removed from the engine, it will not make an effective gas seal if reused.

Several conditions affect the performance of spark plugs, such as fuel-air ratio, engine speed and load, and coil polarity. However, the factors described here are the most common and most important.

Worn out ignition cables and spark plug boots present engine problems which often lead drivers to blame spark plugs. Plugs are replaced, but the problem remains.

Cables which have deteriorated because of high underhood temperature and exposure to grease prevent current from reaching plugs, causing engine misfire. Inspect each cable carefully, looking for cracks in insulation (Fig. 13). If cables are to be replaced, be sure to determine if they are resistance cables which must be used to prevent interference with radio and television. If resistance cables aren't used in your car, then the car probably employs copper cable and resistor spark plugs which perform the same function as resistance cable (Fig. 14).

Be sure that new cables are installed as the old ones were to prevent crossfire which occurs when a spark plug fires out of turn because of induced voltage. Crossfire causes an engine to run rough and backfire. It could lead to major damage.

Crossfire occurs when cables are grouped closely together and run parallel. In some engines, the manufacturer purposely

Figure 15. Your engine may have wires crossed. The result of uncrossing them is crossfire.

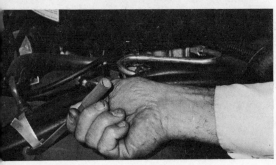

Figure 16. Cracked or brittle spark plug boots should be replaced to prevent flashover.

crisscrosses cables (Fig. 15). Do not straighten them out.

Dried out and cracked spark plug boots will lead to flashover. Examine boots and replace those that are cracked or brittle (Fig. 16).

Since spark plugs rely on the ignition system for voltage, a properly tuned ignition is necessary. Have the ignition tuned up every 12,000 miles, and make sure in particular that ignition timing is set exactly to manufacturer's specification.

The following chart explains conditions you are liable to find when examining plugs and what they mean:

Condition	Meaning	Procedure
All plugs have light tan or gray deposits and electrode wear not exceeding 0.005 inch (Fig. 17)	Plugs are wearing normally	Clean, regap, and reinstall
All plugs have heavy tan or gray deposits and electrode wear of more than 0.005 inch (Fig. 18)	Plugs are worn out	Replace with a new set of the same heat range

Condition	Meaning	Procedure
All plugs are coated with oil (Fig. 19)	Plugs are oil fouled because choke isn't operating properly, plugs are of incorrect heat range, or car's oil control is faulty	Check choke and service and reuse plugs; or switch to hotter plug; or check car's rings and seals, and reuse plugs
All plugs are heavily coated with deposits that flake off easily (Fig. 20)	Brand of gas being used contains additives that leave deposits	Switch to another brand and replace plugs with those of same heat range
One plug has melted electrodes (Fig. 21)	Preignition is occurring in the cylinder	Check for crossfire and intake manifold air leaks. Is plug the same heat range as others? Replace plug
Plug has broken insulator and bent electrodes (Fig. 22)	Foreign object has fallen into the combustion chamber	Major engine work is indicated. Replace plug
Side electrode looks like a question mark (Fig. 23)	Improper tool used to bend electrode during gapping	Replace plug. Use bending bar on feeler gauge to do gapping
Insulator of one or two plugs is chipped (Fig. 24)	Center electrode was bent during gapping, incorrect heat range plug was used, or ignition timing not timed correctly	Verify ignition timing, replace with plug of correct heat range, and gap with proper tool

Figure 17. All plugs normal.

Figure 18. All plugs worn.

Figure 19. Oil fouling.

Figure 20. Additive coating.

Figure 21. Preignition.

Figure 22. Mechanical damage. Figure 23. Ruined electrode. Figure 24. Chipped insulator.

AUTOMOTIVE, STALLING

When an engine that has been running suddenly stalls and won't restart, the problem can often be rectified, at least temporarily, so that you can drive the car to a mechanic. The following outlines what emergency action to take when you are on the road and this happens to you:

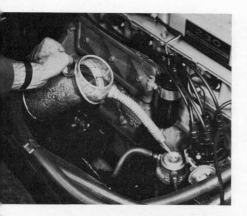

Figure 1. Vapor in the fuel pump can stop gas flow. Cold water will cause vapors to liquefy.

Figure 2. In pouring water over the carburetor, be sure none of it flows into the carburetor.

1. Are you out of gas? This is the main reason why drivers get stranded on the road. There is but one solution: get gas.

2. Did the engine stall when you stopped the car following highway operation? This is often caused by carburetor flooding. Slam the gas pedal to the floor and hold it there as you activate the starter. This will clear gasoline by allowing air to rush into the carburetor. If the engine doesn't start within 15 seconds, allow it to sit idle for about a minute before trying again.

3. Is the weather hot? The stall may have been caused by fuel vaporization, which is blocking the flow of gasoline to the engine (so-called vapor lock). If there is cold water available, pour it over the fuel pump, fuel line, and carburetor. Be careful not to pour water into the carburetor (Figs. 1 and 2). If water is not available, allow the engine to cool down. If vapor lock is the trouble, it will dissipate as heat diminishes.

4. Is it winter? A sliver of ice may have formed in the fuel system and is blocking the flow of gasoline. A quick attempt at repair is to pour some hot liquid (water or coffee, if a thermos is handy) over the carburetor and fuel line. Incidentally, if ice forming in the fuel system does occur, indicating that your engine is prone to such a thing, add a can of fuel system antifreeze (so-called dry gas) to the fuel tank at frequent intervals during the winter. This product can be purchased at service stations.

5. Did the car splash through water just before stalling or has it been raining heavily? Ignition parts may have gotten wet, which will cause the engine to stall. Thoroughly wipe off the distributor cap, ignition coil, and each spark plug with a cloth.

Figure 3. To dry off wet ignition wiring, remove each from distributor and coil (arrow).

Figure 4. Wipe off each spark plug. Also wipe each wire terminal connection dry (arrow).

To do this, remove high tension cables at the distributor cap one at a time and wipe out the tower (Fig. 3). Do the same to the high tension cable that is attached to the coil tower. And remove each spark plug cable by grasping the boot. Wipe off each plug (Fig. 4). Be sure that each cable is pushed back into place firmly. By the way, make certain that you do not pull on the wires themselves, but on the boots covering cable terminals. Cables will be damaged if you tug on them.

6. Make sure that all ignition wiring, specifically spark plug cables, wires going to the distributor cap, and the cable going to the center tower of the coil are well seated. Give each a firm push.

7. Reach up under the dashboard to the ignition switch and jiggle the switch, if the configuration of the dashboard permits this (Fig. 5). The switch may be loose. Shaking it could close the circuit and allow the engine to start. Have the switch tightened or replaced at the first opportunity.

Figure 5. Jiggling a faulty ignition switch may permit current to start its flow again.

*Figure 6. Push in all wires at the bulkhead connector,
which, if loose, will cause stalling.*

8. Another major cause of engine stalling is loose ignition wiring at the bulkhead connector, which is located on the firewall (Fig. 6). If ignition wires work loose while you are driving, the engine will stop dead in its tracks, because current flow to the engine will be halted. Push terminals firmly into the connector.

9. Examine battery cables. If terminals have worked loose from battery posts, tighten them. If terminals are dirty or badly corroded, remove them from battery posts and clean them with a penknife or a battery terminal cleaning tool, which is a valuable tool that you can buy in an automotive supply store for about $1.50. Reconnect terminals to posts, but be sure they are tight.

*Figure 7. If the choke butterfly plate
stays closed, wedge it open with a
book of matches.*

Figure 8. A dirt-clogged carburetor air filter will cause flooding and engine stalling.

Figure 9. Dirt beneath the needle may be dislodged by tapping at th line entry.

10. Remove the carburetor air cleaner and look at the choke butterfly plate. Since the engine is warm, the plate should be wide open. If it isn't, the engine has probably flooded, which caused stalling. A choke plate can become inoperative if the thermostatic spring, that is supposed to pull the plate open as the engine gets warm, becomes weak or breaks. As a temporary measure, wedge the plate open with a block of wood or with a book of matches that you have folded in half (Fig. 7).

11. Examine the carburetor air filter. If it has become clogged with dirt, the air supply to the carburetor will have been impeded, and flooding may have resulted. Remove the filter and try to start the engine (Fig. 8). If it starts, run the car without the filter element until you get to a service station, where a new filter can be purchased.

12. Another cause of stalling because the engine has flooded can be a sliver of dirt (or ice) that has wedged itself beneath the needle valve in the carburetor bowl. Tap the bowl near where the fuel line is attached with the handle of a screwdriver (Fig. 9). This may loosen the dirt and allow the needle valve to close.

13. Check to see if fuel is entering the carburetor by looking down the carburetor throat as you open and close the throttle. Throttle activation can be done by having someone step on the accelerator pedal. It may also be done at the carburetor by you by moving the throttle linkage (Fig. 10). If fuel is getting

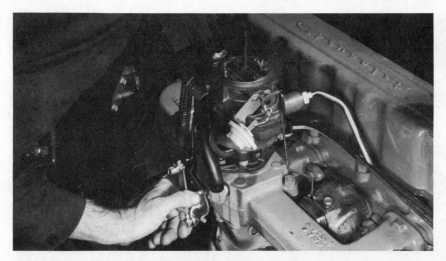

Figure 10. To determine if fuel is getting to the carburetor, activate the throttle linkage.

through to the carburetor, you will hear or see gas being squirted into the carburetor venturi.

If there is gas in the fuel tank, but no gas is reaching the carburetor, then the cause of stalling could be a bad fuel pump or, more likely, a clogged fuel filter. There is nothing that you can do about a bad fuel pump but replace it. However, an emergency procedure can be applied to get the engine restarted if a clogged fuel filter is the cause.

Today's engines normally have an external filter which is positioned in the fuel line between the fuel pump and carburetor. It is held by two clamps. Remove the filter by simply removing the clamps, and replace the filter with a length of ⁵⁄₁₆-inch hose, which is an item that you should carry in your emergency tool kit on the road (Fig. 11). Put the clamps back into position around the hose. This will allow you to get gas to the carburetor. As soon as you arrive at a service station, be sure to buy a new filter.

Figure 11. A piece of ⁵⁄₁₆-inch hose to replace a clogged filter will get you started again.

Figure 12. If the fuel filter is an internal type, you have to disconnect the fuel line.

Engines that don't have an external fuel filter usually have a filter in the carburetor. To get at it, disconnect the fuel line at the carburetor (Fig. 12). The filter is normally positioned at this inlet and can now be taken from place. Reconnect the fuel line. You will be able to run the engine without the filter, but get a new one as soon as possible.

AUTOMOTIVE, TIRE WEAR

Premature tire wear can be avoided if wear is noticed in its early stages and steps are taken to correct the cause. Misalignment of the front end and worn parts in the front end are major reasons for tires to wear out long before they should.

However, the *chief* reason for premature tire wear is avoidable. That reason is operation of tires with improper air pressure (Fig. 1).

Underinflated tires will show maximum wear on the outside edges of the tread. There will be little or no wear in the center

Figure 1. Long tire life is obtained with correct inflation.

Figure 2. **Underinflation:** *tires show heavy wear on the outside and least wear in the center.*

Figure 3. **Overinflation:** *tires show heavy wear in the center and least wear on the outside.*

(Fig. 2). Conversely, overinflated tires show wear in the center of the tread and little wear on the outside edges (Fig. 3).

Tire air pressure should be checked once a week with the tires cold (Fig. 4). Consult the owner's manual for your car to determine how much pressure you should use in your tires, or consult your mechanic or service station attendant.

Practically every driver has at one time or another heard the expressions "toe-in" and "toe-out." These refer to the difference in measurement between the front of the front wheels and the rear of the front wheels. When toe alignment is correct, the front wheels will roll freely without any detrimental force acting upon the tires. If toe is not in alignment, front wheels work against one another, causing tires to scuff abnormally (Fig. 5).

Figure 4. Check tire air pressure frequently. It's your best guarantee of maximum tire life.

Figure 5. Excessive toe-in (left) and toe-out (right) will result in rapid wear to tires.

Figure 6. Excessive camber results in rapid wear on one side of tires on the front of a car.

There are actually two distinct types of toe wear: constant and intermittent. Constant toe wear is caused by an incorrect alignment setting and is corrected by adjustment to specification. Intermittent toe wear occurs when a part in the front end becomes damaged, causing the toe adjustment to bounce alternately in and out of proper setting as the car is driven.

You cannot determine whether an intermittent toe wear problem exists by placing the car on a front end alignment machine, because the vehicle is at standstill and under a fixed load. Intermittent toe wear occurs when the car is driven and the load varies.

Intermittent toe wear, however, reveals itself through tire wear. If several of the tread ribs in the center of the tire are scuffed, but there is little or no wear on the outside edges, the problem is intermittent toe wear. By comparison, if *all* tread ribs show wear, a constant toe wear problem exists.

If the condition is constant toe-in, the outside edges of the ribs will show wear while the inside edges will show a sharp, ragged pattern. If the condition is constant toe-out, the same pattern will be formed, but in reverse. Constant toe wear is corrected by placing the car on a front end alignment machine and having the toe adjusted to specification.

Intermittent toe wear is not as simple to repair. First, the worn or loose suspension component must be found. It could be sagging springs, bad ball joints, loose or worn tie rod ends, worn idler arm bushings, or bent spindle supports or steering arms. The worn or loose part must be replaced.

Another condition that you can uncover by "reading your tires" is camber wear. Camber refers to the inward or outward tilt of the wheel and is the angle formed by the center line of the wheel and true vertical (Fig. 6). The inward tilt of a wheel is called negative camber, and the outward tilt of a wheel is called positive camber. As with toe wear, there are two types of camber wear: constant and intermittent.

Constant camber wear results from improper alignment and is relieved when camber is set to manufacturer's specification. If the outside edge of a tire shows accelerated wear, the specific problem is excessive constant positive camber (Fig. 7). If the inside edge of tire tread demonstrates accelerated wear, the

Figure 7. Positive camber: *tire shows accelerated wear on outside, minimum wear on inside.*

Figure 8. In a static wheel imbalance condition, vertical vibration of the car is created.

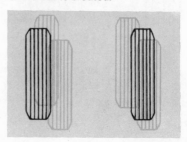

specific problem is excessive negative camber.

A loose or worn part in the front will produce intermittent camber wear. Almost every steering or suspension component that is damaged sufficiently to cause intermittent camber wear will also produce some degree of intermittent toe wear.

When tire wear is caused primarily by a change in camber, that wear will appear as uneven or spotty worn spots that look "knotty." Wear will show up toward the side of the tire. The conditions that cause intermittent wear in camber include worn ball joints, worn bushings in upper and lower control arms, a bent spindle support, or sagging springs.

The shorter radius followed by the inside wheel of an auto during a turn is obtained by introducing a toe change which varies in proportion to the degree of the turn. If this deliberately calculated change were not introduced, front tires would scuff badly. In other words, if the turning radius adjustment goes astray, tire wear will appear normal, except that tires will wear out at a much faster rate. Wear is often heavier at the tread edges. Furthermore, if turning radius is not to adjustment, tires will squeal on turns, including slow speed turns.

The chief causes of turning radius wear are worn tie rod ends and loose idler arm bushings. However, worn ball joints and control arm bushings and a bent steering arm can also contribute to the condition.

One condition that will cause premature wear of tires as quickly as any other is wheel imbalance. There are two types of wheel imbalance: static and dynamic.

Static imbalance causes a car to vibrate vertically (Fig. 8). One or more areas of the tire are forced heavily against the

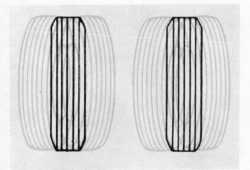

Figure 9. Dynamic wheel inbalance causes horizontal vibration, which creates flat spots.

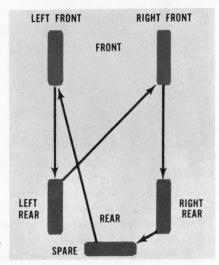

Figure 10. This diagram shows the right way to rotate tires.

pavement with each revolution of the wheel. Dynamic imbalance causes horizontal vibration (Fig. 9). The wheel oscillates, and a scuffing condition is created that soon produces flat spots in the tire.

With static balancing, a weight equal to the heavy spot on the wheel is placed opposite that spot. In the case of dynamic balancing, a weight equal in mass to that on the outside of the wheel is placed at the same point on the inside of the wheel.

Other forces that can contribute to premature tire wear are bad shock absorbers, loose front wheel bearings, and dragging or unequally acting brakes. If a tire problem occurs, be sure that these are checked as well.

Front and rear wheels wear differently even under normal driving conditions, because they do different kinds of work. Tires on one side of a car may also wear faster than those on the other side because of the crown of the road.

For these reasons, tires should be rotated and run in different wheel positions in accordance with car manufacturer's recommendations or every 5,000 miles to equalize wear and thereby increase mileage, handling and riding comfort (Fig. 10). Be certain that you recheck inflation after rotation to get proper front and rear pressure relationship.

AUTOMOTIVE, Upholstery

General overall cleaning of the interior of your car involves vacuuming, dusting with a whiskbroom, and wiping surfaces with a damp sponge or cloth.

Specifically, however, if upholstered areas are dirty, mix a sudsy warm water detergent or soap solution and apply suds to the upholstery with light rubbing. Do not use laundry soap, which contains alkaline.

Remove excess suds with a clean rag that is saturated in clean water. Allow the upholstery to dry.

If the soapy mixture fails to get upholstery clean, use a cleaner made by a car manufacturer or by a chemical company. These are available from new car dealers, automotive parts supply stores, and service stations. Be sure that you get a cleaner made for the type of material in the car.

Interior upholstery materials are either plastic or fabric. Everything which isn't plastic should be considered as fabric, including nylon, orlon, rayon, and viscose. The cleaners you use on plastic or fabric usually differ although there are some all-purpose cleaners on the market which can be used on both.

Fabric cleaner forms a soapy foam that is stronger than plain soap. Cleaners for plastic contain cleaning chemicals.

Fabric and rubber floor carpets may be cleaned the same way as upholstered parts. However, before cleaning, vacuum up loose dirt. If there is oil or grease on carpeting, clean it off with a volatile cleaner as discussed below.

Stains present an entirely different problem from ordinary dust and dirt. Remember that a new stain is easier to clean away than one which has settled, so attack a stain as soon as possible.

The cleaning agent you use, such as carbon tetrachloride or cleaning fluid, is volatile. Handle these with extreme caution. A volatile agent emits toxic fumes. Be sure that you use it outdoors and that the doors of the car remain open. If you accidentally breathe fumes, get into the fresh air as quickly as possible. To keep fumes away from you while using the cleaner, direct the blast from a small electric fan across the work area.

Keep in mind that the cleaning agent will do all the work. Do not rub the stain. In fact, apply the agent with as little pressure as possible.

Moisten a clean pad and gently wet the stain with a circular motion. Allow the cleaner several minutes to evaporate before applying a second application of the agent, if necessary.

The chart below will assist you in removing specific kinds of stains. If you don't know what kind of stain you're encountering, guess at it. Before applying the cleaning agent, dab some of it on to a small patch of upholstery that is hidden from view to make certain that the agent won't cause the material to fade.

Bright trim pieces on the inside of the car may look like chrome, but they are actually aluminum-coated plastic. Never use an auto polish or abrasive cleaner on them. You will rub away the finish.

To clean these pieces, simply wipe off dirt with a damp cloth or sponge and buff with a soft, dry cloth.

Stain	Cleaning Agent	Cleaning Procedure
Blood	Cold water; household ammonia; corn starch and cold water paste	Rub with clean cloth saturated with cold water. If stain remains, apply a little household ammonia with a rag or brush and follow with a cold water wash. Allow the ammonia to settle for two minutes before washing. If the stain remains, make a thick paste of corn starch and water. Apply to the stain. Let it dry. Then, pick it off and brush away particles. Keep applying paste until stain disappears
Candy other than chocolate	Hot water	Soak a cloth in very hot water and rub the spot
Chocolate	Lukewarm water; volatile cleaner	Rub the spot with lukewarm water. Follow with a light rubbing of volatile cleaner
Chewing gum	Ice cube; volatile cleaner	If the gum is soft, lay an ice cube on it until it hardens. Scrape off as much as possible with a dull knife or putty knife. If any gum remains, moisten the spot with volatile cleaner and scrape it off with a knife while the spot is still damp

Stain	Cleaning Agent	Cleaning Procedure
Grease, oil	Volatile cleaner	Scrape away as much as possible with a dull knife or putty knife. Rub lightly with a clean cloth saturated with volatile cleaner. Rub toward the center of the stain to prevent the stain from spreading
Ice cream	Hot water; neutral soap; volatile cleaner	Scrape off excess with dull knife and rub with cloth that has been dipped in very hot water. If stain remains, rub spot with a cloth that has been dipped in warm soap suds. Follow by rubbing with a clean cloth that has been moistened in cold water. Then rub lightly with volatile cleaner
Lipstick	Volatile cleaner	Scrape away excess with a dull knife. Follow by cleaning with a volatile cleaner
Nausea	Neutral soap; volatile cleaner	Sponge the area with a clean cloth that has been saturated with cold water. Follow with a washing of neutral soap suds in warm water. If stain remains, rub lightly with a cloth that has been dipped in a volatile cleaner
Shoe polish	Volatile cleaner	Water-soluble polishes, which are usually white, are easily removed by brushing them vigorously with a dry brush. Paste or wax polish can be removed with an application of a volatile cleaner
Tar	Volatile cleaner	Remove as much as possible with a dull knife or putty knife. Apply volatile cleaner and let it dry. Then, use the knife again to remove stain. Repeat as required

AUTOMOTIVE, WATER LEAKS

The hardest thing about repairing a water leak into a car is finding the leaking area. In most cases, this will be the front windshield or backlite (rear windshield), depending on whether water has shown up in the front of the car or on the rear deck or in the trunk.

To ascertain whether the windshield or backlite is leaking, tape a garden hose to the top of the car and place a can in front of the outlet. The can will allow water to disperse over the entire windshield or backlite (Fig. 1).

Turn on the water, but don't become impatient. If no water shows up in the front, on the rear deck, or in the trunk immediately, conduct the test for at least 30 minutes. It often takes this long. Every so often, rock the car from side to side. Sometimes water accumulates in a seam along the windshield and will start to leak only when you turn a corner.

If water is leaking in through the windshield or backlite, it will have to be sealed by first removing the molding. Never apply sealing compound over the molding. If the molding ever has to come off, the fact that it is sealed will present a greater chance of cracking the glass.

Use a windshield clip tool to remove the molding. This tool costs about $1 and can be purchased in an auto supply store. Don't use a screwdriver. You will crack the glass.

Slip the windshield clip tool beneath the molding and slide it until it strikes a clip. Carefully twist the tool to pop the molding loose (Fig. 2).

When molding has been removed, discard the old clips, which are probably damaged. Obtain new clips by taking one of

Figure 1. In testing for leaky windshields, a can allows wide dispersion of water over glass.

Figure 2. The windshield clip tool is the safest way to remove molding prior to sealing.

Figure 3. Use a quality sealing compound to seal around the entire windshield circumference.

Figure 4. A water leak into the trunk may not become apparent until someone sees it happen.

the old ones to an auto glass dealer. Make sure you get the right kind.

Tap the new clips into place and then apply sealing compound, such as 3M Weatherstrip Adhesive or silicone rubber made by Dow Chemical or General Electric (Fig. 3). Sealer can be purchased in an automotive supply store. Follow directions on the package, but be certain that the area is clean and dry and that a liberal bead is applied. Reattach molding by simply pressing it into place.

In the case of water leaking into the trunk, if the backlite doesn't seem to be leaking, have someone equipped with a flashlight crawl into the trunk (Fig. 4). Close the lid and slowly play a heavy spray of water on the backlite, trunk lid, around the stop lights, and on rear body seams (Fig. 5). The inspector will be able to see from where water is coming. When he spots the leak (or wants a breather), have him tap the trunk lid to tell you to open it.

Figure 5. With someone in the trunk, play a heavy stream of water over possible leak areas.

If water is coming in from around the trunk lid, pry off the gasket with a putty knife, reposition the gasket and glue it back into place with weatherstrip adhesive. If the stoplight housing or a seam is leaking, seal it from inside the trunk with spray undercoating, which you can buy in an auto supply store.

In the case of a leak in the front of the car, if no water appears during the windshield test, play a heavy spray of water from a hose for a minute or two on each area in the front that might be leaking, including the A-post (this is the part of the body on the side of the windshield), drip rails, and each bolt and seam on the firewall. Have someone in the car check to see if water appears. If a leak becomes apparent, seal the leaking part with silicone rubber compound or weatherstrip adhesive.

BATHTUB AND BATHROOM SINK

Sooner or later every homeowner is faced with the problem of what to do about the gap which appears around the perimeter of the bathtub and bathroom sink. This is a result of grout drying out with age, losing its flexibility, and crumbling. Grout is usually used by builders to seal joints between bathroom tile, bathtub and tile, and bathroom sink and tile.

It is important that the sealer which is used around a bathtub and bathroom sink maintain flexibility since the tub and sink shift as settling of a home occurs. Thus, refilling the crack with grout would only lead to the problem again within a comparatively short time. What you need is an elastic bathtub sealer which will maintain its flexibility for many years.

This ability is provided by so-called bathtub caulk which contains silicone or vinyl plastic. Several companies, including General Electric, Dow Chemical, Dap, and Miracle Adhesive, make such a product. It is sold in tubes in hardware stores. A repair made with this sealant will last indefinitely (Fig. 1).

Figure 1. Modern bathtub caulk with silicone rubber or vinyl plastic maintains flexibility.

Figure 2. Clean the joint thoroughly and fill it with sealer. Be sure that no voids remain.

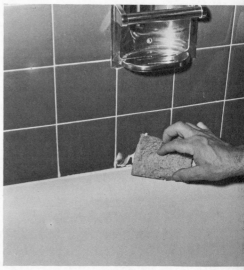

Figure 3. For a neat and smooth finish, gently wipe away excess bathtub caulk with a spatula.

Figure 4. If sealer inadvertently gets on tile, wash it off at once with a sponge or rag.

To use the sealer, the joint area must be thoroughly clean and dry. Remove old crumbling grout by probing it loose from the crack with a thin-bladed screwdriver or similar tool. Use a small wire brush to get all particles loose. A small paint brush will allow you to brush the cavity free of residue. After particles and residue have been removed, be sure to wash the entire joint with rubbing alcohol to remove tub soil and other dirt.

Allow the surface to dry. Then, simply place the nozzle of the tube into the crack and squeeze the sealant into place along the perimeter (Fig. 2). Use a moist spatula or a moist finger to smooth the material, if necessary (Fig. 3).

Silicone and vinyl plastic sealants begin to cure in a few minutes and harden sufficiently in about 1 hour to permit use of the bathtub or sink. The material is thoroughly cured in 24 hours. At full cure it is, of course, 100 percent waterproof.

If you accidentally get some of the material on tile or fixture as you apply it, be sure that you wipe it away with a damp cloth or sponge at once (Fig. 4). Once it dries, you will have to cut the material off. Some sealants are soluble in water in their freshly applied state; others are soluble in mineral spirits and turpentine. Consult the package instructions to determine which applies.

Incidentally, silicone and vinyl plastic sealers can be used for other repairs in the bathroom, such as reinstalling ceramic tile which has come loose, and fastening towel racks and soap dishes to ceramic tile.

BOAT, BOTTOM PAINT

The bottom of your boat must be protected by paint. This is obvious. However, the important question that you should ask yourself is, "Which of the many varieties being sold by marine dealers should I select?"

Use of the wrong kind of bottom paint for particular conditions could result in a paint job which will soon fail, wasting time and money, and possibly damaging the boat.

Bottom paints are of two general types: antifouling and nonantifouling. A nonantifouling paint does not contain a poisonous toxicant. It produces a hard, smooth enamel finish that is less expensive and easier to apply to a hull than an antifouling paint. Thus, you will want to use a nonantifouling paint if it is at all possible.

A nonantifouling paint can be safely employed if you take the boat from the water after each cruise, whether the water is salt or fresh water. Marine organisms that form on the hull will die when out of water.

You may also safely use a nonantifouling bottom paint if you moor your boat in fresh water where current is strong. Fouling organisms don't usually thrive in fresh, moving water.

Boats which are moored in salt water, however, are subject to the most serious threat, and their hulls should be treated with an antifouling paint. Without this protection, a hull can accumulate sufficient marine organisms in 48 hours to seriously hamper performance. A collection of foreign matter on wooden, fiberglass, metal, or plastic hulls will cause a reduction in boat speed. Furthermore, if your boat has a wooden hull that is used in salt water and it isn't protected by antifouling paint, the hull can be destroyed by the termitelike teredo worm.

When an antifouling paint comes into contact with water, it releases a toxicant, such as cuprous oxide, which poisons marine organisms and plants that may cling to the hull. There are five types of antifouling paint: soft copper, vinyl copper, epoxy, copper bronze, and tin base. It is important, as well as economically wise, that you select the right one for conditions.

As a rule, epoxy bottom paint is the most expensive, selling for about $12 per quart. Soft copper is generally the least expensive, selling for about $4 per quart. However, bear in mind that some makes of soft copper paint sell for $13 to $15 per quart. This points up the fact that the price of an antifouling bottom paint is proportional to the amount of toxicant in the paint.

As a rule, once you have put one type of paint on your boat,

Figure 1. To apply a different type of paint, the noncomplimentary paint should come off.

Figure 2. For obvious reasons, wear a respirator as you sand.

try always to use the same type. If the paint doesn't seem to combat organisms adequately, switch to a more expensive paint of the *same* type. For example, if you paint your boat with a soft copper paint that doesn't seem to afford adequate protection, switch to a more expensive soft copper paint which contains a greater concentration of toxicant.

Putting one type of paint over another (epoxy over soft copper, for instance) can cause the new coating to peel because of differences in the compositions of the two paints. This is true even if the two paints are made by the same company and a primer is used.

However, if you must use a different type of paint, the old coating should be sanded off to assure adequate results (Figs. 1 and 2).

The following summarizes the uses and characteristics of each of the different types of antifouling paints:

Soft copper paint has a soft binder that wears away to release the toxicant as the hull slices through the water. Because of the low concentration of poison in all but the most expensive products, soft copper paint is suitable for use on boats that are removed from the water at the end of a few months so that repainting may be done. Boats sailed in temperate climates, for example, where the boating season is comparatively brief are suited for soft copper paint.

Vinyl copper paint possesses a hard binder that wears away slowly. For the most part, it contains a greater concentration of toxicant than soft copper paint and sells for $8 to $10 per quart. It is suitable for boats that are kept in the water for long periods between repaintings, such as those that are sailed in tropical climates.

Epoxy paint has the greatest concentration of toxicant and the toughest binder. It is made to combat extreme fouling conditions but, as noted, is very expensive.

Copper bronze paint is manufactured primarily for sailboats, racing hulls, and other types of speed craft. The paint provides a smooth coating on the hull that gives a minimum of friction. Cost is about the same as copper vinyl paint, but the life expectancy of copper bronze paint is about equal to that of the less expensive soft copper paint.

Tin base bottom paint is designed for use on metal hulls, especially aluminum. The tin toxicant won't cause electrolytic decomposition of the metal as might happen with the copper toxicant that is found in other types of antifouling paint.

When selecting an antifouling paint, consider local fouling conditions. Consult with other boatmen, the harbor master, marine architects, or marina personnel to determine the fouling rate in the area and, thus, the quality of paint you should use. Keep in mind, though, that the density of organisms in water is cyclical. An increase in the salinity of the water, an influx of

Figure 3. For paint to adhere properly, the hull must be free of dirt and foreign material.

Figure 4. To repair a scrape in the new coating, sand the area clean and spot it with paint.

organic sewage, or a change in water temperature can cause an increase in organisms, and you may eventually have to switch to a better grade of paint.

In painting a boat's bottom with an antifouling paint, bear in mind that there are several reasons why the paint can fail prematurely. These reasons are as follows:

• The manufacturer's instructions on how to apply paint are disregarded. Read instructions carefully.

• Paint is applied to an improperly prepared surface. The surface must be dry and free from dirt, oil, and grease (Fig. 3).

• The new coating is scraped when the boat is launched (Fig. 4).

• The boat isn't launched when it should be. Hulls painted with soft copper paint, for example, must be launched almost immediately after painting. See instructions on the paint can regarding this.

• Not enough paint is applied. A minimum of two coats is recommended.

• Paint is applied at the wrong time. Temperature should be 50° to 80°F, humidity should be 65 percent or lower, and the weather should be calm and sunny.

• Aluminum that is being painted for the first time isn't etched as instructed on the paint can label.

The chart below will assist you in determining how much paint you need.

Paint Calculator

Type of Craft	Size	Quantity of Paint*
Dinghy	10'	1 pint
Rowboat	14'	1 quart
Outboard	14'	1 quart
Runabout	18'	2 quarts
Sailboat	20'	3 quarts
Runabout	24'	3 quarts
Utility	24'	3 quarts
Cruiser	25'	3 quarts
Cruiser	32'	1½ gallons
Auxiliary	36'	2 gallons
Cruiser	40'	2 gallons
Yacht	60'	5 gallons

*For *repainting* a hull with two coats. If two coats are to be applied to a *bare* surface, double the quantities given.

BOAT, ENGINE

This section applies to inboard and inboard/outboard (stern drive) gasoline engines. It also deals with the outdrive portion of an inboard/outboard motor. Naturally, a boat powered by a straight inboard engine does not have an outdrive. It is equipped with a marine transmission, which is discussed in a separate section (see Boat, Hydraulic Transmission).

The following services should be performed after 50 hours of engine operation:

• Start the engine to put the fuel and cooling systems under pressure. Examine fuel lines and cooling system hoses for leaks and make sure that all connections and clamps are tight (Fig. 1).

Make sure that cooling system hoses aren't cracked. Squeeze each. If it feels soft and spongy, replace it. The hose is failing and is liable to breakdown while you are under way.

• Bring the engine to normal operating temperature to allow residue inside the engine to suspend itself in the motor oil. If you can reach the crankcase drain plug, remove it and drain off old oil into a container. If the drain plug is not accessible, oil will have to be pumped from the crankcase through the dipstick tube with an oil sump pump.

Clean or replace the oil filter. Most engines use a cartridge filter which has to be unscrewed with a strap wrench (Fig. 2). When installing a new filter, simply screw it on handtight. Do not use a wrench.

Some engines employ an element filter which can be cleaned in kerosene and reused.

Figure 1. Tighten all hose connections and clamps to prevent the loss of fuel and coolant.

Figure 2. A strap wrench, which isn't expensive, is usually required to loosen an oil filter.

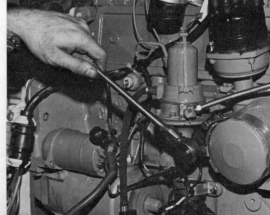

Figure 3. Each flame arrestor should be removed from its carburetor for thorough cleaning.

Figure 4. This is a sediment bowl type fuel filter than can be disassembled for cleaning.

Incidentally, if engine oil pressure suddenly drops as the engine is being operated at high speed, the oil filter is probably clogged. It is a good idea to carry a spare one on board for such emergencies. If one isn't available, head for the dock at low engine speed.

Add the type and grade of oil which is recommended by the manufacturer of your boat in the owner's manual. Generally, marine engines require 5 or 6 quarts of oil.

• If carburetors are equipped with flame arrestors, remove them and clean in mineral spirits (Fig. 3). Allow the arrestors to dry thoroughly before they are reinstalled. Use new gaskets.

Make sure that you do not overtighten a flame arrestor. Overtightening will compress the element and choke off air to the carburetor, causing the carburetor to operate in an over-rich condition. Flame arrestors should be fingertight only.

• Close off the fuel line valve to prevent gas flow and clean or replace the fuel filter. Some engines have a sediment bowl filter at the fuel pump that can be cleaned by unscrewing the bowl, removing the filter, and washing elements in gasoline or kerosene (Fig. 4). If your boat has the type of sediment bowl filter that drops down, keep gas from spilling into the bilge by loosening the screw that holds the bowl and slipping a plastic bag over the bowl. Remove bag and bowl, plus gasoline, together.

Figure 5. To check the positive crankcase ventilation system, hold a finger
over the valve.

Figure 6. A few drops of SAE 10W motor
oil on the wick will help the distributor
function.

The other type of fuel filter used on marine engines is an inline filter which is cut into the fuel line between the fuel pump and carburetor. It has a paper element that cannot be cleaned. This filter should be replaced.

• If your boat's engine is equipped with a positive crankcase ventilation (PCV) system, like the one on your car, it must be cleaned to prevent engine blowby, loss of oil, and shoddy engine performance. Pull the PCV valve from the engine valve cover, start the engine, and place a finger over the valve (Fig. 5). You should feel a strong vacuum. If you don't, remove the PCV valve from the hose and place your finger over the hose. If you now feel vacuum, replace the PCV valve.

• Most marine engine water pumps have prelubricated and sealed ball bearings. They require no lubrication. Some engines, however, have a double-gear type pump which has grease cups in the drive gear housing. Check the owner's manual to determine if your engine is equipped with this kind of water pump. If it is, grease it with water pump lubricant.

Similarly, most modern marine engines are equipped with AC generators (alternators) that require no lubrication and with starter motors that have sealed bearings. However, if you have a DC generator and starter motor which possess oil cups, lubricate them with three or four drops of SAE 30 motor oil.

• Remove the distributor cap and rotor and place three drops of SAE 10W motor oil on the felt wick on top of the breaker cam (Fig. 6). Be careful not to get oil on the distributor breaker points, which should be inspected. If points are badly burned or pitted, replace them.

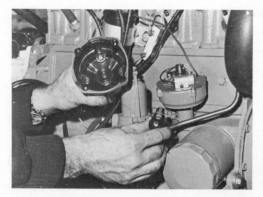

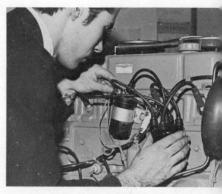

Figure 7. A sound distributor cap and rotor will assure that full current will be available.

Figure 8. Weak ignition cables will rob your engine of current it needs for good performance.

Check the distributor rotor and the contacts inside the distributor cap for traces of arcing (Fig. 7). Rotor and contacts should be clean and bright with no carbon covering them. If either is damaged or discolored, replace the part.

Apply five drops of SAE 10W motor oil to the oil cup on the distributor housing if you find one. Some distributors are to be lubricated; others do not require lubrication.

• Examine spark plug cables and boots carefully for cracks and wear (Fig. 8). If cables or boots are cracked or show signs of deterioration, replace them.

• Remove spark plugs for examination and servicing as outlined in the section entitled Automotive, Spark Plugs. The information concerning automotive engine spark plugs apply as well to spark plugs that are used in marine engines.

• Check the specific gravity of the battery and service the battery as outlined in the section on Automotive, Battery. As with spark plugs, what applies to an automotive battery will apply to a battery that is used in a boat.

• Check drive belts for splits, glazed marks, and fraying. Replace a damaged belt. Check belt tension, which should allow for no more than ¼ inch of free play (Fig. 9). If a belt is too loose, tighten it.

Figure 9. You can usually tell if a drive belt needs tightening by pushing on it by hand.

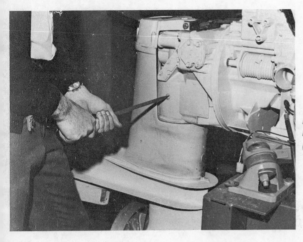

Figure 10. The outdrive you see
is having the upper case drain
plug removed to drain off oil.

To service the outdrive end of an inboard/outboard, the boat
must come out of the water. You will need a lubrication chart,
which is probably included in your owner's manual, because
outdrive units differ from manufacturer to manufacturer. Some,
for example, have one drain plug for oil. Others have more. The
outdrive depicted here, for example, has three separate sections
that have to be checked: a lower unit, upper case, and interme-
diate unit (Fig. 10).

Before draining oil from an outdrive, run the unit for a few
minutes so that lubricant will flow easily. The type of oil that
you put back into the outdrive depends on what type of unit it
is. Most outdrives require an SAE 90 hypoid gear oil, but there
are some that use an SAE 10W-30 or SAE 20W-40 motor oil.
Consult your lubrication chart.

The lubrication chart will also inform you as to the other
parts of the outdrive that require lubrication. The outdrive depicted here, for instance, requires lubrication of trunnions and
swivel bearings (Figs. 11 and 12).

Figure 11. Some outdrives have trunnions on both of its sides that need periodic lubrication.

Figure 12. Consult the lubrication chart
to find out if the swivel bearings need
greasing.

Figure 13. Care of the propeller calls for carefully filing off minor damage from blades.

Many outdrives employ so-called sacrificial anodes which are attached to the housing to protect it from the electrolytic action of salt water. At midseason, these anodes are usually corroded to 50 percent of their original size, which is the limit at which they should be used.

Now, inspect the propeller. File away small nicks and burrs, but do not remove too much metal (Fig. 13). If the prop is badly damaged or cracked, replace it.

Lubricate the propeller shaft with an antiseize compound or a waterproof grease before putting the prop back on.

Finally, give the entire outdrive a close inspection for paint damage and corrosion. Sand or wire brush corroded or marred areas to bare metal and apply an antifouling paint. The color that you need is available in aerosol spray cans from a boat dealer.

BOAT, FIBERGLASS REPAIR

A fiberglass boat is most likely to incur five kinds of damage: gouges, scratches, grazed cracking, wrinkling, and loss of gloss. Each requires a somewhat different method of repair, but before explaining these, it is necessary to discuss for a minute the nature of fiberglass.

The surfaces of most fiberglass boats consist of two layers of material which are bonded together by chemical action. The outside layer is a colored gel coat which is a special smooth resin material that incorporates a concentrated color to provide a finished surface. The layer beneath the gel coat is a polyester resin that adheres to and is reinforced by laminations of fiberglass matting, cloth, or woven roving.

Figure 1. All damaged material must be cleaned away before a permanent repair can be made.

Figure 2. Use a piece of 100-grit sandpaper to roughen the spot to give putty a firm base.

The gel coat and polyester resin are cured with a catalyst that allows them to form a hard, strong mass which is very difficult to penetrate. The only way in which this mass can be damaged is by gouging, and we therefore begin the discussion of how to repair fiberglass by dealing with this type of damage.

Once a fiberglass surface is gouged, the ruptured material has to be cleaned away so that the fiberglass laminations are revealed. Routing of the distressed material can be done with a putty knife or similar tool (Fig. 1).

After clearing away the distressed material, clean off the fiberglass and, at the same time, roughen it with a piece of 100-grit sandpaper so that the repair putty will have a good solid base on which to take hold (Fig. 2). Wash the area down with a cloth that has been saturated in acetone or lacquer thinner, making sure that all dirt and foreign material which would affect adhesion of the repair putty are eliminated.

The repair putty is a polyester compound that can be obtained from a boat supply store. It must be mixed thoroughly with the catalyst which accompanies it (Fig. 3). Follow instruc-

Figure 3. Make sure that putty and catalyst are thoroughly mixed to prevent breakdown.

Figure 4. Apply enough of the repair putty to cover the entire area. Fill the spot full.

tions which come in the repair kit. After mixing catalyst and putty, pack the putty firmly into the routed out hole, building it up to about ⅛ of an inch above the surface of the hull (Fig. 4).

Now, place a sheet of cellophane over the patch to keep the air from it while it cures. Air causes repair putty to breakdown as it dries. Press the cellophane into place with a rubber squeegee.

As you wait for the repair putty to dry, which takes about an hour, mask off the damaged area with paper and masking tape in preparation for the gel coating. Masking assures that adjacent surfaces will not accidentally be coated with the gel finish (Fig. 5).

When the repair putty feels hard to the touch, strip off the cellophane and sand the patch with 220-grit sandpaper until the area is flat and smooth. Use a vibrator sander if one is available (Fig. 6). As an alternative, you can hold the sandpaper by hand, but be sure that the sandpaper is on a sanding block.

Figure 5. Mask off the spot to be coated so that the gel overspray doesn't mar nearby areas.

Figure 6. Use a vibrator sanding machine, if available. It will give the smoothest finish.

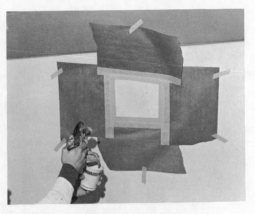

Figure 7. When sanding has been completed, apply the gel coat, with a paint brush if necessary.

Figure 8. Spraying on the gel coat will provide you with the smoothest and most even finish.

Wash the surface with water and sand the area once again, this time by hand with a piece of *wet* 400-grit sandpaper. Wet the paper often. Follow this sanding step with still another sanding. For the final sanding phase, use wet 600-grit sandpaper.

The repair is completed by applying the gel coat. Ideally, this should be the same gel coat used by the manufacturer of your boat so that the color matches. The builder of your boat can tell you where to purchase this coating if you write or phone him.

The gel coat can be applied with a paint brush if a paint spray gun is not available (Fig. 7). However, to obtain the best possible finish, you should use a spray gun (Fig. 8).

The most common problem that owners of fiberglass boats encounter is scratching of the fiberglass surface. To get rid of scratches, wash down the marred area with acetone or lacquer thinner to remove grease and grit that can cause additional scratches while the work is being performed.

Lightly sand the scratch with a piece of wet 400-grit sandpaper (Fig. 9). Keep your eye on the scratch so that sanding can

Figure 9. Scratches in a fiberglass hull are treated with wet sandpaper. Do not press hard.

Figure 10. Use compound to restore gloss to areas from which scratches have been removed.

be halted as soon as the scratch disappears. Be careful not to press too hard on the sandpaper, since it is possible to dig into the gel coat finish.

After sanding, wash the area with acetone or lacquer thinner, and then buff to restore gloss and to remove minor scratches that the sandpaper may have left. Hold the buffing machine at a 45° angle and use a light abrasive rubbing compound, such as Mirro Glaze No. 1. If you buff the surface by hand, use a slightly harsher grit compound, such as DuPont No. 7 or No. 101S (Fig. 10).

Grazed cracks in the gel coat of a fiberglass boat resemble a spider web. They can be removed by sanding the area with 100-grit sandpaper. Use a sanding block to hold the sandpaper.

Make sure that you remove all of the grazed cracks. If any are left, they will spread after the boat has been returned to the water, and your work will have been for nothing.

It will be difficult not to make ripples and indentations in the gel coat as you sand. However, if no ripples or indentations appear, you can spray on a new coating of gel coat as soon as the sanding step is completed. Otherwise, plastic repair putty will have to be used.

Apply the putty with a rubber squeegee, being sure to fill each indentation. Cover the patch with cellophane until the putty hardens. Then sand the area with 220-, 400-(wet), and 600-grit (wet) sandpaper, in turn, until the surface is smooth and even. Complete the repair by applying the gel coat.

Wrinkles in the gel coat are a result of sloppy workmanship in manufacture. Scrape off as many of the wrinkles as possible with a putty knife. Then, sand the area smooth with 100-grit sandpaper to remove the remaining wrinkles. Be sure to use a sanding block.

Figure 11. The best way to restore the gloss to a fiberglass hull is with a buffer and pad.

Wash the surface thoroughly with acetone or lacquer thinner, and mix a quantity of plastic repair putty. Apply it with a rubber squeegee as smoothly and as evenly as possible, and then cover the patch with cellophane until the putty hardens. Sand with 220-, 400-(wet), and 600-grit (wet) sandpaper until the surface is smooth and free from scratches. Complete the repair by applying gel coat.

The gloss of a fiberglass hull can easily be restored. Wash down the surface with acetone or lacquer thinner. Then, with a buffing machine and compound (Mirro Glaze No. 1), buff the surface.

Hold the buffer at a 45° angle and apply little pressure at corners and edges to keep from rubbing off the gel coat. Complete the task by equipping the buffer with a fresh polishing pad. Hold the pad flat against the surface with light pressure and buff to a high gloss (Fig. 11).

BOAT, HYDRAULIC TRANSMISSION

In order to avoid having to completely overhaul the hydraulic transmission in your boat, which will cost from $150 to $400, you should check the transmission oil before every trip and change transmission oil when you change motor oil. This will allow you to uncover a problem in its initial stage, at which point the cost of repair seldom exceeds $50.

To check oil level before a cruise, remove the transmission dipstick. In some transmissions, such as Warner, the dipstick is a threaded pipe plug that is forward of the control lever. It has to be unscrewed (Figs. 1 and 2). On other transmissions, such as Paragon, the dipstick is a bayonet type that resembles the engine oil dipstick. Pull it out (Fig. 3).

Figure 1. In this transmission, a Warner, the oil dipstick is removed by unscrewing a plug.

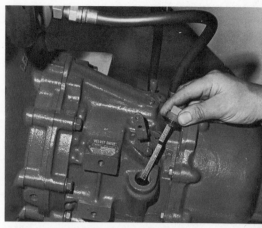

Figure 2. The best way to avert serious expensive transmission damage is to examine the fluid.

Figure 3. In this transmission, a Paragon, the oil dipstick is of bayonet design. Pull it out.

Figure 4. Once the rear flange coupling rusts, it isn't long before the oil seal ruptures.

If the transmission oil level is below the "full" mark, the oil must have gone somewhere. There is probably a defective seal or gasket. Check *engine* oil. Is it *above* the "full" mark on the dipstick? If so, it means that transmission oil is getting into the crankcase through a bad front end plate oil seal.

In most cases, however, loss of transmission oil signifies a defective rear end oil seal. This can be prevented by keeping a tidy bilge.

When water is allowed to build up in the bilge, it swamps the rear flange coupling, causing it to rust (Fig. 4). As the shaft

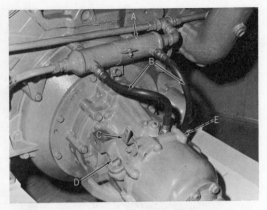

Figure 5. The coupling must remain clean and smooth, so make certain a tidy bilge is kept.

Figure 6. (A) Transmission oil cooler; (B) hoses; (C) control lever; (D) dipstick; (E) drain.

spins, it grinds rust into the seal, causing it to rupture and allowing transmission oil to be lost. The rear flange coupling on which the seal rides must be clean and smooth (Fig. 5).

If the transmission oil is above the "full" mark on the dipstick when you make the before-cruise inspection, it means that water is leaking into the transmission because of a defective oil cooler (Fig. 6). As you know, the oil cooler has the job of drawing in sea water and circulating it to keep the transmission from overheating. Water in the transmission oil can usually be verified by the color of the fluid. If it has turned from its normal reddish color to milky white, the oil cooler has a malfunction and should be replaced.

In replacing the oil cooler, make sure that all contaminated oil is drained from the transmission, that the transmission is flushed to eliminate all traces of water, and that new transmission oil is installed.

The appearance of the transmission oil during the before-cruise examination is important for another reason. If the oil is dark (almost black) and smells like varnish, the clutch plates are starting to burn. This usually happens when transmission oil overheats because of a blocked oil cooler. Remove the hose at the inlet side of the cooler and check inside the inlet for a blockage, such as seaweed and pieces from a plastic bag.

Periodically examine the hoses between the oil cooler and the transmission. Look for cracks. Squeeze each hose. If it feels soft and spongy, replace it. If a weak hose is permitted to remain in service, it may fail at a bad time, such as when you are cruising miles from shore. To remove a hose, simply unscrew it. Hoses are generally held by ⅜-inch pipe fittings (Fig. 7).

Incidentally, hoses should never be painted. Solvents in paint will cause rubber to deteriorate.

Transmission oil should be drained when engine oil is drained, which is after every 50 hours of operation instead of after every 100 hours as recommended in transmission manuals. Some transmission problems just won't wait that extra 50 hours.

Remove the drain plug and allow oil to drain into a clean container. When draining has been completed, examine the oil closely for flakes of metal (bronze and steel) and for sludge. Although it has been used, the drained oil should be crystal clear.

Metal particles or sludge in oil signal a serious problem, such as clutch plate slippage or initial bearing failure. The trouble should be attended to immediately, before it gets worse and costs more money to repair.

Some transmissions, such as Capitol and Warner, use a pickup screen in the drain plug hole to catch foreign particles that circulate in the fluid. When the drain plug (or oil line connection) has been disconnected and the oil has drained, pull the screen from place and examine it for particles and sludge (Fig. 8). Clean the screen in kerosene before putting it back.

Paragon and other transmissions don't have this type of filter. You will have to examine the drained oil.

The owner's manual for your boat will tell you which type of transmission oil you should use. In most cases, it is type A, suffix A automatic transmission fluid, which is the same oil that is used in a car's automatic transmission. You can buy it in a gasoline station.

Fill the transmission until oil shows at the "full" mark on the dipstick. Run the engine for a minute or two at low rpm to circulate oil through the system. Then, shut the engine off and

Figure 7. Inspect hoses often. Replace those that show cracks, or are soft, spongy to touch.

Figure 8. This Warner transmission uses a filter screen. Examine it when oil is drained.

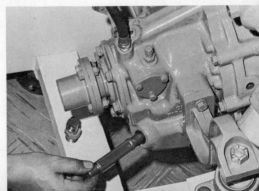

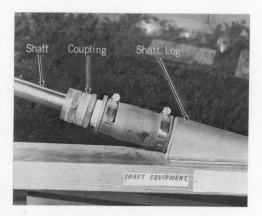

Figure 9. If the shaft is not aligned properly, it will rub the shaft log, causing damage.

Figure 10. Notice the damage to this shaft log which caused a craft to take water and sink.

check the dipstick. Add more oil, if necessary, to bring the level to the "full" mark.

It is important to make sure that the propeller shaft is never misaligned, causing the transmission to be seriously damaged. A prop shaft will go out of alignment if you connect the shaft to its coupling on shore at the beginning of the boating season. When the boat is put into the water, there will be a shift in weight that will cause the shaft to go out of alignment.

The correct way to handle the shaft is to put the boat into the water and allow the hull to take its natural shape before connecting the shaft. With a lapstreak boat, this takes about a week. The shaft in a fiberglass boat can be connected almost immediately after the boat is put into the water.

Coupling of the shaft must be done by someone who knows what he is doing. Play in the shaft must not exceed 0.005 inch or the shaft will whip and damage the transmission. This means that the engine may have to be shifted before the shaft is coupled. If you don't think you can handle the job, leave it to a professional.

Another area that should be examined is the shaft log. This is a component through which the shaft fits. It is attached to the keel or bottom of the hull (Fig. 9). If the log is damaged because of a misaligned shaft, which causes the shaft to rub against the log, enough water will leak into the boat to sink it (Fig. 10).

Every year when the boat goes into the water and the shaft is connected, check the operation of the transmission remote control. Have someone in the cabin shift the control into forward, neutral, and reverse while you, at the transmission, observe that the shift control lever goes squarely and fully into the respective detent. If the lever doesn't engage fully, the boat will cruise, but the transmission will be functioning below normal pressure. This will cause clutch plates to burn. Lubricate the control lever once a year with a few drops of SAE 20 motor oil.

Since hydraulic transmission failure is always preceded by a drop in oil pressure, consider installing a transmission pressure gauge, which costs about $15.

BOAT, REPAIR COMPOUNDS

There are several different types of compounds sold by dealers of marine supplies that are used to seal the joint areas of a boat and for making general repairs. They vary in price and are intended for different purposes. The explanation presented here will allow you to select the kind of compound you need for the job you are doing.

Keep in mind that each of the materials mentioned below differs somewhat from manufacturer to manufacturer. Before using, read the instructions on the label to assure proper application and maximum life.

Bedding compound is an elastic, nonshrinking sealer that keeps water from seeping in around fixtures and in through joints. It is highly adhesive and bonds wood to wood and metal to wood. It also makes an effective seal around glass. Specifically, bedding compound is used to fix cleats, stanchions, windlasses, winches, searchlights, and other hardware to deck and hulls. The material is normally applied with a putty knife (Fig. 1).

Bedding compounds cost about $1 for ½ pint, $1.50 for 1 pint, $3 for a quart, and $10 per gallon. Assuming a thickness of ¹/₃₂ of an inch, one quart of bedding compound will cover about 15 square feet.

Figure 1. A bedding compound, which is highly adhesive, will hold cleats and other hardware.

Glazing compounds are of two types: oil base and resin. Oil-base glazing compound is used to fill hairline cracks and minor grain imperfections in plywood, but it is suitable for use above the waterline only.

Resin glazing compound, which is either polyester or epoxy, is used for repairing gel-coat damage in fiberglass hulls. Both polyester and epoxy glazing compound are two-part mixtures, consisting of a base compound and catalyst that are mixed together thoroughly just prior to use (see Boat, Fiberglass). Once mixed, the material must be applied or discarded since it hardens quickly and cannot be stored.

Polyester glazing compound, which costs about $5.50 in repair kit form, can be used for practically all gel-coat repairs except small ones that will undergo exceptional stress. In this case, the superior holding power of epoxy glazing compound will do the job. Epoxy costs about $7 in repair kit form.

Seam compounds that are designed for use above the waterline only, such as those for filling deck seams, are less expensive than seam compound which is used below the water. A quart of above-water seam compound costs about $3.

The most widely used and strongest seam sealer on the market is polysulfide. It is also the most expensive, costing about $15 per quart. It is used for sealing seams of planked and lapstrake wooden hulls. Polysulfide is the closest thing to a permanent seam sealer ever invented.

Polysulfide comes in both one- and two-part form. The one-part material is available in caulking cartridges or in cans for application with a putty knife (Fig. 2). The two-part material consists of a base compound and catalyst that have to be mixed together. It can be applied with a putty knife.

The major difference between one-part and two-part polysulfide is curing time. Depending upon temperature, two-part

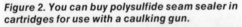
Figure 2. You can buy polysulfide seam sealer in cartridges for use with a caulking gun.

Figure 3. Surfacing compounds are waterproof and can thus be employed below the waterline.

polysulfide cures in 24 to 48 hours. It takes from 3 to 7 days for one-part polysulfide to cure, again depending on temperature. Polysulfide should never be applied at temperatures below 50°F.

If you want a resealing job to last a long time, take pains to properly prepare the surface to accept the compound. Clean out all the old seam filler, and make sure that the seam area is sanded clean and bright. If oil or grease is present, remove it with toluol, acetone, or a solvent recommended by the manufacturer of the seam compound.

Keep in mind that teak and Douglas fir must be primed with a primer recommended by the manufacturer of the sealing compound. These two woods are very oily, and seam compound will not adhere to them if they are bare. Other woods need no priming.

If you are going to paint the craft following application of polysulfide seam compound, make sure that paint and compound are compatible. Consult the label on the compound. If the two are not compatible, paint will begin to peel and blister along the seam.

Since polysulfide seam compound is expensive, you will want to buy only the amount you need. The following formula will assist you in making this estimate:

$$\frac{W \times D \times L}{7} = \text{quarts needed}$$

where W = seam width in inches
D = seam depth in inches
L = seam length in linear feet

Surfacing compounds, in general, have a vinyl-resin base which allows them to dry quickly (in 15 to 30 minutes) and which makes them waterproof. Thus, this compound is suitable for fairing surface imperfections in wooden hulls as well as above the waterline on decks, cabin-trunks, and coamings (Fig. 3). If a

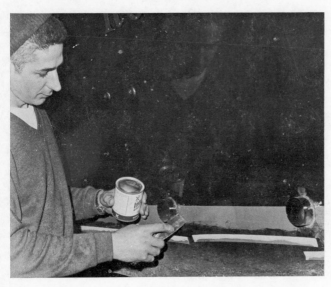

Figure 4. Surfacing compounds will effectively seal around exhaust pipes and other openings.

large surface must be faired, it is suggested that you use trowel cement since it is easier to spread.

Surfacing compound can be used for filling scratches, cracks, and nicks and as a plug compound for sealing nail and screw holes (Fig. 4). It resists impact, doesn't become brittle or chip, and won't shrink. Its price is about the same as that of bedding compound.

Synthetic rubber (silicone) sealer is an excellent but expensive repair material that can be used above or below the waterline as a bedding, glazing, or surfacing compound. It adheres to glass, fiberglass, plexiglass, metal, painted and varnished wood, plastic, canvas, and sailcloth. However, it can't be painted. Since a 3-ounce tube of this material sells for $2, many boat owners use it as a last-resort measure when regular sealers are found wanting.

Trowel cement is used for smoothing large area surface imperfections prior to painting a wooden hull. It is usually employed when the entire hull or a substantial part of it has to be refinished.

Wood fillers are used to fill the grain of open-grained woods so that a smooth surface is provided for painting or varnishing. They are used in particular on a boat's bright work, such as the transom and railings, before these parts are refinished. However, do not use wood fillers if you are going to put one coat of finish over an old coat. Wood fillers must be applied to bare wood.

BRICK

If there is brickwork on the outside of your home, inspect mortar joints between bricks once a year. Spaces between brick and mortar indicate that the mortar has started to shrink. Hairline cracks in the mortar and mortar that flakes free when probed are other indications of damage that should be repaired as soon as possible. This repair is called *pointing*.

If pointing is not done, water will enter the crack or space and cause further deterioration of the joint. In time, the brick will become loose and may fall from place. In addition, water will seep behind the wall.

Repair of brickwork joints requires a bag of ready-prepared mortar mix which can be purchased in a hardware store or lumber yard. Be sure to specify that you want mortar. There are other ready-made premix cement products—sand mix and concrete mix in particular—that should not be used for pointing (see section on Cement). Mortar mix contains lime that lengthens the setting period and keeps shrinkage to a minimum.

Begin the repair by tapping away loose mortar with a cold chisel or an old screwdriver and hammer (Fig. 1). Undercut the crack so that it is wider at the bottom than at the top. This configuration will provide new mortar with a firm base on which to take hold. Then, clean the crack out thoroughly with a wire brush (Fig. 2). Be sure that all particles are removed.

Mix the mortar according to instructions on the package. If the joints between bricks are darker than the new mortar, mix in a little lampblack, which can be purchased at a paint or hardware store (Fig. 3). Add and mix a small amount at a time, comparing the color of the fresh mortar with the old. Keep in mind that a little lampblack goes a long way.

Figure 1. Prepare a joint for new mortar mix by tapping away old mortar. Undercut the crack.

Figure 2. Use a wire brush to assure that the joint is perfectly clean for fresh mortar.

Figure 3. Add lampblack to the freshly mixed mortar to match it to the color of old mortar.

Figure 4. Using a triangular pointing trowel, fill the cavity to overflowing with mortar.

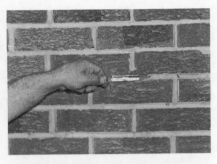

Figure 5. Fashion the joint to the desired configuration with a jointer, as pictured here, or a trowel.

Wet down the cavity thoroughly. Using a triangular pointing trowel, press mortar into the crack until it overflows (Fig. 4). Allow the mortar to set for a few minutes.

Now, use the point of the trowel or a jointer to indent or shape the fresh mortar to the configuration of the joint (Fig. 5.). A jointer is an inexpensive mason's tool that can be purchased in a hardware store. If you accidentally get mortar on brick, remove it with a scrubbing brush and water before it has a chance to set.

To make certain that the fresh mortar doesn't set too rapidly, which could cause it to crumble, wet down the repaired area once or twice a day for about a week. Use the fine spray of a garden hose.

CAMERAS

Although instructions in this section pertain to still cameras, similar procedures may be applied in caring for movie cameras and slide and movie projectors.

The chief enemy of photographic equipment is dirt. If dirt isn't cleaned away periodically, it will find its way into controls and delicate mechanisms and cause problems with such things as the shutter, flash synchronizer, and film advance.

Brush off controls with a soft camel's hair brush, a small good quality paint brush, or a regular photographer's lens brush (Fig. 1). If grime has built up to a point where it can't be brushed away, remove it with a cotton swab that you have dipped in rubbing alcohol. Also use a cotton swab that has been dipped in alcohol to clean off view finder, range finder, and built-in exposure meter windows (Fig. 2).

Figure 1. The brush you use to dust off camera parts should be clean and have soft bristles.

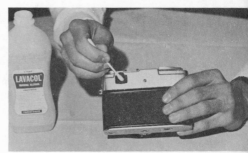

Figure 2. A cotton swab can be used to clean dirt from glass parts, but not from the lens.

The lens, film pressure plate, and mirrors of reflex cameras require special attention. The pressure plate, which is found on the inside of the camera's back, keeps the film flat and smooth behind the lens. To clean it off, brush very gently around it, but exercise care to assure that the plate will not be scratched (Fig. 3). A scratch on the pressure plate will produce a scratch on the film.

Use extreme caution when working with a camera's optics. Employ only that cleaning which is absolutely necessary. Do not overclean the lens. Excessive wiping can damage the antihalation coating and will cause the lens to be scratched.

To clean optics, blow away dust particles with a small rubber ear syringe, which you can buy in a drug store (Fig. 4). Remove any dirt that remains with very gentle brushing with a lens brush. On removable lenses, clean the rear element as well as the front.

If there is a film coating over the lens after brushing, wipe the lens lightly with a lens cleaning tissue (Fig. 5). Use no other material, since it will scratch the lens.

Figure 3. Be very careful when cleaning the pressure plate that you don't scratch its surface.

Figure 4. A small ear syringe is useful for removing dust particles from a camera's optics.

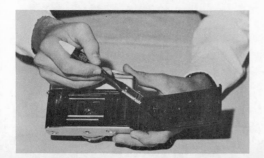

Figure 5. Use very light pressure if you must clean a lens with lens cleaning tissue.

Figure 6. To protect a removable lens when it is not being used, keep it in a case or bag.

Incidentally, when removable lenses aren't in use, keep them in cases or plastic bags with both the front and rear elements capped (Fig. 6.). However, never remove a lens and leave the opening in the camera exposed. Cover the hole with a body cap or keep the lens on the camera. Lenses which remain on cameras should be capped.

Use an ear syringe and gentle brushing to clean mirrors. But never touch or wipe a mirror since you could destroy its precise alignment.

With the back of the camera open, shake the camera gently to dislodge bits of film and paper that may have been torn off around the sprockets. Brush out the interior of the camera carefully. Follow brushing by blowing the camera out with an ear syringe to remove particles that have been loosened by the brush. Never blow out the camera by mouth. Moisture on your breath will collect on parts and may cause rusting.

Do not oil parts of the camera yourself. Leave this task to a professional. If you apply oil in the wrong place, it will gum up mechanisms and cause damage.

Tighten tiny screws in lens barrels and other areas with a small jeweler's or modelmaker's screwdriver that you can buy in a hobby shop. Screws often work loose and fall out, causing serious damage.

To test shutter speed, which slows down as dirt builds up, run a test roll of film through the camera at different exposures. Try some shots with flash and some without. The exposures that are indicated as correct for the test by exposure meter or flashguide should produce the best results. There should be an even gradation of light and dark exposures on either side of the correct exposure.

Another test is to use the same exposure, but at different combinations of shutter speeds and lens openings. If the shutter is working properly, all of the test results will be the same since exposures are the same. If results aren't the same, the shutter timing is off. Usually, a sticking shutter reveals itself at the higher speeds first.

If there is a problem, take the camera to a professional repairman.

CAULKING

The purpose of caulking is to seal cracks around a home through which air and moisture can leak (Fig. 1). During the winter, for example, cold air can penetrate cracks and make a home drafty. During the summer, cool air generated by air conditioning can be lost through cracks, causing an increase in the cost of cooling the home. Unsealed cracks also permit moisture to penetrate to the inside of the house, where it can cause rotting, rusting, and spalling.

Preparing the surface and applying caulk are important tasks. However, they are mechanical, and it is more important to make sure that you have selected the right type of compound for the task at hand.

A caulking compound can be placed into one of two general categories: those that are readily available to the consumer and those which are employed primarily by professional builders.

Latex, butyl, nitrile, and vegetable oil base caulking compounds, which you can buy in hardware and paint stores, lumber yards, and other home supply outlets, will take care of most of the sealing tasks around a home. They are available in cartridges for application with a caulking gun (Fig. 2).

Latex caulk is the most versatile of the consumer-type caulking compounds and the one that you will have the most

Figure 1. An inspection of your home will uncover many cracks that can be sealed with caulk.

Figure 2. Caulk is available in handy cartridges which you slip into a plunger-type gun.

Figure 3. Latex caulking compound is used for practically every sealing task in a home.

Figure 4. Latex caulking can be easily washed off with water if it gets on an adjacent area.

need for. You can use it inside or outside the home, on wood and masonry substrates, over old paint, and under new paint. Specific applications include sealing of baseboard seams, trim and joint cracks, gaps around moldings, wallboard seams, cracks around window frames and wooden storm windows, gaps in exterior wood siding, and gaps around doors and threshold strips (Fig. 3).

The longevity of latex caulking compound is significantly reduced if it is not painted once it has been applied, especially when it is used on the outside of a home. Keep in mind that latex does not adhere well to metal. Use butyl or nitrile compound instead.

Never use latex caulk in cracks which are wider than ¼ inch or those which are subjected to unusual expansion-contraction forces, such as openings in concrete pavements and patios that butt foundations.

Although latex caulk was developed primarily for use with latex (water base) paint, it can be used in contact with any type of paint, including acrylic and oil base. Latex compound has a water base and cures by means of water loss, which causes coalescence. Coalescence is the ability of solids to cling closer together as water evaporates. Latex caulk is therefore subject to some shrinkage, but it is not significant.

Latex caulk is very easy to apply and can be placed on a damp (but clean) surface. Air and substrate temperatures should be 40°F or more. Caulking compound that accidentally gets on an adjacent surface can be cleaned away with a damp cloth or sponge before it dries or cut away with a knife or razor once it has cured (Fig. 4).

As soon as it has been applied, latex caulk can be worked into place or spread with a putty knife or spatula, if necessary, which should be dipped into water often to keep the compound from sticking to the tool. When the compound loses its tackiness, which takes about 15 to 30 minutes, it should be painted.

Latex caulk, if applied properly, will last up to 10 years. Under the limitations noted above, however, it can fail in as little as two years. The compound is nontoxic and nonflammable.

Caution: Latex caulk is often referred to as acrylic. Do not confuse this with acrylic polymeric caulk, which is a construction trade compound that has a solvent base. If you want latex caulk, make sure the cartridge specifies that the product is latex or has a water base.

Butyl and nitrile caulks are solvent base synthetic rubber compounds that have excellent adhesion to unpainted metal and masonry. However, they do not adhere well to *painted* wood and should not be used to fill cracks which are wider than ¼ inch.

Butyl caulk is particularly recommended for sealing cracks between dissimilar materials, such as those between masonry and metal (Fig. 5). Areas of the home where masonry and metal join include chimney flashing and chimney and places where pipes come through foundation and basement walls.

Nitrile caulk is especially suited for sealing cracks that are subjected to a high concentration of water.

Butyl and nitrile can be applied at temperatures of 35°F or higher. Both compounds accept paint, although it is not essential that they be painted. If you decide to paint butyl caulk, leave it exposed after application for a minimum of seven days before painting. Nitrile can be painted as soon as it loses tackiness, which is 10 to 20 minutes after application. Nitrile shrinks as it cures, so refilling of a crack may be necessary.

Vegetable oil base caulk is the oldest and least expensive of the caulking compounds. However, it doesn't provide the performance that the others do, and its life expectancy is the shortest.

Caulking compounds that are normally employed by the

Figure 5. The ability of butyl to adhere to metal and masonry makes it a valuable compound.

building trade are designed for difficult tasks, which include the sealing of cracks and joints that are exceptionally wide (over ¼ inch) and are subjected to unusual expansion-contraction stress. They can be obtained from supply outlets which sell to the construction industry or through paint stores that serve professional builders.

Construction-trade caulks are expensive and should be considered for use by the homeowner only when a consumer-oriented compound fails to do a job.

Construction caulking compounds include acrylic polymeric, polysulfide, and silicone. They adhere well to practically any surface, including glass, metal, masonry, porcelain, and wood.

Acrylic polymeric caulk is very difficult to apply. If the temperature is below 60°F, it is impossible to use. Professionals enhance the flow of the material by heating it to about 120°F. If this is done, be sure to puncture the nozzle seal, but keep the cartridge away from the heat source. All construction trade caulks are flammable and toxic.

Polysulfide caulk has the limitation of not becoming tack-free for about 72 hours. In addition, the surface must first be primed, especially if the caulk is going to be used on masonry. The primer is a special type made for use with polysulfide caulk.

Silicone caulk flows easily, even at temperatures below zero. However, it cannot be used over building materials that may bleed; it cannot be used to seal cracks in a confined space, since it requires atmospheric moisture to cure; and it cannot be applied before a special bonding agent is used on the substrate.

The chart on the next page summarizes the construction-trade caulks and can be used in making a selection. A chart of consumer-oriented caulks is provided on page 118.

To determine whether a surface needs new caulking compound, probe it with a screwdriver (Fig. 6). If the old compound crumbles and falls loose, new caulk is needed.

Figure 6. If old compound falls out as it is probed, you should seal the crack with new caulk.

Figure 7. With a wire brush, brush the surface thoroughly to assure a perfectly clean area.

Construction-trade Caulks

	Acrylic Polymeric	Polysulfide	Silicone
Price (11-oz. cartridge)	$2.50–$2.95	$2.95–$3.65	$2.95–$3.50
Primer required	None	A necessity on masonry	Bonding agent required
Time until tack-free	10–30 min	24–72 hours	1 hour
Ease of application	Difficult	Good	Good
Minimum application temperature	Heat to 120°F	0°F	Below 0°F
Expected life	Up to 20 years	Up to 20 years	Up to 20 years
Adhesion to:			
Metal	Very good	Excellent	Excellent
Wood	Very good	Excellent if primed	Excellent
Old paint	Very good	Do not use	Excellent
Masonry	Very good	Excellent if primed	Very good

Incidentally, if there is no compound in joints of a relatively new home, the builder might have failed to apply it. Cracks should be sealed.

Clean chunks of old caulk out with a wood chisel or an old screwdriver and brush the surface with a wire brush (Fig. 7). To assure complete cleanliness, which is required for good adhesion, wipe the area with a cloth that has been moistened in turpentine or paint thinner (Fig. 8). This will dissolve grease, dirt, and small particles.

Figure 8. Turpentine will dissolve grease and old paint to assure firm adhesion of caulk.

Figure 9. In applying the compound, make sure that a wide bead covers the whole crack.

Consumer-oriented Caulks

	Latex	Butyl	Nitrile	Vegetable Oil
Price (11-oz. cartridge)	$.90–$1.10	$1.00–$1.50	$1.75–$2.00	$.30–$.60
Primer required	Only for metal	None	None	If surface is porous
Time until tack-free	15–30 min	30–90 min	10–20 min	2–24 hours
Ease of application	Excellent	Very good	Very good	Very good
Minimum application temperature	40°F	35°F	35°F	60°F
Expected life	2–10 years	Up to 20 years	Up to 20 years	1–5 years
Adhesion to:				
Metal	Poor	Excellent if unpainted	Excellent if unpainted	Fair-good
Wood	Excellent	Excellent if unpainted	Excellent if unpainted	Fair-good
Masonry	Good	Excellent if unpainted	Excellent if unpainted	Fair-good
Old paint	Excellent	Fair	Fair	Fair-good

It doesn't matter whether you pull or push the caulking gun in applying compound. Handle the gun in the manner which is most comfortable for you. However, make certain that you lay down a wide bead of caulk so that the crack is completely sealed (Fig. 9).

CEMENT

Sooner or later every homeowner is faced with the task of repairing cement or engaging in a project that requires use of a cement product. Perhaps steps or walk have cracked and need repair, or brickwork has to be pointed.

If a comparatively small amount of cement is needed, you will find that a premixed product is the most practical. With a premix, ingredients are mixed in proper proportion. Simply open the bag, pour the contents into a suitable container, and add water.

Figure 1. Sand mix is used for repairing superficial cracks.

Figure 2. Mortar mix is a pliable product that is used between brick for filling joints.

There are several different types of premixes, with each designed for specific purposes. If the wrong product is used for a job, it will soon fail.

Premixed cement products, which are sold in lumber yards and hardware stores, include sand mix, mortar mix, concrete (gravel) mix, and waterproof mix. Although they differ, they have one thing in common: all contain cement which acts as a binder to hold aggregates together.

Sand mix, which contains cement and sand, is used for repairs and projects where a maximum thickness of 2 inches will suffice (Fig. 1). Examples include filling cracks in cement walks, steps, stucco walls and foundations, and laying a base for flagstone and stepping stone.

Concrete (gravel) mix, which contains cement, sand, and gravel to provide extra strength, is used for projects that require a thickness of more than 2 inches. Examples are making collars for posts; constructing steps, wading pools, and walks; and laying a base for built-in barbecue grills and bird baths.

Mortar mix, which contains sand, cement, and lime to make the mixture pliable and easier to spread, should be used for joints between brick, stone, cinder block, and concrete block. For example, use mortar mix for bricklaying and for pointing masonry (Fig. 2).

Waterproof mix is used as a topcoat on surfaces that are subjected to water most of the time, such as concrete wading pools. It contains cement, sand, and a waterproof compound such as polyvinyl acetate. You can make your own mixture by

Figure 3. Special waterproofing and reinforcing compounds are available in hardware stores.

adding a waterproof compound to a bag of sand mix. Waterproof compound, which is sold at lumber yards and most hardware stores, may also be spread on existing cement walks, steps, and other areas to provide a measure of waterproofing (Fig. 3).

A premix should be well blended before adding water. To blend sand mix and mortar mix, turn the bag upside down several times. To blend concrete mix, pour the contents of the bag into a wheelbarrow and work aggregates together with a hoe or shovel.

Premix Cement Calculator

Type of Premix	Packaging	Coverage
Sand mix	11, 25, 45, 80 lb. bags	80-lb. bag covers 8 square feet with 1-inch thick topping
Mortar mix	25, 45, 80 lb. bags	80-lb. bag allows laying of 50–70 brick or 20–25 blocks with a ³⁄₈-inch joint
Concrete mix	45, 90 lb. bags	90-lb. bag makes ²⁄₃ cubic feet of concrete or enough to cover a 12″ × 12″ × 9″ area
Waterproof mix	45, 80 lb. bag	80-lb. bag is sufficient to make a 4′ × 4′ × ½″ topping

To obtain the strongest, most durable mixture possible, add water to a premix gradually and carefully. Read instructions on the bag. Generally, 1 gallon of water to a 90-pound bag is required.

A freshly laid cement product should be cured if the air temperature is 75°F or more, to assure that the water in the mixture will not evaporate too quickly, causing the cement to crumble. To cure cement, spray it with a fine mist of water from a garden hose once a day for about a week.

The chart on the facing page will allow you to estimate how much premix you will need for a task.

CERAMIC TILING

Homeowners who wish to install ceramic tile in bathrooms, powder rooms, and kitchens, or who wish to use tile for other projects, such as countertops, will find that there are two general types of tile: glazed and unglazed. Glazed tile resembles finely polished chinaware, while unglazed tile has a nonluster finish. Both kinds are available in many different sizes, shapes, and colors.

Glazed tile is generally considered wall tile. Unglazed tile, because of its virtual indestructibility, is often regarded as a floor covering. However, unglazed tile has been used to cover walls and countertops with striking results (Fig. 1).

In preparation for laying tile, be aware of the fact that glazed tile of a particular size made by a particular manufacturer is *not* of the exact same size as glazed tile produced by other manufacturers; that is, glazed tile referred to as 4¼-inch square or 6-inch square by manufacturers differ in size from manufacturer to manufacturer. Some may be exactly 4¼-inches square, for example, or ¹⁄₁₆, ⅛, or ¼ inch smaller or larger.

Figure 1. Unglazed ceramic tile normally comes in sheet units and is virtually indestructible.

Figure 2. Carbide-tipped nippers are needed for fashioning tile to fit around protrusions.

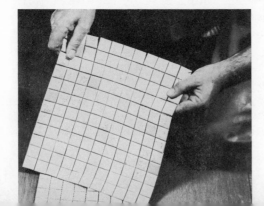

Thus, always use the tile of *one manufacturer* for a particular job to avoid the problem of size discrepancy.

Many of the tools needed for laying ceramic tile are probably available in your workshop. Others can be purchased or rented. Tools you will need are:

• Paint brush.

• Pair of carbide-tipped nippers for nipping out small sections of tile to make the tile fit around protrusions, such as pipes (Fig. 2).

• Carborundum stone for smoothing cut edges.

• Sponges.

• Margin or pointing trowel for mixing grout.

• Notched trowel for spreading mastic.

• Carpenter's level.

• Ruler.

• Window squeegee for removing excess grout.

• Joint striking tool—an old toothbrush handle or rounded stick will do.

• Carbide-tipped drill for drilling holes through tile.

The materials you will need are the following:

• Ceramic primer, if you are tiling an area that will be subjected to moisture. One gallon will cover 225 to 250 square feet.

• Mastic (adhesive) that bears the seal of the U.S. Department of Commerce, attesting to the fact that the material meets Commercial Standard Specification CS 181-52. A gallon of ceramic tile mastic for walls will cover 45 to 50 square feet, while a gallon of mastic for floors will cover about 60 square feet. Note that there is a different type of mastic for walls and floors. Furthermore, be aware that there are different mastics for different wall surfaces. There is a mastic, for example, specifically made for gypsum wallboard, which will not adhere well to plywood. Thus, there is also a mastic for plywood.

• Wall grout. A 25-pound bag will cover 200 to 250 square feet. Be sure that the grout you buy doesn't call for soaking of tiles prior to installation. Dry-method grout is specially treated so that grout doesn't absorb moisture from tile.

• Liquid silicone. If you are tiling a floor, countertop, or other area that will be subjected to heavy soiling, add silicone to the grout as directed on the package. Silicone aids in cleaning.

In addition to regular tile pieces for tiling walls—the 4¼-inch-square size is most commonly used—you will need trim pieces (Fig. 3). Although there are several different sizes and shapes, you will usually be able to make do with four kinds. They are the 2 × 6 inch dry cap (S 4269) that is used as top trim; 2 × 2 inch out-corner trim (SN 4269); 2 × 2 inch fly (in-corner)

Figure 3. To finish off a tiling job, trim tile is needed.

trim (SM 4269); and 4¼-inch bullnose trim (S 4449). The numbers given are standard throughout the industry.

To estimate the number of tiles you will need for tiling the walls of a room, add the length and width of the room and double the sum. Then, multiply this number by the height of the proposed tile installation. The result will be the total area to be covered.

For example, suppose you are tiling a bathroom that is 5 × 7 feet. Add 5 to 7 and multiply by 2, giving you 24. Now, multiply 24 by 4½, which is the standard height of the surface one usually covers with tile in a bathroom, although there are no hard-and-fast rules. Tile as much or as little as you wish. This gives a total of 108 square feet to be tiled.

From this figure, the tile dealer can estimate how many tiles you will need. If you use 4¼-inch-square pieces, for instance, you will require 8 tiles for each square foot. Using the example above, therefore, this would mean about 864 tiles for the installation. This figure allows for windows, doors, and waste. Most tile dealers will allow you to return unused tile for a refund. However, keep several spares in case a block of tile eventually falls from the wall and cracks.

Regarding the ordering of trim pieces, it would be wise to bring the tile dealer a sketch of the floor plan. He will be able to assist you with the type and size trim you need. If you own a Polaroid camera, take a photograph or two of the room and bring that to the dealer.

Ceramic tile can be installed on any surface except tongue-and-groove boards and unseasoned boards which expand and contract and, in time, will cause tile to pop off the wall. Remove all moldings, baseboards, and fixtures from the wall. Scrape away loose plaster and paint, and sand irregular surfaces smooth. Fill holes with patching plaster. If there is wallpaper on the wall, remove it. It is best to use a wallpaper steamer, which you can rent from a paint and wallpaper dealer.

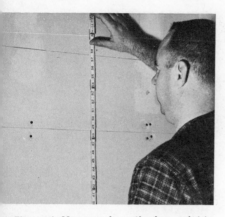

Figure 4. Measure from the low point to where tile is to end.

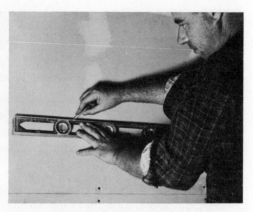

Figure 5. Use a carpenter's level to assure a perfectly straight line.

The wall must be smooth and clean. Thus, if a wall is very rough, you can save much work by covering it with gypsum wallboard. Make sure all joints and corners are taped and cemented.

In a room without a bathtub, use a carpenter's level to find the lowest point along the bottom of the wall. Now, measure up the wall from this point until you reach the height at which you want the top row of tile (Fig. 4). Mark a line. Use a carpenter's level to extend the line around the room, making sure that it is absolutely straight (Fig. 5).

Now, prime the wall if necessary. If moisture in the room is particularly heavy, apply two coats. After primer has dried, apply ceramic tile mastic.

Mastic should be applied in a thin coat, using at first the flat side of the notched trowel. Now, reverse the trowel so that the notched side is used and spread mastic evenly. Ridges must be left in the adhesive (Fig. 6). If insufficient adhesive has been applied so that the wall shows, apply more. Until you become effi-

Figure 6. Apply the tile mastic, stopping at the guideline.

Figure 7. Install tile so that each is embedded in the mastic.

cient at applying mastic, you should do only 10 to 15 square feet at a time.

If the mastic begins to skin over before tile can be applied, scratch the surface with the notched end of the trowel. Apply mastic and tile to one wall at a time. Once mastic is put on the wall, that wall must be completed.

After mastic is put on the surface, lay in the first vertical row of tile. Place the first tile flush with the floor at the lowest point in the room. Extend this row right to the level line, which will be visible through the mastic. Now, simply work out from this row in both directions (Fig. 7).

To anchor the tile properly, press each block into place against the tile next to it and shift it from side to side about ⅛ inch. Then slide it against the previously applied block. This action insures good transfer of mastic to the tile.

If the room has a bathtub, use the top edge of the tub to get the guideline. Find the lowest point along the tub's edge with a carpenter's level. Then, simply follow the procedure outlined above for a room that has no tub.

The row of tile along the top edge of the bathtub is an area that could present a problem later on if you are not careful now. In applying mastic, lap the adhesive onto the edge of the tub to assure that tile will be firmly seated in adhesive. When you apply grout, pay particular attention to the joint between tub and tile. Fill it as full as possible and do not rake it as deeply with the striking tool as you do other grouted lines. This procedure will assure that tile in this critical area will be set more firmly.

Another spot for special attention is around fixtures that fit into the wall, such as soap dishes. After you have cut the area out for the fixture, stuff it with crumpled newspaper or wire mesh. Spread plaster of paris onto the newspaper or wire mesh and over the back of the fixture. Place the fixture in the wall.

Figure 8. A regular tile cutter makes cutting simple. Rent one from a dealer of tile supplies.

Figure 9. You can also employ an ordinary inexpensive glass cutter to cut glazed ceramic.

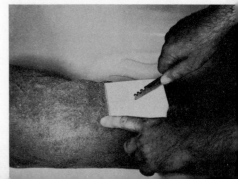

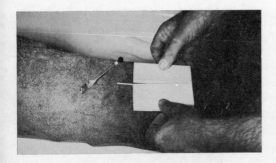

Figure 10. Break the tile along the
scribe mark by pressing it down hard on
a finishing nail.

If fixtures are to be flush with tile, they can be attached to
tile with a special adhesive or by drilling holes for fixture screws
with a carbide-tipped drill.

To cut tile, use a glass cutter or a ceramic tile cutter that you
can rent from a tile dealer. To make straight cuts, draw the glass
cutter or ceramic tile cutter across the face of the tile's glazed
side (Figs. 8 and 9). If you use a glass cutter, break the tile by
centering the scribe over a hard edge, such as a finishing nail,
and pressing on both sides of the scribe line (Fig. 10). If you use
a ceramic tile cutter, the break is made with the cutter's handle.

Be sure to smooth off edges of cut tile with a carborundum
stone before installation.

To cut arcs or notches, make the scribe and break off the
section with a ceramic tile nipper. Take small bites (Fig. 11).
Since most cutouts are covered by an escutcheon plate, a snug-
fitting cutout is not essential.

Mix grout with water to form a paste and sponge this over
the tile, pushing the grout firmly into joints (Fig. 12). Wear rubber gloves since grout contains lye. Flush off any you get on
your skin with plenty of water.

Grout about 25 square feet at a time. Then immediately wipe
the surface of the tile with a window squeegee (Fig. 13). When a

Figure 11. To cut out notches, take small
bites with nippers.

Figure 12. Apply grout, pushing it firmly
into tile joints.

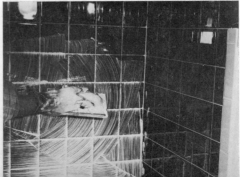

Figure 13. Sweep excess grout off the tile with a squeegee.

Figure 14. Rake joints to give them a professional appearance.

film develops over the tile's surface, immediately rake joints with a striking tool (Fig. 14). Then take water and a sponge or rag and remove the film. If the grout sets before you have time to clean it, moisten a cloth with gasoline and wipe it down.

If liquid silicone has been added to grout, the film must be removed with a rough-surfaced rag, such as burlap or turkish towel, that has been dipped in water.

CLAPBOARD SIDING

Clapboard siding can split or become badly rotted. In any case, damaged boards should be repaired as soon as possible to keep water from penetrating and getting behind walls. This will allow paint on the inside and outside of the home to fail.

A board that has split can be easily repaired with a weatherproof glue, which is available in hardware stores. To apply the glue, carefully wedge, the split apart with a thin-edged tool,

Figure 1. To repair a crack in clapboard siding, squeeze in a liberal application of glue.

Figure 2. Some nails hammered beneath the crack will help to hold it tight while glue dries.

such as a putty knife. Apply liberal quantity of glue into the crack, withdraw the wedge, and push the split parts together (Fig. 1).

The split halves should be clamped so that they hold firmly until the glue dries. To do this, simply hammer in a couple of nails beneath the bottom edge of the damaged piece of clapboard, making sure that the split is tightly closed (Fig. 2). Leave most of the nail protruding. When the glue dries, remove nails.

A badly rotted section of clapboard or a piece damaged beyond repair should be removed and a new section installed. To do this, first carefully pry up the board just above the bad section. Here you may find nails that are holding the damaged piece in place. These have to be removed, but be sure to remove only nails that are hammered into the damaged piece.

To remove nails, wedge a screwdriver or small pry bar beneath the nailheads and try to pull them out. If they won't come out all the way, use a hacksaw blade to cut off the nailheads flush with the board (Fig. 3). After the bad section has been removed, you will be able to pull out the rest of the nail with a pair of pliers.

It is now necessary to cut out the damaged section. Using a saw, vertically score the board about ½ inch on each side of the damaged area (Fig. 4). Cut as deeply as you can without cutting into the board above or below the damaged piece. Now, with a wood chisel, carefully cut out chunks of the bad section.

Be careful not to cut deep enough so that the chisel slices into the tarpaper beneath the board. However, should the tarpaper be damaged, cover the distressed area with a layer of black plastic roof cement. This cement, which is used primarily for making roof repairs, is available in hardware stores.

With the damaged section of clapboard removed, measure the area and cut a new length of clapboard. Before putting the new section into place, paint its backside to assure full protection from weather.

Figure 3. To free the damaged board, saw off nailheads as you carefully lift the top board.

Figure 4. With a saw, score the damaged board vertically to facilitate cutting with a chisel.

Figure 5. When the new piece of clap-board is installed, place nails close to the top edge.

Figure 6. Cracks between sections should be caulked so that water is stopped at the crack.

Slide the new piece of board into place and nail, using galvanized or aluminum siding nails that resist rust (Fig. 5). Before nailing the new board, it is wise to drill small pilot holes to accept the nails. This precaution guarantees that the thin clapboard won't split when nails are inserted.

Countersink nailheads and fill holes with *wood* putty. Do not use glazing putty. When putty dries, sand it smooth.

Finally, close cracks between new and old sections of clapboard with wood putty or caulking compound (Fig. 6). When this has dried, sand smooth. The new section can now be painted.

CONCRETE REPAIRS

Cracks in concrete sidewalks, steps, and driveways should be repaired before cold weather arrives. If water seeps into a crack and freezes, extensive damage could result that will necessitate major renovation.

To repair a crack in concrete, use a cold chisel and hammer to widen the crack (Fig. 1). Wear goggles to guard against flying debris. Widen the excavation so it is wider at the bottom than at the top to provide a firm seat for the repair mixture.

Figure 1. To repair a crack in cement, it must be widened so that compound will have a base.

Figure 2. Loose particles must be cleared from the crack for the repair compound to adhere.

Figure 3. Use sufficient repair compound
to fill the crack full and to extend above
the crack's surface.

Figure 4. After the repair has set, strike
off excess cement.

Brush or wash away all dirt and particles. If particles in
the crack prove stubborn, use a suitable tool to remove them
(Fig. 2).

Prepare the repair compound. In most cases, a premixed
sand mix should be used (see the section on Cement for details).
Wet down the area and fill the crack above the level of the ground
(Fig. 3). Allow the repair to set for about 45 minutes and then
strike the patch. If you desire a smooth finish, use a steel trowel
as the striking tool. If you desire a rough textured finish, use a
wood block (Fig. 4).

Curing is important, especially if the temperature is 75° or
more. Curing assures that rapid evaporation of moisture in the
cement will not take place, causing the patch to eventually
crumble. To cure the repair, simply spray it down with water
from a hose once each day for a week (Fig. 5).

For maximum strength when repairing a crack between a
concrete step and the riser of the step above, after widening the

Figure 5. Curing of the repair will prevent
eventual damage.

Figure 6. On step cracks, widen the
crevice and install nails.

crack, hammer in concrete nails every 2 inches along the cavity (Fig. 6). Be sure nailheads are below the surface so that the repair compound will cover them.

If an entire section of a sidewalk or driveway is in very bad condition, dig up the old concrete down to grade level, but do not discard concrete chunks. Instead, break them up and spread them as a base for new concrete.

If the damaged section is particularly large, enclose it in a form that is made by nailing four pieces of 2 × 4 together. A form keeps the repair material enclosed so that it won't spread before it can dry.

Use concrete mix as the repair compound (see the section on Cement). Pour the mixture into the excavation and level if off by striking it with a board. Follow by smoothing the surface with a wood float that you can buy in a hardware store. Be sure that the patch is cured for a week as explained above.

Repair of a blacktop driveway is done differently from repair of a concrete driveway. Buy a cold patch asphalt for blacktop driveways at a hardware store or lumber yard. Brush away dirt and loose material from the damaged area. If the hole is large, shovel in some gravel to form a base for the patch and tamp it down.

Now, fill the hole with cold patch, working the material around with a shovel to eliminate air pockets. Finally, tamp down the patch until it is compact. Allow the material to set for a few days before driving over it. The end of a 2 × 4 makes an excellent tamping tool.

CONDENSATION (MOISTURE)

Excessive moisture in a home stains walls and ceilings, causes paint to peel from exterior siding, permits mildew to thrive, and causes metal to rust. The best way to stop trouble before it starts is to install a vapor barrier in the walls when the home is being built. However, ripping out walls of an existing home to install a vapor barrier is impractical and expensive.

What can be done, then, to eliminate a condensation problem? This depends on which problem exists. For example, one of the most common troubles created by condensation in a home is peeling of paint from exterior wood siding. This occurs when warm, moist air inside the house penetrates through interior walls and condenses as it strikes the colder inside surface of outside walls. If the outside wall is painted with an impervious coating of paint, specifically an oil base paint, condensation can't escape. Water builds up, causing the paint film to blister. In

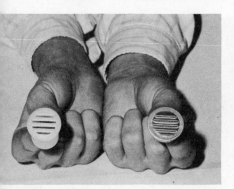

Figure 1. Ventilation louvers are available in plastic (left) or in aluminum with screening.

Figure 2. Ventilation louvers are installed in 1-inch holes that you must drill in siding.

time, blisters burst and paint starts to peel.

One way the problem can be eliminated is to remove paint down to bare wood and repaint the house with an exterior water base (latex) primer and finish coat. Latex paint is a so-called breathing paint and allows moisture to escape through its film. Scraping off paint to bare wood, of course, is a difficult task and should not be attempted unless the peeling condition is extremely bad.

A less painstaking corrective measure is to create an artificial vapor barrier by painting rooms with an alkyd enamel wall paint. This keeps warm, moist air confined to the inside of the house. However, the coating must be complete in order to be effective. Do not leave any area, such as sections behind radiators, in a closet, or behind shelves, void of paint. Warm, moist air seeks the line of least resistance and will penetrate the wall through these unprotected areas.

Another way to correct a paint peeling condition, perhaps the least troublesome method of all, is to install small ventilation louvers in exterior siding (Fig. 1). These vents permit warm, moist air that is trapped by an impervious paint film to escape.

Siding vents can be purchased in hardware stores. Those made of plastic are less expensive than those of aluminum. However, aluminum vents are usually equipped with screening to keep insects from crawling inside the wall. Siding vents can be painted to match the color of the house and are therefore unobtrusive.

Install vents by drilling 1-inch holes into the siding between studs (Fig. 2). Then, simply insert the vent into the hole, but be sure to caulk around the vent to keep water from leaking into

Figure 3. Completely seal the joint around a louver with compound to prevent water seepage.

Figure 4. A ventilation louver placed every 16 inches will get rid of paint-ruining moisture.

the wall (Fig. 3). Place a vent every 16 inches in each course of siding over the area where paint is blistering or peeling (Fig. 4).

The best way to get rid of excessive moisture that is created in kitchen and bathroom is by installing an exhaust fan. However, buying a fan that is not large enough to do an efficient job is a waste of money.

Fans are measured in cubic feet per minute (CFM), which refers to the amount of air the fan can exhaust from a room in one minute. Every fan should have a plate on it that tells its CFM.

To determine the size of the fan you need, multiply the room's length by width by height. This provides the cubic feet of volume. To effectively dissipate moisture from a room, a fan should completely exhaust the air in that room every two minutes. Thus, to determine the CFM of the fan you need, divide cubic feet of room volume in half.

Kitchens and bathrooms are usually painted with a gloss or semigloss enamel. This provides a measure of protection, because this type of paint acts as a vapor barrier.

Condensation could be a problem in a poorly ventilated attic. Moisture forms on cold metal surfaces, such as soil pipes and nails that protrude through the underside of roof boards. The latter situation can be corrected by cutting off nails flush with sheathing (Fig. 5). Use a hacksaw blade or end-cutting nippers.

Figure 5. Nip off nails to prevent moisture from forming on them and dripping in the attic.

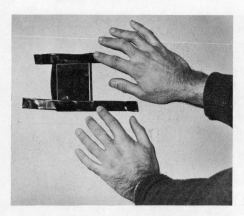

Figure 6. To test for condensation, tape a pocket mirror to the basement wall for 24 hours.

Figure 7. Foam-plastic flexible insulating material will prevent moisture on water pipes.

An attic can be suitably ventilated by adding louvers. The total area of louvered opening should be a minimum of ¼ square inch for each square foot of attic floor space. A minimum of two louvers should be employed, preferably at opposite ends from each other to provide good coverage.

If condensation in the basement is excessive, the area will not be suitable for storage. Condensation can cause mildew. Furthermore, a basement should never be converted into a finished room as long as condensation prevails. If wallboard or paneling is placed over a cinder block or poured concrete wall that is prone to condensation, moisture can eventually seep through to stain wallboard or cause paneling to rot.

Condensation in a basement occurs most often in warm weather, when warm, moist air from outside enters the basement to mix with colder walls and floors and cold water pipes. However, be aware that a wet wall could also be the result of a water leak. A simple test will reveal the real cause of dampness.

Tape a pocket mirror to the wall and allow it to remain in place for a day (Fig. 6). If at the end of this period, the mirror is covered with moisture, you know that the problem is one of condensation.

Condensation can be prevented from forming on basement walls by installation of vapor-barrier insulation material that can be purchased in a lumber yard or home equipment supply store. If condensation is exceedingly bad, the wall should first be coated with a bituminous coating, which is applied like paint.

To install the vapor barrier, nail 1 × 2 inch wood furring strips to the wall with masonry nails. These strips should first

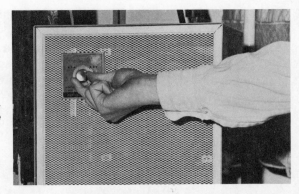

Figure 8. In the end, a dehumidifier with a humidistat is often the
only effective tool.

be treated with a preservative to prevent moisture from rotting
them. The distance between furring strips is determined by the
width of the vapor-barrier material. When strips are in place,
attach the vapor-barrier insulation to them with staples. Paneling or wallboard can now be installed with safety.

Moisture dripping from cold water pipes in the basement
can be prevented by wrapping a foam-plastic flexible insulating
material around the pipes (Fig. 7). This material and adhesive
required to install it may be purchased from plumbing and heating supply dealers.

In its most destructive form, excessive household moisture
causes mildew on clothes, luggage, furniture, books, and other
household furnishings. The best protection (sometimes the *only*
form of protection) is to install an electric dehumidifier, which
draws moisture from the air before it has time to condense.
However, before purchasing one, be aware of the following
facts:

• Although dehumidifiers and air conditioners both reduce
humidity inside a home, a dehumidifier is not an air conditioner.
In fact, just the opposite is true. A dehumidifier will cause the
air temperature in an area to increase. Thus, if dehumidification
is needed in a living area of the home during the summertime, it
would be more practical to buy an air conditioner and not a dehumidifier. On the other hand, a dehumidifier, which is less expensive than an air conditioner, will reduce humidity in those
areas where personal comfort is not a factor, such as in basement
storage areas, attics, and closets.

• Dehumidifiers which are the least costly run continuously.
More expensive models are equipped with a humidistat, which
controls the unit so that it runs when humidity in an area
reaches an undesirable level and shuts off when humidity is
reduced (Fig. 8).

• Depending upon their capacity, humidifiers draw from 10 to 48 pints of water from the air in 24 hours. The size that you buy depends on the volume of space you wish to protect and upon the severity of the moisture problem. It is better to buy a model that is slightly larger in capacity than needed.

Windows and doors leading into an area that is equipped with a dehumidifier should be kept closed for best results.

DOORBELL

A door signaling device consists of a transformer that reduces house electrical service to low voltage (16 volts or less), a pushbutton, wiring, and the signal itself (Fig. 1). When the signal fails to work, check to see that the fuse hasn't blown or the circuit breaker hasn't tripped.

If either has happened, there might be a short on the high voltage side of the transformer. Inspect all wiring that is visible from the transformer back to the fuse or circuit breaker box for breaks in insulation. If you see a frayed spot, wrap friction tape around it.

Replace the fuse or reactivate the circuit breaker. If it malfunctions again, call an electrician immediately and have him test the circuit (Fig. 2). Keep the fuse or circuit breaker off until he arrives. It is a potential fire hazard.

Most often when a door signal fails to function, the problem lies with the pushbutton, signaling device, or transformer, in that order. However, it is suggested that the transformer be tested first to be sure that current is getting to the pushbutton. If it isn't, you will get misleading results if you test the pushbutton.

If your home has a basement, you will probably find the transformer attached to an overhead joist. Notice that the high voltage side is wired with heavily insulated 14-gauge wire,

Figure 1. An example of a basic system, to help you trace a doorbell malfunction.

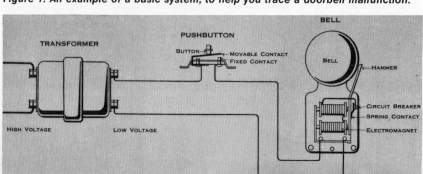

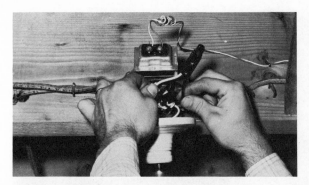

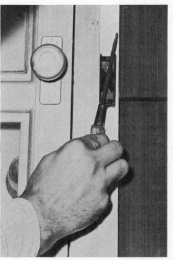

Figure 2. If failure is on the high voltage
side of the transformer, consult an electrician.

Figure 3. To check for pushbutton failure, hold a screwdriver across the two
contact points.

while the low-voltage side is wired with thinly insulated 18-gauge bell wire.

To check the transformer, use a 12-volt testlight which you can buy in a hardware store. Place the probes of the testlight on the low voltage side terminals. Do not touch the high voltage terminals.

If the testlight lights, the transformer is okay. If it doesn't light, you can replace the transformer by first disconnecting the fuse or circuit breaker and making sure that the replacement transformer is of the correct capacity for your signaling setup. To be sure, take the old transformer with you when you buy the new one.

If the transformer is in good condition, test the pushbutton by removing its cover and holding a screwdriver across the two fixed contact points (Fig. 3). If the bell rings, the movable contact plate is probably not making contact with the fixed contacts. Repair this by bending the plate, which is part of the button, so that firm engagement will be made when the button is pushed.

If this doesn't help, replace the pushbutton by unscrewing it from the door jamb, removing the wires connected to it, and reattaching the wires to a new pushbutton.

Sometimes the button will fail because of dirt on the contacts. Clean them off with a cotton swab that has been dipped in mineral spirits. If contacts are rusted, scrape them lightly with a piece of emery cloth.

The signaling device may have failed. To find out, remove the

Figure 4. Occasionally remove rods from the signal for a good cleaning with mineral spirits.

Figure 5. The tops of strikers should be cleaned with a brush that's been dipped in cleaner.

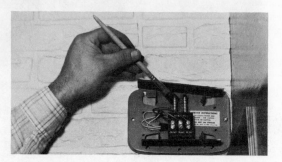

cover and watch the mechanism as someone pushes the push-button. If the hammer or strikers do not function, the electromagnetic coils in the device have probably burned out. Replace the entire signal.

If you have chimes, clean them periodically to assure good performance. Remove the rod or rods and clean them with a rough textured cloth that has been dipped in mineral spirits (Fig. 4). Also brush off the tops of strikers with a small brush that has been dipped in mineral spirits (Fig. 5). Do not use a petroleum base solvent, such as kerosene or gasoline. It will cause rubber pads on strikers to deteriorate.

DOORS

The first thing to do when a door fails to function properly because of misalignment is to tighten *all* hinge screws (Fig. 1). Many times a loose hinge is the reason that a door is out of kilter, causing it to stick at the top or sag at the bottom.

Figure 1. Many times the answer to a door problem is simply to give all hinge screws a turn.

Figure 2. In order to remove a door from the casement, knock out hinge pins as seen here.

Figure 3. Remove screws from the hinge leaf that covers enlarged holes to apply compound.

Figure 4. Fill the holes full, and allow putty to harden completely. Then, replace screws.

If hinge screws do not bite tightly into the wood, replace them with longer, larger screws. However, if screw holes have become enlarged so that no screw seats firmly, remove the door by knocking out the hinge pin (Fig. 2). Unscrew the hinge that has the enlarged screw holes, and fill the enlarged holes with wood putty or plastic wood (Figs. 3 and 4). Allow the compound to dry and harden before replacing hinge and screws

If tightening screws doesn't alleviate the problem, examine the door carefully as you open and close it to determine where the misalignment difficulty is occurring. If it is at the top, place a thin piece of cardboard beneath the upper hinge leaf (Fig. 5). If the door is sagging at the bottom, place the cardboard shim under the lower hinge leaf. Testing will allow you to determine how many shims are needed. For example, if one shim helps but doesn't alleviate the condition, use two or three.

Another major problem that affects a door is swelling because of extreme humidity. If the door sticks, it will probably do so in warm weather. Spray the edges with a silicone spray compound that can be purchased in a hardware store. Most times the swelling condition is such that silicone on the door's edges will relieve the problem.

Figure 5. A misalignment problem can usually be resolved by placing shims beneath hinges.

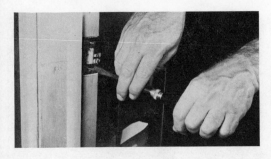

Figure 6. In order to enlarge the striker plate with a file, remove and mount it in a vise.

If it doesn't, though, do *not* plane the door. Planing is a painstaking task, and it is difficult to assure a straight cut. Even if planing is done properly, you may reduce the size of the door so that it will be too loose and rattle when it does dry out.

If the door has swelled, remove it from the frame and place it in a sunny spot for a few days. Make sure it's on a flat surface, and turn it frequently to prevent warping. After the door has dried, apply two coats of varnish to all edges so that moisture won't again attack the wood.

If the door is obviously warped, the only way to correct the problem is to remove the door from its hinges and place it across two sawhorses, or some such support, with the bowed side facing up. Apply about 50 pounds of weight—for example, bricks or a trash can that's partially filled with water—to the bowed area. Remove the weight as soon as the bow straightens, and apply two coats of varnish to all edges.

A door that won't latch is usually caused by the door and frame separating as the foundation settles. This keeps the latch from reaching the striker plate. The problem can often be resolved by placing a cardboard shim beneath the latch plate.

Another cause of trouble may be a misalignment condition between latch and striker. This can be corrected by filing a larger opening in the striker plate so that the latch can enter. Remove the striker plate to do this (Fig. 6).

Sometimes a latch can stick. If this is the case, examine it for rust, paint, and dirt. Clean it with a piece of emery cloth, and squirt some powdered graphite through the keyhole into the lock mechanism. Turn the door knob several times to distribute graphite.

DOWNSPOUTS

The following photographs and captions explain how to treat the downspouts around your home. For a discussion of how to repair gutters, see the section entitled Gutters:

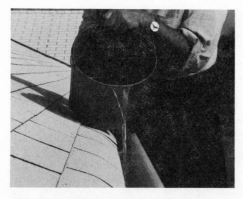

Figure 1. To determine if downspouts are clogged, pour water down. Outflow should be rapid.

Figure 2. If drain is sluggish, direct a high-pressure flow of water down the spout from the top.

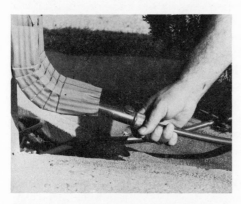

Figure 3. Now, direct water up the downspout from the bottom. Repeat procedure if necessary.

Figure 4. Leaves and other material are kept out of a downspout with this type of guard.

DRAFTPROOFING

A drafty home is uncomfortable and uneconomical. As much as $200 in heat can be wasted during the winter in a home which isn't properly protected against drafts. The methods which you can employ to avert this loss and make your home more comfortable are discussed in this section.

The best method is insulation. Every home has some, but not every home has enough. How can you tell?

Wait for a cold day and place your hand on a wall of a room which faces the outside. Although the wall may at first feel cold, it should start to feel warm within a few seconds. If the wall

Figure 1. To insulate a home, holes are drilled in sheathing.

stays cold to your touch, heat is escaping because of inadequate insulation. Heat can also be escaping through the ceiling. Use the touch test to find out.

The ideal amount of insulation is 6 inches thick in ceilings and 3 inches thick in walls. The ceiling is easily insulated in an existing home if there is an unfinished attic or crawl space into which you can climb. Use either insulation batts that you place between attic rafters or pour loose insulation between rafters. Your hardware store dealer or lumber yard can supply you with these products.

The best time to insulate the walls of a home is when it is being built. If this was not done adequately, however, you may now call in an insulation contractor who will use special equipment to blow insulation material into the walls. This is done by removing siding and drilling holes between wall studs (Fig. 1). A compressor is used to blow loose insulating material through a hose that is inserted into the wall (Fig. 2). Finally, tarpaper and siding are replaced (Fig. 3).

Figure 2. Insulation is blown inside walls by a compressor.

Figure 3. To complete the job, the home's siding is installed.

As you can imagine, this work is expensive, costing between $500 and $1000 for a modest size home. Actual cost depends upon the type of insulating material you select. You have a choice of three.

Rock wool insulation is the oldest type. It is heavy and bulky, and has a tendency to sag. This prevents it from staying in all crevices, which creates dead spots through which heat can escape. Rock wool also absorbs moisture which, in time, will cause the material to rot.

Fiberglass insulation is lighter in weight than rock wool and is better able to fill crevices. It won't sag or retain as much moisture as rock wool. However, it costs about 10 percent more.

Cellulose fiber insulation is the most efficient of the insulating materials. It is the lightest in weight, packs best, and doesn't sag. However, it costs approximately 30 percent more than rock wool.

Don't trust this job to just any contractor. Select one who has a reputation for honesty and competency.

Whether or not a home is adequately insulated, a substantial saving can be realized by weather stripping, which is a method of sealing cracks around doors and windows. There are several different kinds of weather stripping, with each having its own advantages and disadvantages.

Weather stripping for windows can either be glued, pressed, or nailed into place. All are effective in blocking drafts until the window is opened and the seal is broken. Then, the degree of effectiveness is sharply curtailed—more with some weather stripping materials than with others.

Window weather stripping that is glued (adhered) in place is pressure-sensitive tape and adhesive-backed plastic foam. Both are easy to install, but the surface to which the adhesive back will be placed must be clean.

Pressure-sensitive tape is an effective weather stripping material when it is first installed. It is placed directly over the crack and pressed into place (Fig. 4). However, it must be removed before the window can be opened. Once removed, the strip cannot be reused.

Figure 4. To use pressure-sensitive tape, press into place.

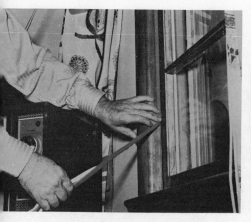 

Figure 5. Adhesive-backed plastic foam weather stripping adheres firmly to window stops.

Figure 6. When caulking is used, the window should not be open.

To install adhesive-backed plastic foam, put the foam against the crack with the adhesive back placed on the window stop (Fig. 5). The window may be opened and closed without removing the strip. However, as the window rubs against the foam, the foam is distorted and the weather stripping loses its sealing ability. Foam weather stripping has a tendency to dry out and shrink in time.

The adhesives of both pressure-sensitive tape and adhesive-backed plastic foam will eventually lose strength, causing the material to pull away from the crack. The two products are relatively inexpensive and are available in a number of sizes.

Window weather stripping that is pressed into place is caulk compound which comes in strips that are peeled off and pressed into the crack with your fingertips (Fig. 6). Caulk is more difficult to handle than the other types of weather stripping, because it takes care to peel it apart without splitting the strip, and it is messy.

Window weather stripping that you nail into place against the crack includes felt, a combination of felt and serrated metal, vinyl, and a combination of vinyl and serrated metal (Fig. 7).

Figure 7. Vinyl weather stripping is one of the most effective materials now available.

Figure 8. Felt and metal door weather stripping is nailed into place so felt covers the crack.

Figure 9. Vinyl weather stripping is also effective in stopping drafts from around doors.

Felt, either by itself or in combination with metal, won't hold its shape after several openings of the window. Vinyl, either by itself or in combination with metal, provides excellent sealing. However, it will eventually dry out and shrink.

In summation, then, although each type of window weather stripping material has some sort of drawback, it is beneficial to use weather stripping in a home. The type you employ depends on your own views. If one type doesn't serve as well as you think that it should, try another.

Weather stripping material for use around door frames include vinyl-metal, foam-wood, plain felt, and felt-metal. Any of these, properly installed, will provide good sealing for a time (Figs. 8 and 9).

Keep in mind, however, that weather stripping for use around door frames should not be used along door bottoms. There are special weather strippings made for the purpose.

The least expensive and least effective but easiest to install door bottom is a simple vinyl and metal strip that is nailed to the bottom of the door (Fig. 10). It glides along the floor as the door is opened and closed, but it can't provide 100 percent effective-

Figure 10. Door bottoms require special types of weather strips.

Figure 11. Determine if drafts exist around mouldings by running your hand along the crack.

Figure 12. It is necessary to use care in removing moulding so that it doesn't split.

ness since some space must be left between the door bottom and the floor to allow you to open the door.

The most expensive door bottoms cost $4 to $5 per door and usually require that the door be removed for installation of the material. One of the most effective types uses a metal threshold equipped with a vinyl bulb and a metal strip that is nailed beneath the door. The strip serves as a cap to keep water from leaking beneath the door.

To install this door bottom, the door must be removed and its bottom cut off to allow a 1-inch clearance between the door's bottom and the floor. The vinyl threshold is installed, and the metal strip is nailed onto the bottom of the door. When the door is reinstalled, the bottom is adjusted to meet the vinyl threshold so that a tight seal is made.

If you have a carpet running to a door, keep in mind that there is also a door bottom that won't interfere with the carpet when the door is opened. This is a spring-loaded door bottom that pops up when the door is opened. When the door is closed, a knob that is installed at one end of the door bottom comes into contact with the jamb moulding to push the door bottom down into place.

In the search for drafts, your hand will serve as an effective detector. Around windows, for example, check to see if cold air is coming in through butt moldings (Fig. 11). As the window settles, the sill and moulding may separate, which will allow drafts to enter. If there is a draft, remove the moulding with a pry bar (Fig. 12). Take care not to crack the moulding. Then, reposition the moulding tightly against the sill and renail with eight-pennyweight finishing nails (Fig. 13).

Figure 13. Reattach the moulding with 8-d finishing nails.

Figure 14. Use a plastic sheet as a storm window when a window air conditioner interferes.

Window air conditioners present a significant draftproofing problem. Since the unit is in a window, you cannot use a storm window.

The first thing to do is to make sure that the exhaust-intake controls are closed. Even with the unit turned off, if ducts are open, drafts will enter.

On the outside, apply caulking compound around unit-window joints. An effective storm window can be improvised by buying a clear plastic sheet and cutting it to the size of the outside window frame. Staple or nail the plastic to the window frame (Fig. 14). An air conditioner cover which fits over the outside of the unit will complete your efforts.

Faulty shoe mouldings along baseboards are also an entryway for drafts. Use your hand to determine if drafts exist. As you did with window mouldings, remove shoe mouldings carefully and reposition them tightly against the baseboard.

Fireplaces that jut into a room are frequently overlooked as a source of drafts. They are always against an outside wall or against a wall that is backed by the garage. Thus, the joint where the fireplace meets the wall could separate, allowing gusts of wind to blow in. To plug this opening, mix some ready-mix sand mix (see the section on Cement for details).

If the joint between the fireplace and wall is very wide, stuff a filler into the gap, such as household aluminum foil (Fig. 15). Now, apply cement.

Figure 15. Ordinary household aluminum foil will fill spaces between a wall and fireplace.

Figure 16. To seal off drafts from the exhaust fan, line the grille with household aluminum.

By the way, fireplace dampers should be closed when the fireplace isn't being used. This is a major cause of drafts.

What about exhaust fans? The outside duct of these has a spring-actuated lid which is supposed to open only when hit by the force of the operating fan. However, they have a way of swinging open when gusts of wind hit them.

If this proves to be a source of drafts, the fan can be lined with aluminum foil (Fig. 16). However, this remedy may be impractical if cooking odors, for instance, can't be dispelled by opening the window for a minute.

One of the best draftproofing mediums, of course, is caulking compound. For a discussion of this, see the section on Caulking.

DRAINS

The best time to correct a clogged drain is when water begins to trickle slowly from the sink. Repair becomes more difficult if the condition is permitted to worsen.

Fortunately, most obstructions become trapped at or near the sink where they are easy to clean out as opposed, for example, to being trapped in the sewer line. The first thing to do if the stoppage occurs in a bathroom sink is to remove the stopper by lifting it out of the sink (Fig. 1). Hair, lint, and other foreign material often become entwined around a stopper, impeding the flow of water into the drain. Clean material from the stopper and test water flow before proceeding further.

Blockages other than those around a stopper are handled

Figure 1. A bathroom sink will become clogged if the stopper has an accumulation of matter.

Figure 2. Every home should be equipped with a plumber's aid. It's effective against clogs.

the same way for bathroom and kitchen sinks. Most times the blockage is nothing more than grease and soap residue which has accumulated over the years. It can often be dissolved with a caustic chemical drain cleaner that you can buy in hardware stores.

Caution: Chemical drain cleaners can cause injury if not used properly, and they are poisonous. Read instructions regarding use and storage that you find on the container.

If chemical cleaning does not eliminate the obstruction, partially fill the basin with water and use a plumber's aid to try to force the obstacle loose (Fig. 2). Place the plumber's aid (plunger) over the drain hole and rapidly pump up and down several times.

If you are working on a double sink, seal one sink while you work on the other. Place a cover, such as a pot lid, over the drain hole. This will prevent water from backing into this sink, instead of remaining in the drain where it will help clear the blockage.

If all else fails to clear the drain, you will have to remove the drain plug, which most traps have (Fig. 3). If one isn't present, the trap itself will have to be removed by unscrewing the large knurled nuts which hold the elbow in place. Wrap tape around the nuts to keep from marring them with the wrench.

Use a drain trap auger (snake) to ream out the obstruction (Fig. 4). The auger is a flexible tool about 25 feet in length that you can buy or rent from a hardware store.

Figure 3. Most drain traps have a threaded plug that can be unscrewed for clearing stoppages.

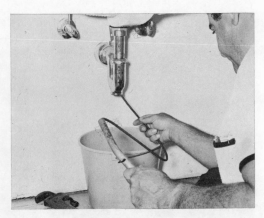

Figure 4. Insert the drain trap auger into the drain plug hole until it strikes the stoppage.

Insert the auger into the hole until you strike the obstruction. Use short, sharp strokes to force the auger through the blockage. If the obstruction is particularly stubborn, twist the auger with a drill-like action (Fig. 5).

When the obstruction has been cleared, replace the drain plug. If you had to remove the trap, wrap packing around the threaded portion of the pipe before reinstalling the elbow (Fig. 6). Packing is an impregnated ropelike material that keeps water from leaking out around the knurled nuts. It is sold in hardware stores.

Clogging of drains is usually avoidable by following a few simple precautions. Keep fats and grease out of the drain. After washing dishes, flush the drain with hot water for about 30 seconds. Regular use of a caustic chemical drain cleaner will virtually eliminate clogging.

Figure 5. Many times you will have to twist the auger in order to get through a blockage.

Figure 6. Before reinstalling the trap, wrap packing around the pipe to stop water leaks.

A clogged toilet drain is handled in much the same manner as a clogged sink drain. Initially use the plumber's aid to try and force the obstruction from the drain. If that doesn't work, use the auger to clear the blockage.

DRYWALL

Drywall (also called plasterboard and gypsum wallboard) has been more widely used than lath and plaster in home construction since the late 1940s. The walls and ceilings in your home are probably drywall.

Drywall is composed primarily of gypsum granules that are compressed between two layers of a heavy paperlike substance. Panels come in 4 × 8 foot sheets and are nailed to 2 × 4 foot wood studs (Fig. 1). Joints between panels are then taped and cemented prior to painting (Fig. 2).

The two biggest problems that drywall presents are nails that pop and cracks which appear primarily around doors and windows. This damage should be repaired before a room is repainted.

Popped nails result when wood studs holding drywall contract as they dry out. Nails are squeezed out of the wood and are pushed up through the drywall. At first, they appear as round areas of raised paint. If the situation is allowed to continue, paint will eventually fall loose to reveal the nailhead.

To repair popped nails, hammer a 1¼-inch drywall nail, which can be purchased in a hardware store, through the drywall panel and into the stud. Position the new nail about 1½ inches below or above the popped nail (Fig. 3). As you drive the nail into place, apply firm pressure to the panel with your hand to bring the panel into firm contact with the stud.

Your final blow on the nailhead with the hammer should

Figure 1. Drywall construction is basically simple. Panels are nailed to 2 x 4 ft wood framing.

Figure 2. Cement and tape are applied over joints to present a smooth surface for painting.

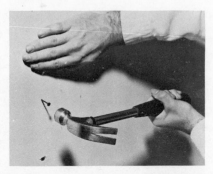

Figure 3. An area which experiences popped nailheads should be reinforced with new nails.

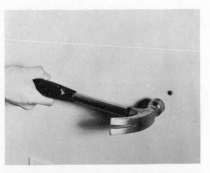

Figure 4. The area surrounding nailheads should be dimpled to provide spackling with a base.

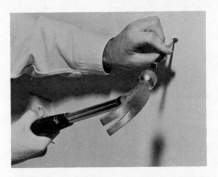

Figure 5. Nailheads that prove too stubborn can be driven home with a sharp blow on a nailset.

Figure 6. After nailheads are set, cover them with spackle. A ready-mix is easiest to use.

drive the head slightly below the surface of the panel and should dimple the surface (Fig. 4). However, be sure that this blow isn't struck too hard or it will cause the gypsum material to crumble.

Now, reset the popped nail. This is done by striking the nailhead so that it is positioned below the panel's surface. If the nail is stubborn and refuses to be reset, use a nailset to drive it home (Fig. 5).

The dimpled areas around the nailheads provide a base for the patching material, which is called spackle. Spackle can be purchased in a hardware store as a powder which is mixed with water or as a ready-to-use prepared compound. The ready-mix costs a few cents extra, but it is recommended that it be used. It is more convenient and eliminates the chore of mixing spackle to the right consistency.

Figure 7. This shows the only compounds needed to repair popped nailheads and small cracks.

Figure 8. To repair cracks using fiberglass, brush on a liberal coat of fiberglass resin.

Apply sufficient spackle to completely cover dimpled areas (Fig. 6). Scrape off excess so patches are flush with the surface of the panel. Allow spackle to dry overnight and then sand lightly with fine-grit sandpaper. Paint can now be applied.

Cracks in drywall occur as the house settles and shifts. Filling a crack with patching material is not recommended. The patch will not last, and the crack will soon reappear because, as the house continues to shift, the repair material will loosen and fall from place.

A permanent repair of a crack can be made with fiberglass cloth which is applied with a fiberglass resin (adhesive). If your hardware store dealer does not have fiberglass, consult a dealer of marine supplies. If you are not successful, the repair can be accomplished with ordinary perforated drywall tape and drywall joint cement (Fig. 7).

To ready the surface, use fine-grit sandpaper to sand the crack and an area about 3 inches on each side of the crack. If you are employing the fiberglass method, apply a liberal amount of resin with a paint brush (Fig. 8). Allow the resin to become tacky and then apply the fiberglass cloth (Fig. 9). Flatten the

Figure 9. The fiberglass cloth is placed over the crack. Make certain that it adheres firmly.

Figure 10. When applying perforated drywall tape, be sure a good coat of cement is used.

cloth firmly into place with a rubber squeegee. When the resin loses tackiness, which takes about 2 hours, brush on another coating. Let this dry for a day before painting.

If you are repairing the crack with drywall tape, apply a liberal swath of joint cement over the crack and to each side of it (Fig. 10). Press tape firmly into place and smooth it down with a broad knife.

During the smoothing process, you will notice that the joint cement comes to the top of the tape through the perforations. This is necessary. Spread cement evenly over the tape and to each side of it. Be sure that there is a coating of cement over the tape even if you must apply more. Allow cement to dry overnight. Sand the area lightly with fine-grit sandpaper and paint.

Major damage to drywall, specifically gaping holes that are accidentally knocked into panels, are easily repaired with a patch that you can fashion from scrap drywall. Follow these steps:

1. Use a keyhole saw to enlarge and round the damaged area to a diameter of at least 3 inches.

2. Cut a backing strip from scrap drywall that is no less than 2 inches larger than the diameter of the hole. If the hole is 3 inches in diameter, the backing strip should be at least 5 inches long.

Figure 11. To repair a gaping hole, cut the hole to a 3-inch diameter and install a brace. (Courtesy of Popular Mechanics*)*

Figure 12. Insert the circular patch so it makes contact with the brace. Spackle the patch. (Courtesy of Popular Mechanics*)*

3. Apply contact or joint cement to each end of the strip and insert it into the hole, positioning it so that it spans the center of the hole (Fig. 11). Hold the backing strip against the wall until it takes hold. Then, allow it to set for an hour.

4. Cut out a circular patch from scrap, making it approximately ⅛ inch less in diameter than the size of the hole.

5. Coat the back of the circular patch with contact or joint cement and insert it into the hole so it contacts the cross strip (Fig. 12). Do not press or you will knock the cross strip from place. Allow the repair to set for 24 hours.

6. Apply spackle over the entire patch, making sure that the joint is filled. Remove excess spackle by scraping it off with a broad knife, and featheredge; that is, smooth the edges of the spackle out so the patching material blends into the panel's surface. Allow the spackle to dry for 24 hours, sand lightly to remove high spots, and paint.

ELECTRIC APPLIANCES AND TOOLS

The modern home contains a variety of electrically operated appliances and tools. For the purpose of repair, each should be placed into one of two categories.

First, there are those that are driven by an electric motor. They include food blenders, food mixers, electric knives, electric garden tools (hedge trimmers, grass shears, edgers, and cultivators), and electric shop tools (drills, saws, and routers).

Then, there are those which utilize heating elements. They include toasters, grills and broilers, coffee makers, and space heaters.

Let's discuss motor-driven equipment first. The small electric motor which drives these appliances and tools is reliable and provides long service. When a piece of equipment fails to function, the problem is seldom a burned-out motor. Instead, the trouble can usually be found at the power cord, motor brushes, or the on-off switch.

Incidentally, if the malfunction is being caused by a burned-out motor, it is usually more practical to replace the piece of equipment with a new one than to have it repaired.

Begin trouble-shooting by examining the power cord. The first thing to do when an electrically driven motor fails to function is to spread the prongs of the plug a bit to assure good contact in the electric outlet. Inspect the cord visually for breaks in the insulation. If the cord is damaged, replace it.

Quite often the wiring inside the cord will be damaged. To determine if this is the case, plug the cord into an outlet and

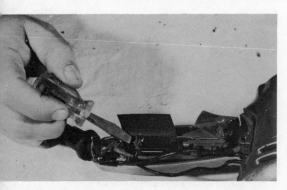

Fig. 1. Disassemble the handle and unscrew the terminals to remove a damaged power cord.

meticulously bend the cord back and forth over its entire length
with the appliance or tool switched on. If the equipment begins
to operate, the cord should be replaced.

It is not possible here to provide step-by-step instructions
on how to replace the power cord or, for that matter, any other
part of an electric appliance or tool. Each appliance and tool
varies from manufacturer to manufacturer in the placement of
parts. However, they are all designed to have power cords,
brushes, and switches replaced. Therefore, the piece of equipment is designed to come apart. If you attempt to do this, proceed slowly and carefully, making note of what you remove
from where.

To replace a power cord of the electric drill seen here, for
example, it is necessary to take the handle apart (Fig. l). Once
terminals are revealed, however, it is a simple matter to take
the old cord off and attach the new one.

By the way, if the power cord passes the test outlined
above, it is possible that the cause of the tool or appliance not
operating is looseness at the cord terminal. To remedy this,
tighten the terminals.

The next things to check are the motor brushes. Brushes
are two comparatively small bars of carbon that press against
the commutator of an electric motor to provide a means of trans-
mitting electricity to the motor. Brushes wear with use.

In many appliances and tools, brushes can be removed from
the equipment without having to take the case apart. You will
find slotted retainers on each side of the equipment. Unscrew
them slowly, maintaining inward pressure (Fig. 2). Brushes are
under spring tension and will fly loose if not held as they are
removed (Fig. 3).

If brushes cannot be removed externally, you will have to
take the case apart and find the brush retainers.

Figure 2. If your equipment has large slotted retainers, remove them slowly to replace worn brushes.

Figure 3. Note that brushes are equipped with springs. Keep pressure on the brush as you remove it to keep it from flying loose.

Brushes should be considered worn if they are less than ¼ inch in length (Fig. 4). Replace brushes in pairs. They may be purchased at hardware stores or at a dealer who sells appliances or tools.

You can tell if the on-off switch has gone bad by the way it feels. If it fails to click and feels sloppy, it should be replaced. This involves gaining access to the switch and removing it.

If a tool or appliance begins making a grinding noise as it operates, you should apply fresh lubricant as soon as possible. The dealer who sells your make of tool or appliance can advise you which lubricant to use.

Some appliances and tools can be lubricated through lubrication holes in the equipment's case. With others, such as the drill seen here, it is necessary to remove the gear end of the tool or appliance and apply lubricant directly (Fig. 5).

Figure 4. Brushes should be at least ¼ inch in length. If not, they should be replaced.

Figure 5. When lubrication is required, it may be necessary to remove the cover over the gears.

If the equipment continues to make noise after lubrication, shut it off at once and consult a professional repairman. Bearings are probably damaged and should be replaced. Continued use in this condition will result in serious damage.

The chief enemy of appliances that use heating elements is dirt. When a problem occurs, disconnect and clean the unit as thoroughly as possible. Use a small brush to get into crevices to clean away food particles.

If cleaning the unit doesn't improve its operation, check the power cord as was described above. If this fails to solve the problem, there is a bad thermostat or a burned-out element. The appliance should be disassembled. However, before you allow a professional repairman to fix the unit, get an estimate of cost. It may prove more economical to buy a new appliance.

EMERGENCIES, WINTER

There are five serious household emergencies that often occur in winter that are difficult, if not impossible, to repair permanently because of bad weather. They are a roof leak, frozen water pipe and drain, a burst water pipe, and a broken window.

Since these emergencies will cause serious damage as well as discomfort and inconvenience to your family, it is imperative that some remedial action be taken, if only of a temporary nature. The following offers you some solutions:

Roof leaks appear as damp spots on ceilings. If snow, ice, or cold temperature prevents a permanent repair from the roof side, the problem must be tackled from inside. This involves two tasks: you must find from where the leak is originating, and then you must employ a compound that will stop the leak until a permanent repair can be made.

Keep in mind that roof leaks are devious. The actual leaking area may not be over the room whose ceiling is being spotted. Water travels. Thus, to find the actual origin of the leak, go into the attic or crawl space and examine the rafters. Water enter-

Figure 1. Trace dampness back along the rafter until the exact area of leakage is found.

Figure 2. Latex caulking compound makes an effective repair, if temperature is above 40°F.

Figure 3. Press the caulking compound into and all around the leak to assure a tight repair.

ing the house through a hole in the roof will run down rafters, which are usually pitched. Find the wet rafter and trace dampness back up the rafter to the point of origin (Fig. 1).

A relatively small hole can be effectively sealed with latex caulking compound if the temperature in the attic is 40°F or above (Fig. 2). Latex caulk adheres strongly to wood and cures in about 30 minutes. Apply a thick dab and spread it with a wood spatula or putty knife beyond the edges of the leak (Fig. 3).

If the temperature in the attic is below 40°F, latex caulk cannot be used. In this case, employ white silicone rubber compound, which is available in hardware stores. It can be applied at temperatures below 0°F. However, its curing time is 24 hours. Apply a liberal amount and spread the compound with a wood spatula or putty knife.

If the leak is so massive that it can't be stopped with caulking compound, use Instant Patch, which is an asphalt-glass-fiber compound that can be applied to a wet surface. This thick emulsion material can be spread over the leaking area with an old paint brush (Fig. 4). The material takes about 24 hours to dry for maximum effectiveness.

Figure 4. If the roof leak is massive, spread Instant Patch over it with an old paintbrush.

After patching a roof leak, examine the area every two or three days to assure that the temporary repair is holding. Apply additional repair compound, if necessary. However, keep in mind that this patch is not permanent. When weather permits, the roof should be repaired properly (see the sections on Roofs and Flashing Repairs).

Frozen pipes result when water in a pipe in an unheated basement freezes. Frozen pipes can also result when homeowners neglect to shut off and drain a pipe which supplies water to an outside faucet.

A frozen pipe, of course, will block the water supply to faucets. Furthermore, there is danger that the pipe will crack as ice expands. Therefore, before attempting to thaw a pipe, inspect it closely for cracks. If a pipe is cracked, shut off the water supply, thaw the pipe, and apply a temporary repair to seal the crack as explained below. This repair will be effective until a plumber arrives.

There are several ways to thaw a frozen pipe. The quickest method is with a propane torch. However, a torch should only be used if the pipe is exposed and not near a joist. Use of a flame near a joist presents danger of fire.

Open all water faucets served by the frozen pipe and move the torch along the pipe until the blockage is relieved and water begins to flow from the faucets (Fig. 5). Keep the torch moving at all times. Never concentrate the flame on one spot. This could cause water in the pipe to start boiling, which will result in increased pressure that could burst the pipe.

If the frozen pipe runs along a joist, the safest way to thaw it is with a heat lamp or a photographic lamp and reflector (Fig. 6). Make sure the faucets served by the pipe are open and set

Figure 5. Use a propane torch if the frozen pipe is not near a joist. Keep the torch moving.

Figure 6. A photolamp and reflector are safest to use when the pipe is nailed to a joist.

Figure 7. Sufficient heat will be generated by a drain cleaner to melt ice clogging the drain.

Figure 8. Temporary repair of a cracked pipe is made with retort cement and plastic tubing.

the lamp so that its rays shine on the pipe. Leave the lamp in place for several minutes. Then move it to another section of pipe until the condition is relieved.

Frozen drains that prevent dissipation of sink and toilet wastes can be thawed by pouring boiling water down the drain. If this method is ineffective, a chemical that is used to clean drains should be applied (Fig. 7). Drain cleaning chemicals generate a good deal of heat.

You can prevent drains from freezing by mixing an equal quantity of kerosene and automotive antifreeze and pouring the mixture down the sink or toilet before cold weather strikes. This mixture will settle in the drain trap and provide effective freeze-proof protection. Two quarts of solution is sufficient for a toilet. Use two pints in sink drains.

Cracked water pipes that cannot be repaired immediately by a plumber can be repaired temporarily with furnace and retort cement, a length of plastic aerotube pipe insulation, and hose clamps. These items can be purchased at a plumbing supply store.

Coat the crack with a liberal amount of the cement and wrap a length of insulation, slit lengthwise, around the pipe (Fig. 8). Secure the insulation with the clamps.

Broken windows that are difficult to repair because of cold weather can be sealed temporarily with a plastic storm window. This is a large sheet of polyethylene which is sold in hardware and department stores.

Simply tack or staple the plastic sheet to the window frame

and tape its edges with plastic tape. This sheet makes a weather-tight seal that will provide protection until the window can be replaced.

Naturally, the repair materials mentioned in this section should be purchased and stored in the home before winter starts. The following list will summarize what they are:

1. Latex caulk and white silicone rubber compound for small roof leaks.

2. Instant Patch for massive roof leaks.

3. Propane torch for thawing an exposed frozen water pipe.

4. Heat lamp or photoflood lamp and reflector for thawing a frozen pipe that is attached to a joist.

5. Caustic drain cleaning chemical for thawing a frozen drain.

6. Furnace and retort cement, plastic aerotube pipe insulation and hose clamps for repairing a cracked water pipe.

7. Plastic storm window and plastic tape for broken windows.

ENGINE, TROUBLESHOOTING

This section deals with troubleshooting of one-cylinder gasoline engines which drive yard and garden equipment, including self-propelled and riding lawn mowers, tillers, leaf blowers, sweepers, tractors, chain saws, and snow blowers. The section that follows discusses how to repair and maintain this equipment. To begin with, some definitions are in order.

Troubleshooting, which is the single most important area to master, means to zero in on a malfunction. Before you can solve a problem, you have to know its cause. Even if you don't wish to tackle repairs yourself, by knowing what is causing a breakdown you can be very specific in dealing with a mechanic, thus assuring that unnecessary repairs won't be made.

Repair means to fix. Replacing parts and making adjustments to solve an existing problem are considered repairs.

Engine overhaul, which should be left to a professional mechanic who has the necessary tools, is not discussed. How-

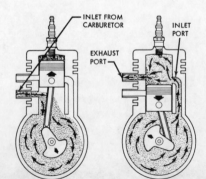

Figure 1. Two-cycle operation.

ever, practically every case of small engine failure, which are the ones we deal with in the next section, can be resolved with a minor repair, comparatively speaking.

Maintenance, which includes tuneup, refers to the care you give a small engine to avert a breakdown. Maintenance involves replacement of parts that are on the verge of failure and checking to see that adjustments are within specification.

Two additional terms you will encounter often in this discussion are two-cycle and four-cycle. Your single-cylinder engine is one or the other.

Two-cycle engines take in fuel, compress and ignite it, and exhaust waste gases in two strokes of the piston—up and down (Fig. 1). The ignition (power) stroke occurs during every revolution of the crankshaft.

Four-cycle engines accomplish intake, compression, ignition, and exhaust in four piston strokes, with the power stroke occurring during every other revolution of the crankshaft (Fig. 2).

Although two-and four-cycle engines differ in operation, much about their troubleshooting, repair, and maintenance is the same, because they possess several common parts, such as carburetors and magnetos. However, it will be important to keep in mind whether your equipment has a two- or four-cycle engine. Differences between them will be emphasized.

If your engine is made by Briggs and Stratton, Kohler, or Wisconsin, it is four-cycle. If it is a Jacobsen engine, it is two-cycle. Jacobsen, incidentally, is one of the few manufacturers of yard and garden equipment that makes its own engines. In other words, the manufacturer of the equipment and the manufacturer of the engine are not usually the same, so consult the nameplate attached to the engine to determine which company produced it. By the way, four-cycle engines used on some models of Jacobsen equipment are not made by Jacobsen, but by other

Figure 2. Four-cycle operation.

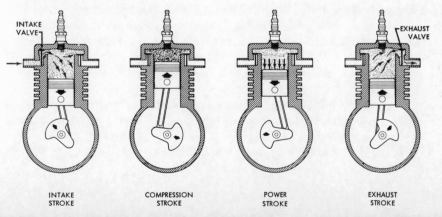

| INTAKE STROKE | COMPRESSION STROKE | POWER STROKE | EXHAUST STROKE |

Figure 3. In two-cycle engines, gas and oil are mixed together, then poured in the fuel tank.

Figure 4. In four-cycle engines, oil is poured into a crankcase, just like in your automobile.

companies, such as Lauson-Tecumseh. Jacobsen manufactures two-cycle engines only.

Two-cycle engines used in Lawn Boy self-propelled mowers are manufactured by the company that makes the mower, Outboard Marine Corp. However, Lawn Boy riding mowers use either Briggs and Stratton or Lauson-Tecumseh four-cycle engines.

If your engine is made by Clinton or Lauson-Tecumseh, it could be two- or four-cycle. These companies make both.

A major difference between two- and four-cycle engines is in their lubrication. Two-cycle engines are lubricated by oil that is mixed in and flows into the cylinder with gasoline (Fig. 3). Four-cycle engines are lubricated by oil from a crankcase that is distributed to engine parts by pressure, splash, or a combination of the two (Fig. 4). Lubrication is discussed in greater detail in the section dealing with Engine, Repair and Maintenance.

Before you troubleshoot an engine, you should have trouble. The following is a list of the major problems that affect small engines:

1. Engine doesn't start or is hard to start.
2. Engine overheats.
3. Engine cuts out while running and won't restart.
4. Engine misses under load or lacks power.
5. Engine surges (gallops).
6. Engine backfires.

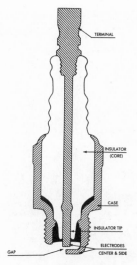

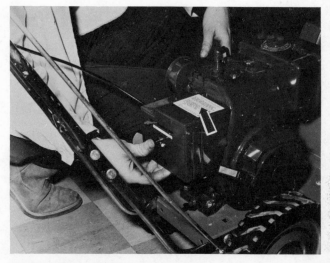

Figure 5. The spark plug is a major cause of engine failure.

Figure 6. Many engines have the starting procedure printed on a decal stuck to the engine.

7. Engine vibrates excessively.

8. Engine knocks.

Each of these problems, with the exception of engine knock and excessive vibration, is caused primarily by trouble in one of four areas: ignition, spark plug, fuel, or compression.

Technically, the spark plug is part of the ignition system. However, it is treated separately for two reasons: first, because a bad or incorrectly gapped spark plug is a chief cause of small engine failure; second, because a bad spark plug that is causing the engine to malfunction may be the result of a more serious problem that will not be resolved by simply replacing the spark plug (Fig. 5). An examination of the spark plug will show what that problem is.

The first thing to do when your engine starts to give trouble, unless that problem is engine knock or excessive vibration, is to localize the trouble to one of the four areas. However, before doing this, stop for a minute and determine whether you have followed instructions in the operator's manual on how to operate the engine (Fig. 6). The best troubleshooting technique in the world will not help you if the problem is human and not mechanical.

To isolate the trouble, proceed in the following manner:

1. *Check ignition output.* Most small engine problems are caused by a breakdown in the ignition system. There are two basic types of system: magneto and battery ignition. Your en-

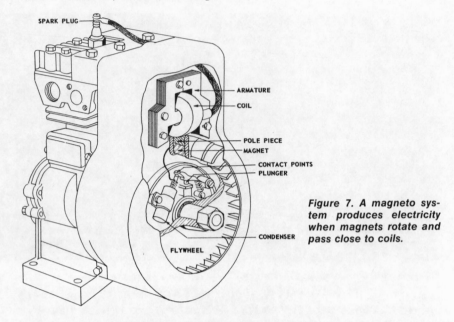

SPARK PLUG

ARMATURE

COIL

POLE PIECE
MAGNET

CONTACT POINTS
PLUNGER

CONDENSER

FLYWHEEL

Figure 7. A magneto system produces electricity when magnets rotate and pass close to coils.

gine is equipped with one or the other.

Battery ignition is ill-named, because self-start magneto systems employ batteries, too. So, to lessen confusion, let us refer to "battery ignition" systems as "ignition coil" systems.

Most single-cylinder engines have magnetos. Exceptions include some larger horsepower Wisconsin, Kohler, and Lauson-Tecumseh four-cycle engines that are used in garden tractors. They use an ignition coil system.

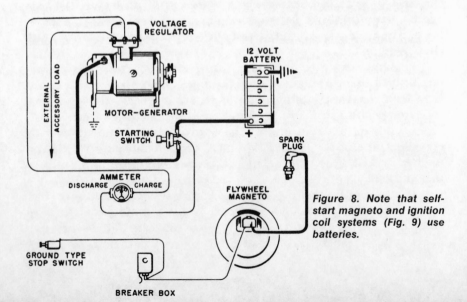

VOLTAGE
REGULATOR

EXTERNAL
ACCESSORY LOAD

12 VOLT
BATTERY

MOTOR-GENERATOR

STARTING
SWITCH

SPARK
PLUG

AMMETER
DISCHARGE   CHARGE

FLYWHEEL
MAGNETO

GROUND TYPE
STOP SWITCH

BREAKER BOX

Figure 8. Note that self-start magneto and ignition coil systems (Fig. 9) use batteries.

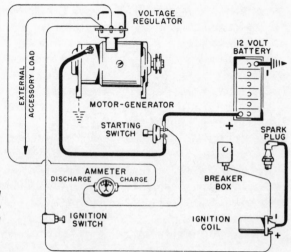

Figure 9. An ignition coil system is quite similar to the ignition system in an automobile.

The difference between magneto and ignition coil, simply stated, is that once the engine is running, a magneto makes its own electricity (Fig. 7). A properly operating magneto system provides about 15 kilovolts to the spark plug. To get an engine with a magneto started, you use either manual (rope) starting or electric (battery) starting (Fig. 8).

With the ignition coil system, a regular automobile-type ignition coil, which is basically a transformer, replaces the magneto (Fig. 9). A modern ignition coil system has a 12-volt battery (charged by an AC generator) providing current to the ignition coil, which steps the 12 volts up to about 25 kilovolts at the spark plug.

Both magneto and ignition coil systems employ breaker points which act as a switch to concentrate full voltage at the spark plug at the time that it is needed to fire the fuel mixture. A different innovation used on some garden tractors with four-cycle engines is breakerless ignition, which employs solid state devices instead of mechanical breaker points.

With breakerless ignition, which provides current approaching 50 kilovolts at the spark plug, the timing of the spark is permanently set. With breaker points, timing can go astray, which will cause an engine problem.

To test a *magneto system,* buy an 18-millimeter spark plug at a gasoline station and open the electrode gap to between 5/32 inch and 3/16 inch. Remove the high tension lead from the spark plug that is in your engine and attach it firmly to the test plug. The spark plug in the engine can stay in place while the output test is being conducted.

Place the plug on the engine head next to a clean ground, such as a bolt. Keep the plug from slipping by placing it beneath a cable, such as the choke cable, or by attaching it with a vise clamp. Do not hold the plug or high tension lead in your hand while the test is being conducted. You could receive a shock.

Crank the engine. If sparks jump the plug gap, the magneto output is satisfactory. Ignition is not the cause of your engine problem. However, if there is no spark, the engine malfunction is being caused by a breakdown in ignition (Fig. 10).

Perhaps you are curious as to why you are told to use a separate spark plug for testing magneto output rather than simply removing the spark plug from the engine and using that. The wide gap of the test plug provides a more accurate indication of magneto output.

A 14-millimeter spark plug (most single-cylinder small engines use a 14-millimeter spark plug) that is gapped to 0.028 inch, which is a normal gap for this plug, requires a magneto output of only 7 kilovolts for a spark to jump the electrode gap. If you open the electrode gap of an 18-millimeter spark plug to $^{5}/_{32}$ to $^{3}/_{16}$ inch, about 10 kilovolts are required for spark to jump the gap. A magneto ignition system that is in good operating condition provides about 15 kilovolts of electricity to a spark plug. Thus, if your magneto cannot provide a widely gapped test spark plug with sufficient voltage to make spark, it informs you that the magneto has broken down or is in the process of doing so.

Conversely, a less accurate method of measuring ignition output must be employed when testing the *ignition coil system*. Conduct this test in the same manner as you do the magneto system test, but use the engine's spark plug rather than a test plug. An ignition coil system should develop about 25 kilovolts. The comparatively small amount of voltage required to make spark with a wide gapped test spark plug does not justify use of this plug for this test.

Figure 10. As you crank the engine, check spark at the plug to verify an ignition failure.

Figure 11. The spark intensity tester is needed for checking of breakerless ignition setups.

If spark occurs as you crank the engine, you can assume for the time being that the ignition system is okay. However, if other tests (spark plug, fuel, and compression) show these areas to be in good condition, then suspect that there is a problem in ignition and come back to it.

Incidentally, if spark doesn't appear at the plug while testing ignition coil system output, replace the plug with a new one that is properly gapped before ripping into the ignition system. A bad spark plug will prevent spark.

To test *solid state (breakerless) ignition* you will need a spark intensity tester for solid state ignition. Spark occurs so rapidly that you cannot see it jump the spark plug gap. Besides, grounding of the spark plug as you do when testing magneto and ignition coil systems can damage solid state components. One company that makes a spark intensity tester is Snap-On Tools of Kenosha, Wisc.

To use the tester, disconnect the cable from the spark plug and attach the test instrument's lead to the cable's metal terminal. Touch the point of the test instrument to ground as someone cranks the engine (Fig. 11). If the test light flashes, the ignition system is in good working order.

2. *Check spark plug condition.* If your engine won't start, is hard to start, misses, or lacks power, check the spark plug (Fig. 12). Look for a cracked insulator, burned electrodes, and heavy carbon deposits. If any of these conditions exist, get a new spark plug.

Make sure that electrode gap is to specification (Fig. 13). Set it with a spark plug feeler gauge as explained in the section dealing with Automotive, Spark Plugs. For two-cycle engines, the gap is set to 0.028 to 0.033 inch, depending on manufacturer's specifications. For four-cycle engines, the gap is 0.025 to 0.028 inch, depending on manufacturer's specifications. Consult your owner's manual for the exact specification.

Figure 12. To remove the spark plug from an engine, make sure the socket is the right size.

Figure 13. Use a regular spark plug feeler gauge only to adjust the plug's electrode gap.

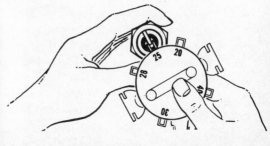

Figure 14. Spark plugs that are showing normal wear should be cleaned, filed, and regapped.

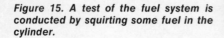

Figure 15. A test of the fuel system is conducted by squirting some fuel in the cylinder.

Critical examination of a spark plug's firing tip can lead you to the cause of an engine problem. The following are some of the most commonly encountered conditions and what they mean:

• *Normal wear*. If the spark plug has brown or greyish tan deposits and there is some electrode wear, it means that the spark plug is wearing normally. Clean off deposits with a small wire brush, file the electrodes square and bright with an ignition point file, set electrode gap with a spark plug feeler guage, and reuse the plug (Fig. 14).

If the spark plug shows extreme electrode wear and a pitted insulator, you have kept it in use too long. It is worn out. Get a new plug.

• *Carbon fouled*. A carbon fouled spark plug will have dry, fluffy black deposits on the tip. The condition usually results when the engine is operated with an over-rich fuel mixture. This is normally caused by over-choking or a clogged air cleaner that restricts air flow to the carburetor. It could also be caused by an incorrect fuel mixture adjustment.

Another reason for carbon fouling of the plug is poor ignition output that results in a reduced voltage condition, which is causing misfire. Check for bad breaker points, a weak coil and condenser, and worn ignition cable.

• *Oil fouled*. An oil fouled spark plug means that there is internal engine trouble in the form of worn piston rings or valve stems.

• *Burned electrodes*. The chief cause of this is operating the engine while it overheated, but be aware that improper ignition timing and a lean fuel mixture will also cause electrodes to burn.

When reinstalling the spark plug into the engine, be sure that it is seated properly. If it is too loose, gases will escape. If it is too tight, the plug will be damaged. To install the spark plug, seat it by hand and then turn it one-half turn with a socket.

3. *Check the fuel system.* In testing the fuel system to try to uncover an engine malfunction, you have to make sure that fuel is getting to the carburetor and, if so, that is is getting through the carburetor and into the cylinder. To do this, squirt some fuel into the cylinder from a clean trigger-type oil can (Fig. 15). Only two or three squirts are needed. Insert the spark plug and try to start the engine. If the engine starts, runs for a few seconds, and then stops, the trouble is in the fuel system.

To determine if the stoppage is ahead of the carburetor or in the carburetor, examine your carburetor for a bowl. Many carburetors with bowls have a drain valve in the base of the bowl next to the main adjustment screw. Press this valve. If fuel doesn't leak out, there is an obstruction in the fuel tank or fuel line (Fig. 16).

If there is no drain valve and the fuel system has a fuel line that connects from the fuel tank (or fuel pump) to the carburetor inlet, unhook the line at the carburetor (Fig. 17). If fuel drips out, it means that fuel is getting to, but not through, the carburetor.

Figure 16. Press on the drain valve. If no fuel shows, there is a blockage in the fuel line.

Figure 17. If there is no drain valve disconnect the fuel line to check for presence of fuel.

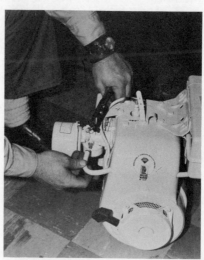

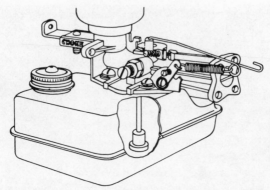

Figure 18. A setup that is common to small engines is having carburetor and tank connected.

If your fuel system is the type that has the carburetor and fuel tank connected to each other, fuel is fed directly from the tank to the carburetor through fuel pipes that are attached to the carburetor (Fig. 18). This is done by the creation of low pressure in the carburetor while the piston in the engine is on its downward stroke. In any event, if the test indicates that a fuel failure exists, the carburetor will have to be disconnected from the fuel tank (Fig. 19). Check the screens in the fuel pipe to determine if they are clogged. If they aren't, the carburetor needs to be overhauled.

Engine trouble is also caused by fuel system flooding. If the engine doesn't start after cranking, remove the spark plug and examine the tip. If it is wet with fuel, the engine is flooding, or an ignition or compression problem exists. Make ignition and compression tests as explained in this section to determine which condition prevails.

4. *Test compression.* If the ignition and fuel systems of your engine are apparently in good condition and you have installed a new spark plug, the engine will still fail to function properly if

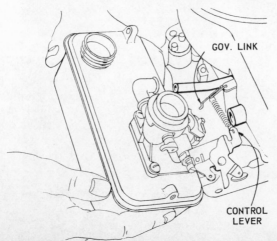

GOV. LINK

Figure 19. Carburetor and fuel tank are removed as a unit from the engine and are separated.

CONTROL LEVER

Figure 20. Only a compression gauge can tell you whether the engine has internal problems.

it has low compression. Compression is the ability of the piston to compress fuel to the point where it will ignite and burn to provide full power.

Compression in a single cylinder engine is extremely important. Without the correct amount of compression, the engine would be hard to start and would not develop maximum horsepower. Compression is a result of engine "tightness." An engine loses compression when it loses its ability to seal. Loss of compression results if there are leaks around rings, pistons, cylinder, and valves, or if there is a ruptured gasket.

The only accurate way of checking compression is with a compression gauge (Fig. 20). If you don't have one and don't wish to buy one (a gauge costs about $7), perhaps you can borrow one from the gasoline station that you patronize.

Remove the spark plug and hold or screw in (depending on what kind of compression gauge you use) the gauge into the spark plug hole. Crank the engine several times until the gauge reads as much as it is going to read (Fig. 21).

Figure 21. Hold the compression gauge in the cylinder and crank until you get the best reading.

If you are checking a two-cycle engine, the gauge reading should be a minimum of 60 pounds per square inch. If you have a four-cycle engine of 4½ horsepower or less, the compression reading should be at least 65 to 70 pounds per square inch. If you have a four-cycle engine of more than 4½ horsepower, the minimum compression you should get is 70 pounds per square inch.

Once you have isolated the general area of engine failure (ignition, carburetion, or compression), you can now proceed to make repairs.

ENGINES, REPAIR AND MAINTENANCE

As was pointed out in the preceding section, once a small engine problem has been isolated to the fuel or ignition system or to compression, the condition can often be remedied by the homeowner. This section outlines the order in which repairs should be made.

Luckily, most malfunctions can be corrected with a simple repair. However, if a repair is outside your scope of experience or tool availability, seek the services of a small engine repair shop.

As emphasized in the preceding section, before doing anything, make sure that the spark plug is in good condition and gapped to specification. You may not have to make any further repairs.

Failure to start or hard starting. If this condition exists because fuel is not getting to the engine, check the following in the order presented:

1. Is there fuel in the fuel tank?

2. Are you starting the engine according to manufacturer's instructions?

Figure 1. If carburetor mounting bolts are loose, the volatility of the fuel is affected.

Figure 2. As the engine starts, the choke should close (A), but should open after starting (B).

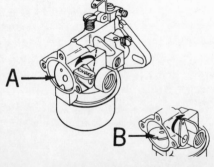

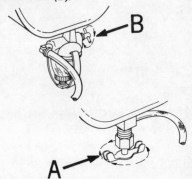

Figure 3. Use carburetor cleaning solvent to unbind chokes.

Figure 4. Unscrew the shutoff valve to get at filter (A) or disassemble the sediment bowl (B).

3. Is fuel contaminated? Drain an eye-dropper amount from the fuel tank and drop it into your hand. If water or dirt remains after fuel evaporates, remove the fuel tank, discard old fuel, and slosh the tank clean with kerosene.

In two-cycle engines, the oil used in the fuel mixture will not evaporate. However, if water is present, you will see droplets in the oil after gasoline evaporates. If dirt is present, oil will feel gritty as you rub it between your fingers.

Never use fuel in your engine that has been stored for any length of time. It may not vaporize and could leave varnish on carburetor parts. Avoid trouble. Always fill the tank with fresh fuel.

4. Check the fuel line for damage. Replace it if it is kinked. Remove the line and blow through it. If it is obstructed, clean it out or get a new one.

5. Is air leaking into the fuel system because of loose bolts? Tighten all carburetor mounting bolts and fuel line connections (Fig. 1).

6. If the choke plate isn't closing fully as you start the engine, clean dirt from around the plate and shaft with carburetor cleaning solvent (Figs. 2 and 3). Make sure, too, that the choke cable, if there is one, is neither kinked nor broken.

7. Is the fuel filter clogged, obstructing fuel flow? Engines that employ float-type carburetors generally have a wire mesh screen fuel filter in the tank-to-fuel-line shut-off valve (Fig. 4A). Remove it by unscrewing the adapter, and wash it in gasoline. Do this when the fuel tank is empty.

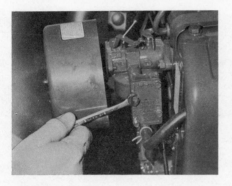

Figure 5. If your engine has a fuel pump, tighten cover bolts.

Figure 6. Air filter cleanliness is important to an engine.

On large engines, the standard filter is a sediment bowl which houses a ceramic element. Shut off the fuel valve, drop and clean the bowl, and swish the element in clean gasoline (Fig. 4B).

8. Is the fuel pump shot? If your engine has a fuel pump, which it must have if it doesn't possess a gravity feed fuel system, it will be found on the fuel line between fuel tank and carburetor. However, diaphragm carburetors have the fuel pump built into the carburetor. You can't see the diaphragm element unless the carburetor comes off, which has to happen if you suspect fuel pump failure.

Fuel pump trouble is not too common, but it does happen. Pumps fail mainly when cover bolts work loose, and the pump begins to pull in air. This thins out the fuel mixture, so make sure that bolts are tight (Fig. 5).

Fuel pump diaphragms can also develop leaks, but they don't normally fail immediately to the point where they stop pulsating, which would keep the engine from starting. Rather, an engine with a faulty fuel pump diaphragm will stall when accelerated as a result of insufficient fuel delivery at higher speeds. If this happens, inspect and, if necessary, replace the diaphragm.

9. If you haven't yet uncovered why the engine is starving for fuel, the trouble is undoubtedly inside the carburetor. Unfortunately, this book cannot go into detail on how to disassemble and clean the carburetor, since there are several different variations. However, the task is relatively simple if you have instructions. These can be obtained by writing the manufacturer of your engine, giving him the engine's model and serial numbers.

The fuel system can keep the engine from starting by flooding it. In this case, check the following:

FILL TO LEVEL
MARK WITH SAME
OIL AS ENGINE

Figure 7. Oil bath air filters are common to small engines.

Figure 8. Try tapping the float bowl to free the needle valve.

1. Does the choke open fully as soon as the engine starts? If not, repair it as described above.

2. Is the engine flooding because of a dirty carburetor air cleaner? This is a common condition. There are seven basic types of air cleaner elements that are used on small engines, as follows:

a. Polyurethene. Wash in detergent solution and oil with SAE 30 motor oil (Fig. 6).

b. Paper. Replace when dirty.

c. Oil bath. Discard old oil, clean in kerosene, and add fresh oil (Fig. 7).

d. Aluminum foil. Wash in kerosene.

e. Felt. Wash in soapy water.

f. Metal cartridge. Tap lightly to loosen dirt. If very dirty, replace.

g. Fiber. Blow dirt out with compressed air.

3. Is dirt holding the needle valve open? This is indicated if fuel drips from the carburetor. Consider this possibility if you have a float-type carburetor. Often, tapping the bowl lightly with a screwdriver handle will remedy the problem (Fig. 8). If this doesn't help, the carburetor will have to be disassembled for cleaning.

4. Is the carburetor out of adjustment? Specific adjustment details, which vary from carburetor to carburetor, will have to be obtained from the manufacturer. Meantime an approximate adjustment may be made, assuming that the carburetor doesn't have fixed main mixture and idle mixture jets, which can't be adjusted.

To adjust the main mixture and idle mixture needles, turn them in until they are fingertight. Then, back them out one turn.

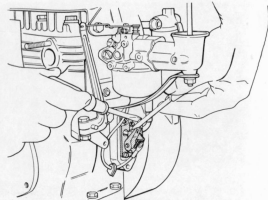

Figure 9. The idle speed is adjusted by turning the screw in.

Figure 10. To get at external breaker points, simply remove the cover over the point box.

To adjust the idle speed, back out the screw and then turn it until it just touches the throttle lever. Continue for one full turn more (Fig. 9).

If the engine doesn't start because of ignition failure, the reason is usually a bad spark plug or breaker points (assuming you don't have solid state ignition). Often, a major obstacle to ignition repair is getting at points.

There is no difficulty if your equipment has external breaker points which are kept in a box attached to the engine and which are revealed by simply removing the cover (Fig. 10). Larger engines used in garden tractors, such as those manufactured by Wisconsin and Kohler, use external breaker points as part of an ignition coil system.

If breaker points are internal—that is, beneath the flywheel as they are in magneto ignition systems—then the problem is to remove the flywheel. Before going through this trouble, make sure that the cause of ignition failure is not some minor thing,

Figure 11. It is often necessary to tap a wrench bar with a hammer to free the flywheel.

Figure 12. It may be necessary to employ a flywheel holder to keep the flywheel from moving.

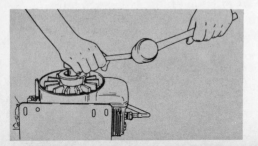

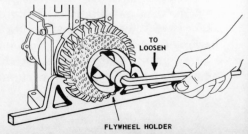

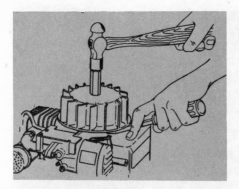

Figure 13. With some flywheels a knock-out puller is employed.

1. FASTEN FLYWHEEL TO FLYWHEEL WITH TWO SELF TAPPING SCREWS

2. TURN DOWN THESE TWO NUTS TO LOOSEN FLYWHEEL

Figure 14. With some flywheels a fly-wheel puller is employed.

such as the engine stop device being in the "off" position, a weak battery, or a wet spark plug cable.

The way in which you remove the flywheel depends on which kind the engine has. There are two general methods.

With most flywheels of two-cycle engines, the flywheel nut can be removed with a socket wrench. If the nut proves stubborn, tap the wrench bar with a soft hammer (Fig. 11). If the flywheel turns as the nut is being removed, you will have to use a flywheel holder.

On flywheels of most four-cycle engines, the flywheel must be held with a flywheel holder as the nut is removed (Fig. 12).

With the flywheel nut off, you now have to remove the flywheel. On some, you have to install a knockout puller, hold the flywheel firmly, and rap the puller with a hammer to jar the flywheel loose. This method is generally employed on engines smaller than 3½ horsepower (Fig. 13).

Other flywheels (those that have holes in them for the purpose) are removed with a flywheel puller (Fig. 14). This method is generally used on engines of 3½ horsepower and larger.

With the flywheel removed, check all ignition leads for tightness and cleanliness. Make sure no high tension wire is shorting out.

Examine breaker points and replace them if they are burned or pitted. If frequent breaker point replacement is necessary, the condenser is faulty. Replace it.

Check point gap. Correct gap in most cases is 0.020 inch, but verify this specification with your owner's manual (Fig. 15).

If the ignition system now fails to produce spark, all ignition parts, such as coils, condenser, and magnets, should be tested on an analyzer, and the ignition timing adjusted to specification. Leave this to a professional repair shop.

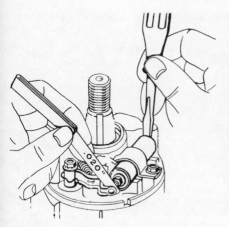

Figure 15. With the flywheel removed points are adjusted.

Figure 16. Make it a point to clean debris and dirt from between cooling fins frequently.

Compression failure is caused most often by a problem that requires major engine overhaul, such as a scored cylinder, sticking piston rings, sticking valves, or defective crankshaft oil seals. However, before plunging into this, listen carefully as you crank the engine.

If you hear a hissing noise, check the spark plug for looseness or damage. The hiss could be caused by the fuel mixture escaping from around a loose or bad plug. If the plug is okay, then the hissing is coming from a loose cylinder head or bad cylinder head gasket.

Engine overheats. Check the following in this order:

1. Is the engine being used for a purpose it is not designed for and thus being overloaded?

2. If a four-cycle engine, is the crankcase filled with oil? If a two-cycle engine, are you using the correct oil/gas ratio as specified by the manufacturer? If not, you are asking for trouble. There is no more frequent cause of two-cycle engine malfunctioning than incorrect fuel mixture ratio.

Are you using the oil specified by the manufacturer? In most cases, oil designed for outboard motors should never be used. It thickens to the consistency of grease when hot. Always use the oil recommended by the manufacturer of your engine and a regular grade of gasoline marketed by a well-known company.

3. Is air flow obstructed? Are cooling fins clogged? Your engine must breathe. Make sure nothing stops that (Fig. 16).

4. Is the carburetor set too lean?

5. Is ignition timing off? This is not too critical in a small

engine. Usually, if breaker points are properly set, timing will be correct.

6. If all else to this point has failed to overcome overheating, then there is probably a buildup of carbon in the combustion chamber which needs to be cleaned out. The engine will have to be dismantled.

Engine cuts out while running. Look for the following (method of repair in most cases is dealt with above):

1. Out of fuel?
2. Contaminated fuel?
3. Excessive engine heat on the fuel line may be causing a vapor lock condition. Pour cold water over the fuel line and carburetor, but take care that none gets into the carburetor. Try to start the engine. If it starts, the trouble is vapor lock. Make sure that nothing is obstructing air flow around the engine and that cooling fins are clear.
4. Is the vent hole in the fuel tank cap clear? Clean it out with a piece of wire of proper size, but take care not to enlarge the hole (Fig. 17).
5. Ignition failure?

Engine misses. The reasons for this are as follows:

1. Contaminated fuel.
2. Spark plug gap too wide or the plug is damaged.
3. Loose ignition wires.
4. Pitted or worn breaker points.
5. Compression failure.

Engine surges (gallops). Look for the following:

1. A plugged vent hole in the fuel tank cap.
2. Carburetor flooding. Maybe the throttle linkage is dirty and sticking. Clean it off with carburetor solvent and lubricate with a thin coating of white grease. If this doesn't prove to be the cause of the flooding, refer to the information above that deals with flooding.

Figure 17. Fresh gasoline and an open vent hole in the fuel tank cap are necessary factors.

Figure 18. Vibration that can cause serious engine damage results if mounting bolts loosen.

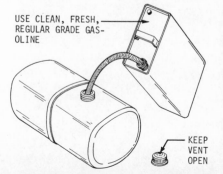

USE CLEAN, FRESH, REGULAR GRADE GASOLINE

KEEP VENT OPEN

Figure 19. Make it a practice to tighten bolts periodically.

Figure 20. In this machine, exhaust ports are revealed when the muffler is disconnected.

3. Governor parts sticking. Clean dirt off of linkages.

Engine backfires.

1. Is fuel contaminated?

2. Is the fuel mixture too lean?

3. Is timing (breaker points) to specification?

4. If no repair to this point has helped, the problem is a sticking valve, and the engine has to be disassembled.

Engine vibrates excessively. Vibration in small engines is always present, but doesn't become serious until it causes mounting bolts to loosen (Fig. 18). This, in turn, leads to even greater vibration that can eventually result in major engine damage.

Tighten up on all bolts and fasteners. This should be done periodically (Fig. 19). If vibration isn't reduced by this, then check the balance of associated equipment, such as cutting blades. If vibration is still troublesome, then you had better suspect that it is being caused by a bent crankshaft.

Engine knock. If checking for the causes of overheating and for contaminated fuel doesn't relieve engine knock, then do the following:

1. Make sure timing isn't overadvanced.

2. Make sure the flywheel is tight.

3. Remove the cylinder head and clean carbon from the head and piston crown.

4. Do an engine job. There is a bad connecting rod.

Maintenance. Periodic care of a small engine is a wise course of action. Often, it will help avert one of the problems discussed in this section.

The engine owner's manual details exactly how to keep your engine in good running condition. The following are the most important points on which to concentrate and how often to do them:

1. Check the oil level of four-cycle engines every day that the equipment is used.

2. Clean out engine shrouds and exhaust ports before every use (Fig. 20).

3. Change the oil of four-cycle engines with the proper grade and weight every 25 hours (*hours* refers to hours of operation).

4. Tighten all body bolts and fasteners every 25 hours.

5. Clean or replace the air filter every 50 hours. However, clean oil bath filter systems every 25 hours.

6. Clean the fuel filter every 100 hours.

7. Service the spark plug and breaker points every 100 hours.

FAUCETS, INDOOR COMPRESSION TYPE

Fixing a leaky compression faucet in the kitchen, bathroom, or utility room is an easy task once you identify its design. A compression faucet is used in fixtures that have separate controls for hot and cold water. One-handle faucets, which are discussed under a separate heading, are not of the compression type.

Also discussed under a separate heading are outdoor water faucets. Although these are compression faucets, they differ somewhat from indoor compression faucets. Compression faucets get their name from the fact that a compression washer is employed to control the flow of water.

A compression faucet utilizes a stem as its main part. This is basically a screw which, when turned down, forces a washer against a seat to shut off the flow of water. When the washer or washer seat is damaged, water will drip from the spout (Fig. 1).

If water is leaking from around the stem, the packing washer or O-ring seal is damaged. The purpose of the packing washer or O-ring seal (a faucet has one or the other) is to stop water from flowing up the stem, which will cause the stem to corrode. If the faucets in your home were installed immediately after World War II, they probably use packing washers. Faucet

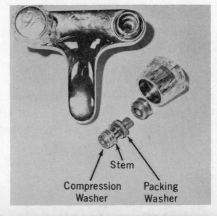

Figure 1. A compression faucet has a stem with washer to control water flow from the spout.

Stem

Compression Washer   Packing Washer

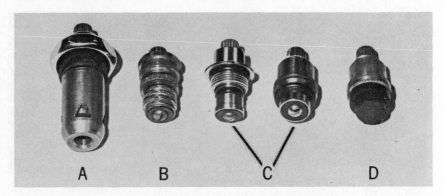

Figure 2. Different faucet designs are (a) renewable barrel, (b) packing washer, (c) O-ring seal, (d) neoprene diaphragm.

manufacturers began employing O-ring seals in the early 1950s.

Between the time that the packing washer was introduced and the O-ring seal replaced it, a renewable barrel faucet was developed (Fig. 2). Although this type utilizes a packing washer, it is unique in that the barrel and stem are screwed together so that when the stem is removed, the barrel is also removed. The two can then be separated by unscrewing them.

This design allows you to replace the barrel if it becomes damaged without having to replace the entire faucet. With other faucet designs, the entire faucet must be replaced if the barrel is damaged.

Although this approach to faucet design may seem logical, the renewable barrel faucet hasn't proved practical. If a washer seat is damaged, which is a common occurrence that is inexpensively repaired in other faucets, the entire barrel of the renewable barrel faucet must be replaced, since you cannot separate the seat from the barrel. This proves to be quite costly.

In the late 1960s, a new compression faucet design eliminated the use of the compression washer and O-ring seal. A one-piece neoprene diaphragm that fits over the tip of the stem like a cap is used instead (Fig. 2). The brim of the cap performs the function of the O-ring seal in that it prevents water from traveling up the stem. The crown of the diaphragm acts as a washer to control the flow of water.

Since faucets that employ compression washers and O-rings (or packing washers) predominate, we will discuss how to repair these. The procedure, however, is similar when repairing other types, specifically the newer diaphragm design.

In repairing a faucet, proceed slowly. Remove each piece in order. Do not force any part.

Figure 3. In this installation, the screw that holds the handle is removed with a screwdriver.

Figure 4. If the handle proves stubborn, gently tap it loose.

The usual order of removal is: cap screw, handle screw, handle, gland nut that holds the stem, and stem (Fig. 3, 4, and 5). Naturally, before starting repairs, turn off the water.

If water has been leaking from around the stem which, as explained above, indicates that the packing washer or O-ring seal is damaged, slip the washer or O-ring off the stem or out of the gland nut (Fig. 6). Make certain that you get the correct size packing washer or O-ring by bringing the old part to the hardware store.

If the stem utilizes an O-ring, lubricate the new O-ring with a little heat-resistant grease before installation. This will assure long O-ring life. Faucets with O-rings should be disassembled and O-rings lubricated in this manner once every two years to prevent O-ring deterioration.

As explained above, if water is dripping from the spout, the compression washer or the seat is damaged. Remove the old washer by unscrewing it from the stem and replace it with a new one of the same size (Fig. 7). Use a new screw and make

Figure 5. Remove the gland nut. Wrap tape around the chrome nut to prevent marring the finish.

Figure 6. In this installation, the packing washer is contained inside the faucet's gland nut.

Figure 7. To replace a washer, remove the screw. Get the correct size and use a new screw.

Figure 8. An inexpensive seat wrench is necessary to unscrew the faucet seat from its place.

certain that it is tight. If the washer is left loose, the faucet will chatter when water is turned on.

If the faucet continues to drip with a new washer, replace the seat. The seat is removed from the barrel with a seat wrench, which you can buy in a hardware store for about $1 (Fig. 8).

If washer and seat incur frequent damage, the cause is probably high water pressure. High water pressure is defined as that which is 65 pounds per square inch or more. To halt this problem, have a plumber install a pressure-reducing valve, which is not too expensive and which will reduce the frequency of repairs. A reducing valve will also help to quiet noisy plumbing, which frequently results from high water pressure.

When reassembling the faucet, be careful that you do not overtighten the gland nut, which can damage the faucet by distorting the threads of the stem and barrel. Once this happens, you will have to replace the entire faucet. Run the gland nut up fingertight and then turn it three-quarters of a turn with a wrench, but no more.

Figure 9. To get at a spout's O-ring, loosen the gland nut.

Figure 10. Remove and discard the worn O-ring in favor of a new one of the right dimension.

If water leaks from around the base of the spout of a swing-type kitchen faucet, you can assume that the O-ring in the spout needs to be replaced. Wrap some friction tape around the gland to protect the chrome and loosen it (Fig. 9). With the spout removed, simply discard the old O-ring and replace it with a new one of the same size (Fig. 10).

FAUCETS, NONCOMPRESSION TYPE

Single-handle faucets in kitchens and bathrooms do not use stems with compression washers as do compression faucets. However, repair of a damaged single-handle faucet is basically a simple task.

A single-handle faucet may utilize a lever or a push-pull control. In any event, its basic design is either a tipping valve or a removable stem.

Tipping valve faucets employ a cam and two spring-loaded valves which control the flow of hot and cold water (Fig. 1). When you turn off the water, the cam and tipping valves disengage, allowing the valves, which are under spring tension, to close over their respective seats and stop the flow of water.

When water is turned on and the faucet handle is positioned directly in the center, the cam engages both tipping valves and opens them an equal amount to permit an even mixture of hot and cold water. To make water warmer or colder, the handle is moved to the left or right, respectively. This permits the cam to put more force on one tipping valve and less force on the other to allow one valve to open a greater amount than the other (Fig. 2).

Seat damage is the one problem that affects a tipping valve design most often. It becomes evident when water begins to drip from the spout.

Occasionally, a piece of dirt will lodge itself on one of the seats, preventing the tipping valve from closing. Thus, before

Figure 1. Note the cam. It is not engaged with either valve. Thus, the faucet is turned off.

Figure 2. Here, the cam is putting more pressure on the hot water valve, less on the cold.

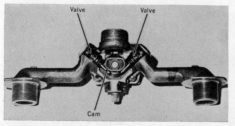

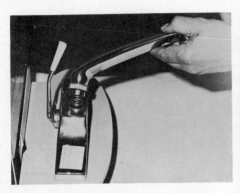

Figure 3. Begin disassembly by unscrewing the faucet's spout.

Figure 4. Lift the cover off, which reveals the slotted nuts.

you disassemble the faucet to replace the seat, quickly open and close the faucet several times to try and flush dirt away. Activate the faucet handle first to one side and then to the other.

If this doesn't work, proceed to replace the seat. Although there are several different faucet designs, one-handle faucets with tipping valves are generally repaired by first unscrewing and removing the spout (Fig. 3). Now, take off the cover. It may be held by a screw or two, so look for them.

When the cover has been removed, you will notice two slotted nuts, one covering the hot water valve and the other covering the cold water valve (Fig. 4). Unscrew these nuts and remove the tipping valves (Fig. 5). Now, unscrew the seat with a seat wrench that you can purchase in a hardware store. Replace seats with new ones and reassemble the faucet.

The removable stem design used in single-handle faucets is a barrel that is inside a sleeve. Both barrel and sleeve contain a series of machined ports that allow water to flow at a controlled temperature. As the stem is rotated in one direction or the

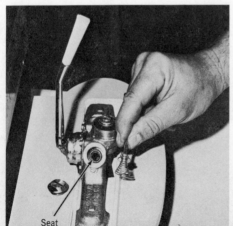

Seat

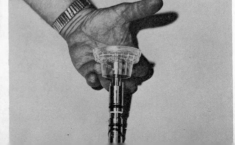

Figure 5. Lift out the tipping valve. Unscrew the valve seat.

Figure 6. Note the O-rings of this removable stem design. Replace the stem if O-rings leak.

other, some ports are opened and some are closed to permit hot and cold water to mix or one to take dominance over the other.

The removable stem control utilizes a complex series of O-ring seals which keeps water from leaking from the spout. If the faucet begins to drip, it means that one of these O-rings is damaged. The entire stem should be replaced since it is very difficult to replace O-rings (Fig. 6).

You should lubricate O-rings with a thin coating of heat-proof grease once every two years to keep them from early failure. Grease can be purchased in a hardware store.

FAUCETS, OUTDOOR COMPRESSION TYPE

Compression faucets on the outside of a home are repaired somewhat differently from those on the inside. However, the task is easier, because there is one basic design of outdoor compression faucet.

An outdoor faucet will drip water from the spout or from around the stem when it is damaged. If water comes from around the stem, tighten the bonnet with a wrench (Fig. 1).

If this doesn't stop the leak or if the leak is coming from the spout, the faucet should be taken apart to do three things: (1) replace the washer; (2) install a new stem packing washer; (3) smooth down the washer seat.

Turn off the water supply to the faucet and remove the stem by unscrewing the bonnet (Fig. 2). The washer is attached to the stem. Remove it and replace it with a new washer of the correct size (Fig. 3). If you don't know the size, bring the stem to the hardware store.

Figure 1. Leaks from around the faucet stem can often be stopped by tightening the bonnet.

Figure 2. To restore the faucet to good condition, remove the stem by unscrewing the bonnet.

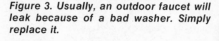

Figure 3. Usually, an outdoor faucet will leak because of a bad washer. Simply replace it.

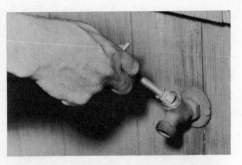

Figure 4. Packing washers are installed on most outdoor faucets. Simply slip a new one on.

Figure 5. A seat-dressing tool removes burrs and nicks which will cause the washer to fail.

Use a new brass screw to attach the new washer. Make sure that the screw is tight. A loose washer will cause faucet chatter when the water is turned on.

An outdoor faucet employs either a packing washer on the stem or regular string-type packing to keep water from leaking from around the stem. Regular packing is an impregnated string-type material that compresses when the bonnet is tightened down. If the faucet uses regular packing, wrap a length of the impregnated material around the stem directly below the bonnet and reinstall the stem.

Most outdoor faucets use a packing washer (Fig. 4). To replace this washer, remove the handle and bonnet from the stem and simply slip the old packing washer off. Then, slide a new one of the correct size back on the stem.

Before replacing a stem, use a seat-dressing tool to remove burrs and nicks from the washer seat. A damaged seat will chew up a new washer and cause rapid failure.

A seat-dressing tool can be purchased in a hardware store for about $1.50. Insert it into the barrel as far as it will go, hold it straight, and turn it twice (Fig. 5).

Now, reinstall the stem. Tighten the bonnet with your fingers and then turn it one full turn with a wrench. Turn on the water. If water drips from around the bonnet, tighten the bonnet about one-half turn more. Do not overtighten.

FIREPLACE

Wood-burning fireplaces require little maintenance and practically no repair. The main job is to sweep the chimney occasionally. This is no longer the dirty task it used to be because of a cleaning agent called Chimney Sweep, which is available in hardware stores. However, if Chimney Sweep is to be effective, it should be used at least once a year so that there is no extreme buildup of soot.

Start a small fire in the fireplace and sprinkle Chimney Sweep powder onto the fire. Allow it to burn. As fumes exit through the chimney, they will dissolve soot from around the damper and in the flue.

If soot has built up inside the flue for several years, a more extreme method will be required. Attach a length of tire chain to a rope and dangle it down the chimney from the roof. Be sure that the damper is closed to keep particles from flying into the room and pull the chain rapidly up and down against the sides of the flue. This will break deposits loose.

When you have dislodged as much soot as possible, open the damper slowly to allow soot to drop into the firebox. Sweep it out the ash drop door. Complete the cleaning operation by using Chimney Sweep.

If the damper isn't opening as wide as it should, soot is probably clogging it at pivot points. If cleaning with Chimney Sweep doesn't help, clean off as much soot as possible from around the damper and damper pivot points with a wire brush.

Fireplace brick which has become stained with smoke is unsightly, especially that brick which is facing into the room. Stains often can be cleaned off by scrubbing with a scrub brush and a strong detergent solution. If this fails, dilute one part of muriatic acid, which you can buy in a hardware store, with five parts of water. Wear rubber gloves to protect your hands and scrub the brick with the solution. Then be sure to rinse it off with clear water.

FLASHING

Flashing refers to material (usually aluminum, galvanized steel, or copper) that the builder of your home installed at roof joints to stop water from leaking into the house. Joints are those that are formed where the chimney meets the roof, where vent pipes go through the roof, in valleys (i.e., where two roof planes meet), and where a roof butts against a wall.

Flashing can fail for several reasons. For example, perhaps the builder didn't install the material properly, or perhaps he used dissimilar metals in contact with each other. Installing aluminum flashing with galvanized nails, for instance, causes corrosion that will eat away the flashing.

Flashing can also fail because of shifting of the house. A frame structure will settle, but the chimney will stand firm. If

Figure 1. Weak flashing often reveals itself by gaps between flashings and crumbling mortar.

Figure 2. To reinforce the mortar joint, spread on a liberal application of Instant Patch.

there is excessive movement, flashing is liable to loosen (Fig. 1).

When flashing fails, the roof will leak. It is not often possible to determine whether a leak is caused by weak flashing or a bad roof. The least costly and easiest procedure, then, is to inspect the roof visually. If no damage, such as torn shingles, is apparent, reinforce the flashing to determine if that will stop the leak. Roof repairs should be the last resort (see the section on Roof).

Material you will need to reinforce flashing (replacing old flashing with new is neither practical nor necessary) includes asbestos felt or fiberglass flashing, black plastic roof cement, and Instant Patch, which is a quick-setting roof repair compound. These products can be purchased in a hardware store or from a supplier of roofing materials.

To reinforce flashing around a chimney, wire brush the mortar joint where the top of the flashing is inserted into the chimney. Coat the joint with a liberal application of Instant

Figure 3. After applying roof cement, install flashing material. Be sure corners overlap.

Figure 4. Vent pipe gaps such as this should be repaired with flashing and black roof cement.

Figure 5. Make sure you apply a good coating of roof cement on top of the flashing material.

Figure 6. First apply roof cement, then flashing, then more cement to seal roof-wall areas.

Patch, which will seal the area (Fig. 2).

Now, spread a liberal amount of black plastic roof cement over the old flashing. Pay particular attention to corners. Cut four pieces of asbestos felt or fiberglass flashing material to the size of each side of the chimney. Make sure pieces are cut so that corners will overlap. Wrap pieces around the chimney so that they cover old flashing (Fig. 3). Follow by coating corners with black plastic roof cement to make a watertight seal.

To reinforce flashing around vent pipes, apply black plastic roof cement around the entire base of the pipe and halfway up the pipe (Fig. 4). Cut a piece of fiberglass or asbestos felt to conform to the configuration of the pipe. Cut a series of slits along one edge of the material to make it easier to install. Now, draw the material around the base of the pipe (slit side at the base), wrapping it tightly and pressing the slit tabs firmly into the cement (Fig. 5). Overlap the ends and apply a liberal amount of cement over the patch.

Along valleys and at roof-wall joints, apply roof cement down the entire length, extending the cement about 2 inches to each side of the joint (Fig. 6). Cut flashing to size and press it firmly into the valley or joint. Be sure that the material anchors itself firmly, especially at edges. Complete the job by spreading a coat of roof cement over the entire length of the flashing material, paying particular attention to edges.

FLOORS, NOISY

Whether or not you are going to refinish the hardwood floors in your home (see section on Floors, Refinishing), you will

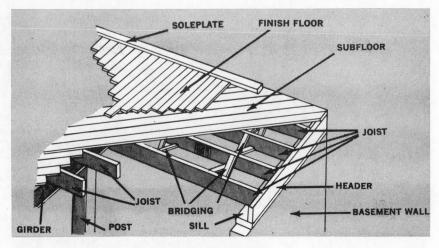

Figure 1. This diagram will assist you in identifying the parts of your home's hardwood floors. (Courtesy of Popular Mechanics)

want to tackle the problem of a noisy floor. However, the cause isn't always readily discernible. Thus, a trial-and-error procedure is often required.

In seeking quiet hardwood floors, it is only logical to proceed from the most likely to the least likely cause. The repair procedures discussed here are presented in that order. Use Fig. 1 to identify the parts referred to in the text.

Hardwood finish flooring is tongue-and-groove; that is, the tongue of one strip fits into the groove of an adjacent strip. The chief cause of floor squeaks are strips of finish flooring that have dried out. This causes shrinkage, which allows the tongue of one strip to move and rub against the groove of another, producing squeaks.

If squeaks are isolated to a few spots as the floor is walked on and are not numerous, they can frequently be silenced by forcing powdered graphite into the joints between flooring strips (Fig. 2). You can buy powdered graphite in a hardware store or at an automotive supply store.

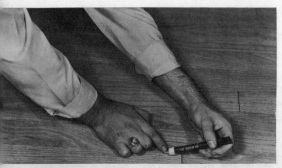

Figure 2. Squeaky floorboards can often be silenced by applying graphite between joints.

In some instances, many strips might be affected, producing squeaks over an entire floor area. These may be too numerous and too scattered to treat individually. In this case, it is best to seal the entire floor with a penetrating floor sealer, which can be purchased in a hardware store.

Brush the sealer over the floor with a paint brush, working in the direction of the wood's grain. Apply a liberal coating, especially between strips in joints. If you are seeking to silence a parquet floor, which has an indiscriminate grain pattern, apply the sealer in any direction.

Allow the sealer to settle for a few minutes and wipe off excess with a clean rag, working the cloth across the wood's grain. Allow the sealer to dry for 24 hours. If you are not going to sand the floor in preparation for refinishing, apply a floor finish which you can buy in a hardware store. Several types are available. They are described in the section on Floors, Refinishing.

Apply the finish by brushing across the wood's grain. However, as you complete each section, gently run the tip of the brush's bristles in the direction of the wood's grain for a few strokes. This is done to highlight the floor's appearance.

There are other reasons that floors squeak. For example, isolated squeaks will result when subflooring dries out and shrinks away from joists. Assuming that the squeak develops on the first floor of a home and can be attacked from the basement, first find the squeaking area. Have someone walk slowly over the floor as you listen from below.

When the noisy spot has been pinpointed, drive a shim between the subfloor and joist (Fig. 3). This will close the gap which has formed between the two elements. If the shim will not penetrate, there is no gap. Conversely, if the gap is too wide, you may have to insert several shims, side by side.

Coat each shim with a good quality wood glue before driving it into place. Wood shingles made ideal shims, because they are beveled on one end and this makes them easier to drive into place. Buy shingles in a lumber yard.

Figure 3. A shim driven between joist and subfloor will close a gap and silence a squeak.

Figure 4. When bridging strips touch, push a saw between them and shave wood to form a gap.

Figure 5. Bridging strips that can be wiggled by hand should be nailed firmly to the joists.

Another cause of noise is bridging that touches so that the two wooden elements rub against each other when weight is put on them from above. There must be a gap between cross pieces. If they touch, pass a saw between them and shave off wood (Fig. 4).

Examine each cross piece to make sure it is nailed tightly. If you can move or wiggle a strip by hand, hammer in several nails until the piece is anchored solidly to its joist (Fig. 5). The purpose of bridging is to strengthen the floor structure by preventing joists from twisting.

Warped flooring strips and flooring strips that are loose because of inadequate nailing will make noise when they are walked upon. The affected area may also vibrate. Pinpoint the noisy area as described above and have someone stand on the spot as you drill a pilot hole through the subfloor and into the hardwood floor (Fig. 6). Be sure to stop drilling before the bit passes through the surface of the finished floor.

One way to assure that the bit won't go through the floor is

Figure 6. Drill a pilot hole in the subfloor and finish floor so that screws can be employed.

Figure 7. A No. 10 1-inch screw driven through a warped floor will help to straighten it out.

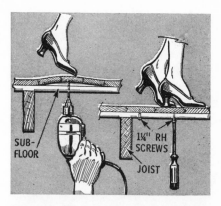

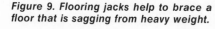

Figure 8. *This cross-sectional view will help further explain the drill-screw repair method. (Courtesy of Popular Mechanics)*

Figure 9. *Flooring jacks help to brace a floor that is sagging from heavy weight.*

to fashion a depth stop. Drill through a small block of scrap wood so that 1 inch of the drill bit protrudes. Leave the depth stop in place on the bit and drill into the subflooring. When the block of wood touches the subfloor, stop drilling.

After drilling the pilot hole, drive a No. 10 1-inch or 1¼-inch roundhead screw into place while someone keeps his weight on the noisy spot from above (Fig. 7). You may have to insert four or five screws to completely silence the squeak (Fig. 8). However, if four or five screws don't quiet the squeak, you are either screwing into the wrong board or else the squeak cannot be eliminated in this manner.

A hardwood floor will often sag when heavy furniture is placed on it. Brace the floor from below with a commercial floor jack, which costs about $8 in a lumber yard. Place the jack against the joist in the affected area and tighten up on it (Fig. 9).

If squeaks occur on the second floor so that they can't be attacked from below, you will have to try to quiet them by driving flooring nails into flooring strips from above. This assumes that the powdered graphite method explained before doesn't do the job.

The major task involved in surface nailing is to locate the joist near the noisy area. You cannot nail into the floor in an indiscriminate manner.

One way of finding the joist is to tie a magnet to a string and pass it over the area. When you feel a tug on the string, you will know that you are above a concentration of nails and, therefore, over a joist.

Drill a small pilot hole through the floors and into the joist at an angle. Hammer in an annular-ringed flooring nail, which has a countersunk head. Try a second nail if one doesn't silence the noise. However, do not pepper the area. If two nails fail, give it up as a lost cause.

When nails are in place, fill holes with wood putty and dab the spot with shellac or varnish.

FLOORS, REFINISHING

Refinishing hardwood floors is not a difficult task. The homeowner who undertakes the job will save himself a considerable amount of money by not having to hire a professional.

Special equipment will be needed, specifically a drum sander and a hand-held power edging machine. These can be rented from a paint store, hardware store, or a tool rental shop. Sandpaper for both machines will also be needed: No. 3½ (2½ or 3 if the floor is parquet), No. 1½, and No. 2/0 (Fig. 1).

Ask the dealer who rents you the machines to show you how to fit them with sandpaper. He can also give you other information concerning how to operate the sanders.

Before you start to sand the floor, remove all furnishings from the room and carefully inspect the floor for protruding nailheads and cracks. Reset nails. Now, fill holes and cracks with a putty compound made for hardwood floors (Fig. 2). You can buy this in a hardware store. If the floor squeaks, make repairs as explained in the section on Floors, Noisy.

Figure 1. Equipment and supplies that you will need to refinish hardwood floors include a drum sander and sandpaper.

Figure 2. Fill cracks with a hardwood floor putty compound that is available in hardware stores.

Figure 3. Fitting the drum sander with sandpaper involves loosening of holders and insertion of the paper into holding slots.

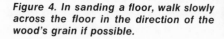

Figure 4. In sanding a floor, walk slowly across the floor in the direction of the wood's grain if possible.

Fit the drum sander with a sheet of No. 3½ (coarse) sandpaper (Fig. 3). Now, starting at a wall, walk *slowly* across the floor to the opposite wall (Fig. 4). Make sure that you go in the direction of the wood's grain.

Now, walk backwards so that the machine passes over the *same* path. Continue sanding in this manner, making certain that each pass overlaps the previous pass by 2 to 3 inches.

It is very important to keep the sanding machine moving at all times when the drum is in contact with the floor. If you should stop, the floor will be scratched or gouged. Most drum sanders are equipped with a lever that can be used to raise and lower the drum (Fig. 5). If the machine you are using does not have a lever, tilt it back toward you to raise the drum off the floor before you stop your movement.

Figure 5. To avoid gouging the floor, raise the drum by using the lever, if one is available.

Figure 6. The hand-held power edging machine is used to sand around the edges of the floor.

If the floor that you are sanding is parquet, the same method described above should be used. However, since it is not possible to follow any set grain pattern, a No. 2½ or 3 sandpaper, which is of finer grit than No. 3½, should be used to minimize the possibility of scratches.

After the main body of the floor has been sanded, fit the hand-held power edging machine with the same grit of sandpaper that was used in the drum sander and sand the borders of the room where it was not possible for the drum sander to go (Fig. 6). Use light pressure on the machine and, if possible, follow the grain of the wood.

Some areas are not accessible to either the drum sander or edging machine, such as corners and spots around radiators. Here, a manual floor scraper will have to be used. Be sure that all of the old floor finish is scraped away.

The floor is now ready for a second sanding with the drum sander, which should be fitted with a piece of No. 1½ sandpaper. Sand in the same manner as before. Follow this sanding with the edging machine around the room's borders. The edging machine should be fitted with No. 1½ sandpaper.

The third sanding step is absolutely essential if you are to obtain a perfectly smooth surface. The final sanding is done with no. 2/0 (fine) sandpaper. Follow the same procedure as before.

After sanding has been done, wipe off window sills, door ledges, and moldings with a damp cloth, and vacuum the floor thoroughly. It is essential that the entire room be free of dust before the floor finish is applied. If any dust falls on the wet finish, an otherwise professional looking job will be ruined.

The finish must be applied to a newly sanded floor as soon as possible (Fig. 7). Delay will allow moisture to penetrate into the pores of the bare wood, causing white spots and allowing the finish to chip, peel, and wear away prematurely.

Figure 7. Apply finish to the newly sanded floor as soon as possible to prevent damage from moisture.

You have a choice of finish tones. If you prefer to keep the floor a natural grainy color, apply the finish material directly to the wood. If you wish a darker tone, apply an oil stain to the floor according to the manufacturer's instructions. Oil stain for floors may be purchased in a hardware or paint store. Allow the stain to dry overnight. Then rub it down with clean, dry clothes before applying the finish coat.

There are four kinds of floor finishes from which to choose: shellac, varnish, penetrating floor sealer, and synthetic resin varnish.

Shellac dries fast, is easy to apply, and wears well if waxed regularly and kept free of moisture. Varnish dries slower than shellac and will scratch if not protected by wax. However, it is more water resistant and offers a higher gloss. If shellac or varnish is used, a paste wood filler must be applied to the floor to seal the pores before the finish is applied.

Penetrating floor sealer is an all-around finish that is somewhat more expensive than shellac and varnish. It is easier to apply, because it contains substances that penetrate the pores of the wood. Thus, a separate paste wood filler is not necessary.

Synthetic resin varnish is the most durable of all floor finishes, but the most expensive. It should be used only if conditions are extreme. These finishes are used primarily on school gym floors and in other high traffic areas. A floor that is finished with synthetic resin varnish requires only occasional mopping and seldom, if ever, needs waxing.

Regardless of the finish that you use, be sure to follow the manufacturer's instructions regarding application. Always let the final coat dry thoroughly before you walk on the floor.

FLOOR TILE, LAYING

When old floor tile becomes too badly battered to permit easy replacement of individual blocks or you simply desire a change in decor, you can install new tile by placing underlayment-grade hardboard on top of old tile and laying new tile on the underlayment. Underlayment is available in 4 × 4 foot and 3 × 4 foot sheets in lumber yards.

The use of underlayment allows you to lay new tile over old without having to remove the old tile, which is a difficult, time-consuming job. However, you should never install new tile right on top of old tile. The new tile will not stay in place. Furthermore, as temperature and humidity cause old tile to expand and contract, wide cracks will appear along the seams of the new tile.

The most popular types of tile are vinyl-asbestos, vinyl, and asphalt, with vinyl-asbestos being the one which is most widely used by homeowners. Vinyl-asbestos is generally less costly than vinyl (but more costly than asphalt) and is grease-resistant, easy to maintain, and fairly durable. Vinyl-asbestos tile is available in $1/16$-, $3/32$-, and $1/8$-inch thicknesses, and in 9 × 9 and 12 × 12 inch squares.

Vinyl tile offers the widest range of colors, sizes, and designs. However, it is the most costly of resiliant floorings for the home. Vinyl tile is grease-resistant and about as durable as vinyl-asbestos. It is available in 0.080 gauge, and $1/16$- and $1/8$-inch thicknesses. Sizes are 9 × 9, 12 × 12, and 9 × 18 inch.

Asphalt tile is available in $1/8$-inch thickness and 9×9 inch squares only. It is offered in a limited selection of colors and designs. Since it is not grease-resistant, asphalt tile is not recommended for use in the kitchen or in other rooms, such as in laundry rooms, where foreign matter is liable to drop on it. However, it has usefulness in playrooms, patios, and basements.

The chart included in this section will assist you in buying

Figure 1. This chart will assist in determining the number of tiles required for the job.

Square Feet	Number of Tiles Needed			Square Feet	Number of Tiles Needed		
	9 × 9″	12″ × 12″	9″ × 18″		9 × 9″	12″ × 12″	9″ × 18″
1	2	1	1	60	107	60	54
2	4	2	2	70	125	70	63
3	6	3	3	80	143	80	72
4	8	4	4	90	160	90	80
5	9	5	5	100	178	100	90
6	11	6	6	200	356	200	178
7	13	7	7	300	534	300	267
8	15	8	8	400	712	400	356
9	16	9	8	500	890	500	445
10	18	10	9	600	1068	600	534
20	36	20	18	700	1246	700	623
30	54	30	27	800	1424	800	712
40	72	40	36	900	1602	900	801
50	89	50	45	1000	1780	1000	890

Allowance for Waste	
1–50 sq. ft. — 14%	
50–100 sq. ft. — 10%	
100–200 sq. ft. — 8%	
200–300 sq. ft. — 7%	
300–1000 sq. ft. — 5%	
Over 1000 sq. ft. — 3%	

Figure 2. Every crack and gouge should be treated with filler to be sure the floor is level.

Figure 3. Hammer nails through bumps to level the area so that tile will have a flat surface.

tile so that you do not purchase more than you need (Fig. 1). Let's cite an example of how to use the chart.

If you have an area of 240 square feet that you wish to cover with 9×9 inch tile, the chart shows that you should order 356 tiles for 200 square feet and 72 tiles for 40 square feet—a total of 428 tiles. Allow an extra 7 percent or 30 tiles for waste and spares for a grand total of 458 tiles. Spares should be kept in the event that a tile block has to be replaced in the future (see the section on Floor Tile, Replacing).

Before laying underlayment, inspect old tile for gouges and cracks. Fill these with floor patch and crack filler (Fig. 2). Follow mixing instructions given on the package.

Now, run your hand over the surface of the old floor. If you feel bumps, drive a nail or two directly through them. This is done to restore the floor to a level condition so that a flat surface is available for new tile (Fig. 3).

File the edges of each underlayment board to remove burrs

Figure 4. Before installing underlayment, file burrs from its edges so panels will lie flat.

Figure 5. Leave a slight space between underlayment panels to compensate for size variation.

that could keep underlayment from lying flat, thus presenting an uneven base for tile (Fig. 4). In putting the underlayment into place, make sure that edges aren't butted too tightly together. Leave about a 1/64-inch space (about the width of a pencil point) between edges to allow for expansion (Fig. 5). Furthermore, stagger seams to avoid having four corners meet at one point. Tile placed on top of a four-corner intersection will tend to shift.

Use 4d (d stands for pennyweight) coated cement nails, ringgroove flooring nails, or 7/8-inch divergent chisel staples to fasten underlayment. These are available in hardware stores. Underlayment panels are usually marked with small Xs to denote where nails should be driven. If these guides aren't present, space nails about 4 inches apart. Drive nailheads flush with the board's surface.

Naturally, underlayment will have to be cut to fit around outside corners and other protrusions. A sabre saw makes short work of this task, but be sure to file edges to remove burrs (Fig. 6).

After underlayment is installed, the floor has to be marked off to provide guidelines that will assure that tiles are laid in a straight line. Determine the center points of two opposing walls and hammer in a tack at one end of the room. Tie a string that has been rubbed in chalk to the tack.

Now, extend the string across the room to the center point of the opposite wall and snap a chalk line down the center of the room (Fig. 7). Do the same thing between the other two walls so that the room will be divided into quarters.

Figure 6. Use of a sabre saw to make irregular cuts makes short work of a tedious, tough task.

Figure 7. Be careful that chalk lines are snapped straight. If not, tile will also be crooked.

Figure 8. Laying test rows of tile is important to ascertain that tile will fit border areas.

Figure 9. Measure the distance between test tile and wall to be sure border size is right.

Using the chalk lines as a guide, lay two test rows of tile which are perpendicular to each other (Fig. 8). When this has been done, measure the distance between each wall and the tile closest to the wall (Fig. 9). This distance should not be less than 2 inches nor more than 8 inches. If it is either, readjust the center line so that the last tile is about 4½ inches from the wall. The purpose of this is to avoid having a strip of tile along the wall that is less than 2 inches in width.

Pick up the test tile and spread tile adhesive (mastic) over one quarter of the room. Work in one-quarter segments to prevent the job from getting overbearing. The dealer from whom you buy tile can recommend a suitable adhesive to use with it. Use adhesive sparingly and follow instructions on the can carefully.

Allow adhesive to dry thoroughly. Generally, you will know that it is dry by touching it with your fingers. If it is tacky (or dry) but doesn't stick to your fingers, tile can be laid.

Figure 10. Lay tile into place carefully. Do not slide tile. Do ¼ of the room at a time.

Figure 11. To obtain tile for the border, first place a tile on top of an installed square.

Figure 12. Place another tile on top of that and push it to the wall. Now, mark the tile.

Starting from the determined center point, lay tile along the chalk guideline at first, and then extend out from this straight row. Be sure to *lay* tiles into place. Do not slide them (Fig. 10). If adhesive oozes up from between the tile, remove it immediately with fine steel wool. To fit tile properly around the perimeter of the room, lay a loose tile on top of one of the tile blocks which is in the row nearest the border (Fig. 11). Lay another loose tile on top of that, butting it against the wall and use its outer edge as a guide to mark off the tile below (Fig. 12).

Now, cut the marked tile. The result will be a piece of tile which will fit exactly into the border. Vinyl-asbestos and asphalt tile should be heated over a stove to make them pliable enough to cut with scissors. Vinyl tile can be cut without heating.

FLOOR TILE, Replacing

You may think that the main drawback to replacing one or more damaged blocks of resilient floor tile is the inability to secure replacement tiles that are of a matching pattern. Although it is good practice to buy and save some extra tiles when a new floor is installed, failure to have done so should not prevent repair (Fig. 1).

Figure 1. Plan ahead. Buy some extra tile of the same pattern when laying a new tile floor.

If you cannot get replacement tile of the exact pattern, you can make an attractive repair with tiles of contrasting color that form a design. This works especially well when the repair is being made in the center of the floor. In side areas, a strip of contrasting tiles is eye-appealing.

There are five different types of resiliant floor tile: vinyl-asbestos, asphalt, vinyl, rubber, and linoleum. To remove damaged vinyl-asbestos and asphalt tile, the block must be heated to loosen the adhesive. The fastest but least safe heating method is a propane torch. Make certain that you keep the flame moving constantly to avoid overheating one spot, which could present a fire hazard.

Another way to loosen tile by heat is with an ordinary steam iron that is set to its hottest setting. Place a damp cloth over the tile to keep the iron from sticking and place the iron on top of the cloth.

If you are making extensive repairs—that is, replacing many tiles—the best way is with an electric heating plate. This is a professinal tool which you can rent from a dealer who sells tile and linoleum supplies.

As the tile is being heated, pry in from the seams with a putty knife. If the tile should stick at any one point, concentrate your heat source at this point.

Vinyl, rubber, and linoleum tiles don't require heating. To remove them, use a linoleum knife to cut around the seams so that the tile is freed at the edges. A linoleum knife may be purchased at a hardware store or at a dealer of floor tile and linoleum supplies.

After seams are loosened, the tile can then be cut out with a hammer and wood chisel. Work from the center of the tile out toward the edges to avoid damaging adjacent tiles and do not gouge the floor with the chisel.

When tile has been removed, scrape off as much of the old adhesive as possible from the floor and examine the floor for high and low spots. These must be leveled or the replacement tile will be placed on an uneven surface and traffic over the tile could cause it to crack.

A high spot—that is, wood slivers that are sticking up—can be cut down with a chisel or shaved with a plane. Depressions should be filled with wood putty so that they are made flush with the floor. Allow putty to dry thoroughly before installing new tile.

To install new tile, be sure that you use the adhesive which is recommended for that tile. There is a recommended type of adhesive for every type of tile. Consult with your dealer and

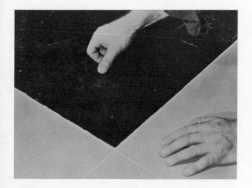

Figure 2. Most tile adhesives will feel tacky but not stick to the thumb when dry enough.

Figure 3. Use a kitchen stove to get vinyl-asbestos and asphalt tile pliable for cutting.

Figure 4. Vinyl floor tile is easy to handle. It requires no heating. Vinyl-asbestos does.

Figure 5. Whether heat is required or not, modern resilient floor tile is easy to fashion.

bring him the replacement block of tile if necessary. Apply adhesive exactly as directed on the can (Fig. 2).

Now, press the tile into place firmly. Use a piece of dowel or a regular tile roller to assure firm contact. Concentrate particularly on the edges. If edges aren't held tight by adhesive, they will curl.

If vinyl-asbestos or asphalt tile must be cut to make it fit, it should be heated over a stove (Fig. 3). This will make the tile easy to cut with scissors (Fig. 4). Other types of tile can be cut and trimmed without heating them (Fig. 5).

FOUNDATION

As a home settles, cracks often develop in both the foundation and the cellar walls. Visible cracks on the outside of the house should be repaired promptly before they allow water to seep into the crack, where it will eventually build up sufficient pressure to cause a leak into the basement.

Cracks in basement walls should be repaired as well to prevent water that could build up inside the wall from leaking into the cellar and also to reinforce an outside repair.

To determine the extent of a foundation crack, dig down below grade level. If the crack is present only near the top of the ground, undercut it with a hammer and cold chisel to provide a base to which repair compound can take firm hold. Wire brush away all loose dirt and chips and wet the crack with water from a hose (Fig. 1).

One of the best repair compounds you can use to seal a foundation crack is hydraulic cement, which sets quickly, has good strength, and is waterproof. Mix the material as instructed on the can and pack it into the crack, making sure that you cover the entire crack with a liberal amount of cement (Fig. 2).

In digging down below grade level, if you find that the crack extends below the surface of the ground, there is a relatively simple repair method that you can try. It is not practical, of course, to dig much beneath grade level since many times cracks extend clear to the foundation's footing.

Incidentally, if water begins to leak into the basement through a crack in the wall, you can figure that there is a crack in the foundation, not visible to you, through which water is coming. This repair method should be applied.

The repair involves use of Gold Bond Hydro-Stop, which is manufactured by National Gypsum Co. and is available in hardware stores and lumber yards. This is a latex compound that works its way into a crack where it sets and seals.

If you can't see the crack and can't determine its exact location, project its approximate location by lining it up with the crack in the basement wall through which water is coming. It

Figure 1. It is important that debris from a foundation crack be cleaned away before repair.

Figure 2. Try to find the end of the crack by digging below grade. Use plenty of compound.

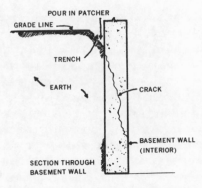

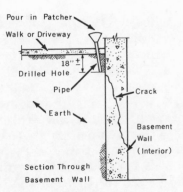

Figure 3. If ground is exposed, dig a hole near foundation and apply Hydro-Stop to seal crack.

Figure 4. If the ground is covered, drill a hole through the walk. Apply Hydro-Stop as seen.

isn't necessary to pinpoint the exact location since Hydro-Stop spreads itself over a fairly wide area.

When the location of the crack has been determined, dig a hole near the foundation to a depth of about 6 inches. Fill the hole about halfway with water (Hydro-Stop isn't able to penetrate hard or dry soil) and pour the solution into the hole (Fig. 3). Spray the Hydro-Stop with water from a garden hose nozzle which is set for a fine spray. This will keep the solution from skinning.

Most foundation cracks will be sealed with an application of 2 gallons of Hydro-Stop. Apply 1 gallon, wait 24 hours, and then apply the second gallon.

However, never apply Hydro-Stop when soil temperature is below 55°F.

To test the adequacy of the repair, soak the ground with a hose in the vicinity of the crack and check to see if leakage shows up on the inside of the basement.

Figure 5. Start the repair of basement wall cracks by widening the crack for the compound.

Figure 6. Apply a liberal coating of Quick Plug, which will effectively repair the damage.

What do you do if the area above a foundation crack is covered by a sidewalk or driveway? First, find the approximate location of the crack as explained above and drill a ½-inch or larger hole directly through the sidewalk or driveway as close as possible to the wall. Insert a rod and poke a hold through the soil to a depth of about 18 inches. Insert a funnel into the hole and pour in water and Hydro-Stop as explained above (Fig. 4). After the treatment has been completed, the hole in the sidewalk or driveway can be patched with a cement mixture.

Cracks in a basement wall are easy to seal. First, widen the crack with a cold chisel and hammer to give the repair compound a firm base. (Fig. 5). Apply a product called Quick Plug, which is an excellent repair compound for this application (Fig. 6). You can buy it in a hardware store or lumber yard.

FURNACE

Your home's heating system consists of two sections: a burner where a fuel, such as oil or gas, is burned to create heat and a delivery system which circulates heat throughout the home. This delivery is done either by hot water, steam, or forced air. When there is a furnace malfunction, begin by checking the burner section.

Oil burner checks. 1. Check thermostat operation by setting the thermostat 5 degrees above the indicated room temperature. If the burner doesn't start and the thermostat is an automatic day-night control, make sure that the cycle hasn't been reversed.

Remove or open the thermostat cover and check the dial control. If the unit is a sealed mercury type, which seldom gives trouble, reinstall the cover. However, if the thermostat has a contact point control which is exposed, dirt may have gotten on the points, preventing contact. Pass a new dollar bill or a clean business card between the points. Now see if raising the thermostat will start the burner.

2. Check emergency switches. One may have accidentally been turned off. Most oil burners have two switches. One is usually placed on the burner, while the other is often located at the head of the basement stairway. Familiarize yourself with the location of emergency switches and be sure that they are turned on if the oil burner turns off.

3. Check the fuse or circuit breaker (Fig. 1). Vibration may in time cause a fuse to loosen. Make sure it is tight. If the fuse has blown, replace it with one of equivalent value. If a fuse insists on blowing or a circuit breaker trips repeatedly, there is an

Figure 1. A blown fuse or tripped circuit breaker is common.

Figure 2. When your oil burner shuts down, press the overload switch, which is on the motor.

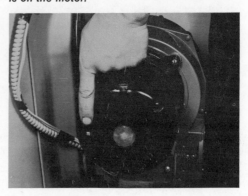

electrical malfunction. Call a serviceman.

4. Check safety switches. Oil burners as a rule have two: the overload switch and the stack control relay. They prevent furnace damage if a problem develops in the electrical circuit.

The overload switch, which is often painted red, will be found on the motor housing (Fig. 2). Press it one time only. If the motor does not start, activate the stack control relay one time only (Fig. 3). This switch is found on the smoke pipe or the burner housing.

If the burner doesn't start or starts and stops, call a serviceman. There is an electrical problem.

If your oil burner was installed after 1965, it may be controlled by a photoelectric cell. If this gets dirty, the burner won't operate. Remove the photoelectric cell from its housing and carefully wipe it clean with a cloth (Fig. 4). Replace the part and activate the stack control relay.

Figure 3. The stack control relay is another safety switch to activate if a breakdown occurs.

Figure 4. A photoelectric cell of a modern oil burner is kept inside a housing on the burner.

5. Check the oil supply. Don't trust the oil gauge if there is one on the furnace. It may be stuck, showing that there is oil. Tap the gauge gently.

If procedures thus far have failed to reveal the cause of the oil burner malfunction, check the delivery system (see below). **Gas burner checks.** 1. Check thermostat operation as discussed above.

2. Check the emergency switch. A gas burner has only one. It is normally positioned on the furnace.

3. Check the fuse or circuit breaker.

4. Check the gas pilot. If it is not burning, relight the pilot as explained on the instruction plate which is attached to the furnace. A pilot light which doesn't stay lit may be clogged with dirt or carbon. Tap the pilot burner lightly with the handle of a screwdriver and try to light it. If it doesn't light, call your local gas company. Gas companies as a rule provide free service when gas-operated equipment breaks down.

Checking the delivery system. A faulty delivery system will cause a shutdown of the burner or will allow the burner to continue operating while no heat is delivered. The following is an explanation of how to check each of the various delivery systems:

Hot water systems use a circulator to distribute hot water. If a circulator needs lubrication, it will not operate although the burner section of the furnace will continue to run. Instructions on the circulator explain how to lubricate the machinery.

If the circulator fails to operate, check to see if there is a reset button on the housing. Press it once. If there is no button, give the unit a sharp slap with the palm of your hand. If the system doesn't function, call a serviceman.

Steam systems have a boiler gauge that should be checked when the burner shuts down. If the water level is too low, the burner will shut off and not start again until the boiler is refilled. However, never refill a hot boiler. It may crack. The burner should automatically turn back on when the boiler gauge indicates that the boiler is half filled.

Figure 5. A dirty air filter is a major cause of lack of heat.

Forced air systems have filters that will become clogged with dirt which reduces heat flow (Fig. 5). Filters should be replaced often to allow the unit to operate efficiently.

A broken fan belt may be a problem. If a belt breaks, buy one of the same size at a hardware store. Place it on the blower motor pulleys and tighten the adjusting nut, which is normally found behind the pulley motor. A properly adjusted belt has ½ inch to ¾ inch free play.

A blower motor that is not functioning properly will refuse to run or will cycle on and off in brief spurts. Turn off the burner and call a serviceman.

FURNITURE REFINISHING

There are seven steps involved in applying a new finish to a piece of furniture: stripping, repairing, filling, sanding, staining, finishing, and waxing. Each step must be done carefully and with patience if professional looking results are to be obtained. **Step 1 — *Stripping the old finish.*** Remove hardware, such as metal handles, from the furniture and apply a stripping agent (Fig. 1). Follow application instructions on the container. Several suitable stripping agents are Solventique, Kut-Kote, Deft, Strypeeze, Double-X, Wil-Bond, DuPont's Paint and Varnish Remover, Wash-Away, Kleen Strip, Sure-X, and Wonder Paste.

These solutions are usually applied with a paint brush. Use short, gentle strokes to achieve uniform density over the surface. Pay close attention to crevices, turnings, and curvings.

Allow the solvent to set for about 15 minutes or 30 minutes if the finish is very old. Now, scrape away a portion of the finish from a small section. Use a putty knife. This will allow you to determine whether the finish will come off easily or if you should allow the solvent to do its work for more time.

If the bare surface becomes exposed with little effort, you can remove the finish from the entire piece of furniture. However, if not, allow the stripping agent to set for an additional 15 minutes.

Figure 1. Apply the stripping agent carefully. Be sure that every section is well covered.

Figure 2. Note the position of the putty knife. It will remove waste without harming the wood.

Figure 3. Remove the old finish from coves, edges, and beads by use of a stiff-bristle brush.

Figure 4. The blanching operation is peformed with a No. 2 steel wool pad and detergent.

Figure 5. After washing, residue is removed from the furniture with a window squeegee.

To remove the old finish, use light but firm pressure on a putty knife (Fig. 2). Take care not to dig or gouge the wood. Use a stiff-bristle brush to remove the old finish from edges, coves, beads, and curved detail (Fig. 3).

Now, blanch the wood which raises the wood fibers to permit a more thorough removal of residue. Fill a container with water and detergent, and wash the furniture with a No. 2 steel wool pad that you dip frequently into the detergent solution (Fig. 4). When the furniture has been washed, wipe off water with a rubber window squeegee (Fig. 5). Wash the furniture again, but this time use clear water and a No. 2 steel wool pad. Dry the furniture as thoroughly as possible with clean rags.

Figure 6. Complete the blanching step with a thorough washing with turpentine. Let dry.

Figure 7. Fill gouges and nicks with a good quality wood putty that has been mixed properly.

The final step in blanching is to wash the wood with turpentine. Be sure the turpentine covers the entire surface. Rub it into the wood with a No. 2 steel wool pad (Fig. 6). This will remove residue entrenched in wood fibers that stripping didn't remove. Allow the furniture to dry for 24 hours.

Step 2 — Repairing. You will probably notice imperfections in the wood, such as dents and depressions. These should be repaired. Minor scars can mar the appearance of an otherwise excellent refinishing job.

Gouges and nicks can be repaired with a wood putty, such as Schalk, Deshler, Poly-Chemical, or Durham (Fig. 7). Follow directions on the can. In most cases the putty, which comes in powder form, will have to be mixed with water and packed into the dent with a putty knife. When putty dries, sand it smooth.

If a dent is small, it can often be straightened with steam rather than putty. Wet the damaged area with hot water, lay a heavy moist cloth over it, and place a hot steam iron on top of the cloth. Remove the cloth and iron often to determine when the wood has swelled sufficiently to fill the dent.

If you are working with veneer and find a blister, slit the blister down its center with a sharp razor blade. Be sure to follow the grain of the wood.

Now, lift the sides of the split carefully, apply a little Presto-Set or Elmer's Glue beneath them, and carefully press the wood into place. Cover the repair with a weight such as a book and allow it to dry overnight. Next day, sand the glue line very lightly if excess glue has oozed out. This is done to get rid of unsightly crust or bead.

Figure 8. Weak drawer bottoms can be strengthened with a few wooden blocks and strong glue.

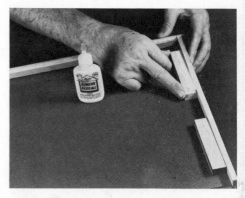

Figure 9. Reinforcement blocks for drawers are placed two to each side. Attach them firmly.

If drawer bottoms are weak, reinforce them with wood blocks about 3 inches long. Place two of the blocks to a side. Coat each block with wood glue (Fig. 8). Then, position them so that maximum reinforcement will be provided (Fig. 9). Wipe off excess glue and allow the repair to set for a day or so until the wood blocks have attached themselves firmly.

Step 3 — Filling. Does a paste wood filler, which you can buy in a hardware or paint store, have to be applied to furniture? This depends on whether the wood is open grain or closed grain.

If you have an open grain wood, the pores of the wood must be filled to obtain a smooth surface for stain. If filler is not applied, too much stain will be absorbed. If the wood has a closed grain, treatment with a wood filler is not necessary.

The chart below will assist you in determining if the furniture's wood is open or closed grain. If you cannot identify the wood, take a sample (such as a drawer) to a lumber dealer and ask him.

SOFT WOODS (Closed Grain) No Filler Required	HARD WOODS (Closed Grain) No Filler Required	HARD WOODS (Open Grain) Filler Recommended
Poplar	Ash (white)	Oak
Redwood	Elm	Chestnut
Larchwood	Birch	Mahogany
Spruce	Cherry	Walnut
White Pine	Maple	
White Fir		

Figure 10. At first, apply wood filler across the wood's grain; then in the grain's direction.

Figure 11. When wood filler has lost its gloss, wipe away excess compound with a clean rag.

Before using paste wood filler, mix it with a little turpentine until the filler becomes of a consistency that can be applied with a paint brush. Use a soft-bristle brush and apply the filler *across* the grain of the wood; then reverse direction and apply filler *with* the grain (Fig. 10).

Wood filler will lose its gloss in 15 to 20 minutes, which means that it is dry. At this time, remove excess filler lying on the wood's surface with a wad of burlap cloth. Rub across the grain at first. Then rub *lightly* in the direction of grain (Fig. 11). Wait several hours before disturbing the surface again.

Step 4 — Sanding. This step is necessary to rid the wood of blotches and scratches that will mar the finish. Handsanding with a sanding block is the safest way of doing this (Fig. 12). Power sanding, if not done with extreme care, will damage the wood.

Sanding is done in two steps. Use a No. 2/0 sandpaper for initial sanding. When the wood has been sanded smooth, wash the entire piece of furniture with water and allow it to dry. This washing will raise depressed grain and fiber endings to permit you to obtain a glass-smooth finish with the second sanding step. This second step is done with a No. 4/0 sandpaper. After sanding has been completed, wipe the furniture clean with a soft rag or, better yet, vacuum it to get rid of dust.

Figure 12. Sanding is an important step. Do it patiently and carefully. Use a sanding block.

Figure 13. Stain can be applied with a clean rag. Be sure all areas are completely covered.

Figure 14. Use of a paint brush gives you better control than a rag when applying the stain.

Design areas, such as beads and coves, require special close attention. Fold the sandpaper and trace the design until the surface becomes as smooth as you can possibly get it. Naturally, you won't be able to use a sanding block.

Step 5—Staining. There are different types of stains, specifically, water, alcohol, and oil. However, it is strongly suggested that you use oil stain only. It works slower than the others, thus giving you maximum control over the result.

Apply stain with a brush or piece of cheesecloth (Fig. 13). If you use a brush, employ short, even strokes (Fig. 14).

If you want to determine the result that you will get, obtain a scrap piece of wood of the same type you wish to stain from a lumber dealer and stain that first. Use a watch to time various lengths of application.

The longer that the stain is permitted to set, the darker will be the result. Thus, wipe it off with a clean rag when you believe that you have achieved the desired result. If the stain is too dark as it comes from the can, dilute it with a little turpentine to lighten it.

Steps 6 and 7—Finishing and waxing. After the stain has dried (give it 24 hours), rub the piece of furniture with a tack cloth to remove lint. You can buy tack clothes in a hardware store.

Figure 15. The topcoat provides long-lasting protection. Apply from the center to each edge.

Figure 16. Refinishing is completed with a light coating of a good quality furniture wax.

Now, apply a clear protective topcoat with a paint brush, working from the center of the furniture to each edge (Fig. 15). Be careful that the coating does not drip over an edge. Protective coatings are available in flat, eggshell, semigloss, and high-gloss finishes.

Allow the topcoat to dry (give it 24 hours). Now, wax the furniture with a good quality furniture paste wax (Fig. 16). Apply wax with a folded, damp cloth. Use only a light application, allow the wax to dry, and buff.

GARAGE DOOR

The reasons that an overhead garage door will fail to operate properly include incorrect adjustment, loose hardware, binding, and friction. Before attempting to make repairs, identify the type of door that you have.

An extension-spring door has springs along both horizontal tracks (Fig. 1). A torsion-spring door has a torsion spring wrapped around a shaft that extends across the top of the door and is equipped with cables that wind on winchlike drums that are attached to the same shaft on which the torsion spring rides.

Figure 1. A garage door of the extension spring type is identified by springs along the tracks.

Figure 2. To avoid problems caused by friction, lubricte moving surfaces with SAE 20 oil.

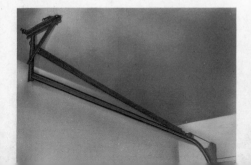

Figure 3. Clean dirt from the tracks of an overhead garage door.

Figure 4. Apply Lubriplate to each track to prevent binding.

Friction is the number one problem that strikes overhead garage doors. As soon as trouble occurs, lubricate critical areas. In fact, to avert a problem, these areas should be lubricated once every six months.

Lubricate pulleys, ball bearings, door rollers, and hinge pins (Fig. 2). Use SAE 20 weight motor oil to lubricate each, but keep in mind that only a drop of oil is needed. Do not overlubricate.

Another critical spot to lubricate is inside the tracks, especially at curved sections. Be sure that dirt is cleaned from each track, and then apply a thin coating of Lubriplate, which is a waterproof product that is not affected by weather (Figs. 3 and 4). You can buy Lubriplate in an automotive supply store.

If lubrication fails to resolve the problem of friction, examine the door and door stops to determine if paint has been rubbed away in any spot (Fig. 5). If it has, the door should be moved away from the door stops.

If the track is equipped with brackets that have bolts, loosen the bolts and move the track away from the door about ⅛ inch (Fig. 6). Tighten the bolts. If tracks have brackets that are

Figure 5. To determine if the door requires readjustment, examine the door stop for rubbing.

Figure 6. To readjust a door that is equipped with brackets, loosen bolts and move the track.

Figure 7. To compensate for added weight to extension spring doors, first prop the door open.

Figure 8. The S-hooks are moved forward to increase tension.

welded, it will not be possible to make this adjustment.

Examine the door to determine if there is a moisture problem. Indications of this are small cracks and checks in the paint. If the door has become too heavy because of moisture, wait for a dry spell and hope that lack of precipitation in the area will cause moisture to evaporate. Now, sand the door thoroughly on both sides to remove cracked paint and repaint the door with a good quality exterior house paint to keep it from absorbing moisture once again.

If this doesn't work and you have an extension-spring door, it is possible to compensate for the added weight that a door may incur by adjusting the springs. Prop the door open with clamps or by placing a ladder beneath it (Fig. 7). If this is not done, the door will fall once springs are detached.

Most doors are anchored by S-hooks. To increase spring tension, move hooks forward a hole at a time and test the door (Fig. 8). On other doors, springs are adjusted by moving the back end of the extension spring over a notched bar. On still others, adjustments are made with an eyebolt and nut through the rear track hanger.

A door is properly adjusted when, with its bottom 1 to 2 inches off the ground, it will rise or fall by itself. When more than 1 or 2 inches off the ground, a properly adjusted door will rise slowly. When less than 1 or 2 inches off the ground, a properly adjusted door will fall by itself.

Do not attempt to adjust a torsion-spring garage door. These are dangerous to handle and require the use of special equipment. Consult a professional serviceman if the door is damaged.

GARBAGE DISPOSERS

The average life of a garbage disposer is about 10 years. When the motor burns out, it is more practical to replace the unit than to fix it. The purpose of this discussion, therefore, is to explain how to take care of a garbage disposer so that you will achieve maximum use from it.

Those parts of a garbage disposer which do the job of pulverizing garbage are dull-edged shredders that are attached to a table (Fig. 1). The table revolves at approximately 1700 revolutions per minute to fling waste against the shredders. The shredders pulverize the garbage into tiny particles which are then discharged through holes into the drain pipe where they are flushed into the sewerage system (Fig. 2).

There are two types of garbage disposers to choose from: continuous-feed and batch-feed. With a continuous-feed unit, waste can be deposited into the disposer through a flexible rubber cover while the disposer is running (Fig. 3). A continuous-feed garbage disposer is turned on and off by a wall switch that is usually placed on the wall just above the sink.

Figure 2. The garbage disposer fits beneath the kitchen sink and is connected to the drain.

Figure 1. Shredders pulverize garbage into minute particles as the table revolves rapidly.

Figure 3. The continuous-feed disposer is characterized by a flexible rubber drain covering.

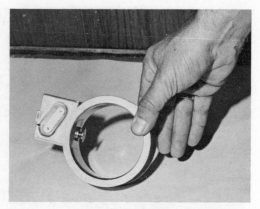

Figure 4. A batch-feed unit operates when the cover engages an on-off switch in the drain.

Figure 5. The control that you see in the drain opening is the unit's on-off control switch.

Batch-feed garbage disposers run only when a cover is placed over the drain opening and turned to lock position (Fig. 4). When the cover is turned to unlock, which must be done before the cover can be removed to feed waste into the unit, the disposer automatically shuts off.

The on-off switch for a batch-feed garbage disposer is inside the drain opening (Figs. 5 and 6). Thus, with a batch-feed unit, you cannot dispose of more than one load of garbage at a time. However, many families with children prefer the batch-feed unit because of the protection afforded by the cover-activated switch.

One problem that bothers homeowners who are comtemplating the purchase of a garbage disposer is whether one can be installed if the home has a septic system. According to the Robert A. Taft Sanitary Center of the U.S. Public Health Service in Cincinnati, Ohio, a garbage disposer can be used with a septic system if the septic tank meets the following standards:

Number of People Living in Home	Minimum Capacity Of Septic Tank
4	750 gallons
6	900 gallons
8	1,000 gallons
10	1,250 gallons

The capacity of a septic tank can be determined by consulting with the builder of the house or with the town engineer.

Figure 6. Here, the switch is uncovered. If the unit fails to run, have the switch checked.

Garbage disposers will not cause a septic system's absorption field to flood. The average absorption field handles about 50 gallons of water a day per person. The average garbage disposer uses 6 gallons of water a day, which is equivalent to one flushing of a toilet's water closet or an 80-second shower.

When operating a garbage disposer, keep the cold water running. Do not turn off the water until grinding has been completed. Cold water causes grease and fat to congeal into tiny globules that will flow easily into the sewerage system. Hot water, on the other hand, should not be used to flush the system. It will melt grease which will coat the drain line and eventually create a stoppage.

Garbage disposers are self-cleaning. However, it's a good idea to fill the sink with cold water periodically and allow it to drain out all at once. This flushes the drain line and gets rid of waste and detergent scum.

Do not use chemical drain cleaners in any drain that is equipped with a garbage disposer. Chemicals will damage the unit.

Never allow food scraps to remain in a disposer for any length of time. Wastes produce odors. And never feed metal objects, cartons, rubber, glass, crockery, rags, strings, or plastic into a disposer. They will damage the unit and clog the drain line.

If a dishwasher is connected so it drains through a garbage disposer, allow the disposer to operate for several seconds before starting the dishwasher, to flush away wastes that could cause discharge water from the dishwasher to backup. After a dishwasher has completed its cycle and has shut off, run the garbage disposer for several seconds to flush away particles that may have been discharged into the disposer by the dishwasher.

*Figure 7. This particular garbage dispos-
er is equipped with automatic reversing
capability.*

*Figure 8. With this unit, reverse rotation
is manual. Note the reverse rotation
control.*

*Never operate a garbage disposer and dishwasher at the same
time.*

To prevent a foreign object from dropping through the drain
opening into a garbage disposer where it can cause jamming,
keep the cover over the unit at all times. If by accident the unit
should jam, there are two ways of clearing the obstacle.

Some units have an automatic reverse-action switch that
kicks the table into reverse when the jamming object causes
table speed to slow down below a normal speed (Fig. 7). This
reverse action will usually loosen the clogging object. Other
units have a reverse-action switch which must be manually operated when jamming occurs (Fig. 8).

If reversing the direction of the table does not clear jamming, shut off the unit and fish the object out with a pair of
pliers or ice tongs. If your unit is batch-feed, be careful that your
hand does not touch the activating switch.

Modern garbage disposers have built-in overload protection.
If a unit jams for more than 30 seconds, an overload switch that
works like a circuit breaker automatically shuts off current to
keep the unit's motor from burning up. If you notice that overload protection has been activated, shut off the on-off switch
and free the jamming object.

Some models automatically reset themselves when the overload switch cools. With others, however, you have to wait 5 minutes to allow the switch to cool and then reset the switch by
pressing a reset button. Be sure to read the instruction manual
which comes with your garbage disposer.

GARDEN HOSE

There is no reason to discard a garden hose if it should spring a leak or is otherwise damaged. Repairs can be made quickly and easily with items that are available in a hardware store. This is true for both plastic and rubber hoses.

If plastic hose should develop a small cut, for example, try to patch it with plastic adhesive tape. Overlap the cut by about 1 inch, and wrap the tape tightly. Repeat the application to provide a double layer of tape.

If damage is major and tape doesn't stop a leak, plastic hose can be repaired with a plastic hose mender coupler. You must know the inner diameter of the hose when you buy the coupler. Most garden hoses have an inner diameter of $1/2$ or $5/8$ inch.

A mender coupler is a male-female fitting. To attach it, first remove the piece of damaged hose with a sharp knife or hacksaw (Fig 1). Keep the cut edges as square as possible. To assure square edges, wrap some tape around the hose on each side of the damage. It will serve as a guide for cutting.

Before you install the mender coupler, soften the hose by inserting both pieces into hot water (Fig. 2). Now, push one part of the mender coupler into one end of the plastic hose, and the other part into the other end of the plastic hose (Fig. 3).

The mender coupler comes equipped with two ring clamps. Put these around the hose so that they are positioned over the mender coupler pieces and tighten them so that the pieces will be held firmly. Complete the repair by attaching the male end of the mender coupler to the female end (Fig. 4).

Figure 1. To repair a plastic hose, cut away damaged area with sharp knife.

Figure 2. Insert the ends of the hose into hot water to make them pliable.

Figure 3. Insert the parts of the mender coupler into the ends of the hose.

Figure 4. Join the two pieces of hose by screwing the mender coupler together.

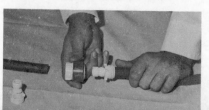

If the water tappet coupling of a plastic hose is damaged, the repair is similar to that just described, except that the repair hardware consists of a female fitting only. Follow the procedure we have just described: cut away the damaged coupling, soften the end of the hose, insert the coupling, and tighten with a clamp.

Repair of a leaky rubber hose is done either with a metal clincher or a clincher coupler, depending on the length of the hose and the location of the damage. If the hose is short (25 feet), use a metal clincher, which is a one-piece fitting. If the hose is long (50 feet) and the leak is near the center, use a clincher coupler, which is a two-piece fitting consisting of male and female parts. The two-piece fitting allows you to separate the hose into two sections for easy storage.

To make the repair with either of the two types of hardware, remove the damaged section of hose with a sharp knife or hacksaw. Keep cut edges as square as possible. Insert the hardware, being sure that it is of the correct size for the hose (either ½ or ⅝ inch). There is no need to heat the cut ends of rubber hose, which is sufficiently pliable to be cut easily. Now, hammer down the metal prongs of the coupler until they clinch the hose securely. A damaged water tappet coupler for a rubber hose is replaced with similar hardware in the same manner.

GARDEN TOOLS

Keen-edged garden tools make work easier. This is why you should hone tools with the proper sharpening device when it becomes necessary.

Keep in mind, however, that you shouldn't put a knife-edge on a garden tool. If you have doubts concerning the degree to which a blade should be honed, examine the blade of a new tool of the same kind at a garden supply store.

Grass shears are restored to good condition with a fine round-edge slipstone. Spread the blades and run the stone along the edges until both blades are of the same bevel and smoothness.

Sod-cutting spades and hoes are given a keen blade with a utility file. Apply the file at an angle that is parallel to the bevel of the edge. Stroke in small circles along the entire edge (Fig. 1).

An ax that is very dull or has a badly nicked edge should first be treated with a mill file. Mount the handle of the ax in a vise and use diagonal strokes, pushing against the slope of the edge.

Now, to put a keen edge on the blade, use a round ax stone.

Figure 1. The blade of a spade should not be razor-sharp. File the edge with circular strokes.

Figure 2. Dirt brings rust. Be sure that the tool is perfectly clean before you store it away.

Use a circular motion and try to maintain a uniform bevel on both sides of the blade so that a wedge-shaped edge is produced.

A sickle can be given a keen blade with a sickle stone. Apply the convex side of the stone at the angle of the cutting bevel and stroke in both directions along the entire edge.

Note that a burred edge will be created on the other side of the blade. This is easily removed by running the flat side of the sickle stone over the blade.

The life of garden tools will be greatly extended if they are prepared for storage in the correct manner after the gardening season ends.

First, clean off the working end of the tool. Brush away caked dirt, rust, and other foreign matter with a wire brush (Fig. 2).

Now, clean off wooden handles. If they are not protected by paint, apply a coating of linseed oil. If paint has rubbed away so that raw wood shows, repaint the handle.

Make sure that handles are tight. If a handle is held by bolts, tighten the bolts. Garden tools that have the working end pressed into the handle can be tightened, if loose, by tapping the working end back into the handle (Fig. 3).

Complete storage preparation by applying a thin coating of

Figure 3. Tap the working end of the tool back into the handle with sufficient force only.

Figure 4. Apply penetrating oil to metal parts. Spread it thin to prevent rusting in storage.

penetrating oil to metal surfaces (Fig. 4). This will keep the metal from rusting.

Store tools in a clean, dry area. If possible, hang them up.

GUTTERS

Gutters can become clogged with debris, which will cause water to overflow and flood the foundation of a home. This can cause shrubbery to wash out and water to leak into the basement. Gutters will also overflow if downspouts become clogged (see section entitled Downspouts).

You should clean the gutters of your home twice each year—in late fall after leaves have fallen from the trees and in late spring to remove granules that have washed down into the gutters from composition roof shingles. If granules are dry, sweep them up with a vacuum cleaner (Fig. 1). If granules are wet and heavy, scoop them out with a small garden shovel and deposit them into a pail which you can carry to the roof with you. Use of a pail avoids having to make frequent trips up and down the ladder.

You can keep your hands free for work by suspending the pail from a hook that you attach to a rung of the ladder. Hooks for this purpose are available in hardware and paint stores.

Wood gutters will leak when seams spread and when rot causes holes. Galvanized gutters will leak when rust eats through the metal. Aluminum and vinyl gutters don't develop these problems.

The use of fiberglass resin and fiberglass cloth facilitate the repair of wood gutters which have *not* been treated with paint or preservative. Fiberglass products can be purchased from a dealer of boating supplies. Cloth is available in various widths to fit most size gutters.

Caution: The fiberglass method cannot be used on any but a

Figure 1. Remove shingle granules, which will clog a gutter, with a vacuum when they are dry.

Figure 2. Clean gutters thoroughly with a wire brush before repairing them with compounds.

Figure 3. Fiberglass products seal leaking areas in wood gutters and prevent future rotting.

Figure 4. Use aluminum foil and plastic roof cement to repair treated wood or metal gutters.

raw wood surface. If a gutter has been coated with paint or a preservative, use the alternate repair method explained below.

To make repairs with fiberglass materials, clean debris from the gutter and thoroughly scrape the entire surface with a wire brush or sandpaper (Fig. 2). Remove dust particles with a vacuum. The surface must be absolutely clean and dry otherwise fiberglass cloth will not adhere.

Brush on a liberal application of resin, using an inexpensive or old paint brush that can be thrown away (Fig. 3). Allow resin to become tacky. Now, line the trough with fiberglass cloth. Press the cloth firmly into place and apply another coating of resin to the top of the cloth.

A leaking wood gutter that has been painted or treated with preservative or a rusted galvanized gutter can be repaired effectively with ordinary household aluminum foil (heavyweight grade) and black plastic roof cement, which you can purchase in a hardware store.

Thoroughly clean the damaged area with a wire brush or sandpaper and vacuum up particles. Now, spread on a thin coating of black plastic roof cement, extending the cement out on both sides of the damage to cover an area larger than the patch. Mold a piece of aluminum foil to fit the gutter's configuration and size and press it firmly into the cement. Follow this with another application of roof cement to the top of the aluminum foil patch. Be sure that all the foil is covered by cement (Fig. 4).

HOME LUBRICATION

It has been estimated by the Panef Manufacturing Co. of Milwaukee, Wisconsin that Americans spend $200 million annu-

Figure 1. Most home appliances require regular lubrication in order to give maximum service.

Figure 2. The variety of items in a home that can use lubrication periodically is great.

ally to have home appliances repaired. A considerable portion of this sum could be saved if homeowners were more conscientious about lubrication (Fig. 1).

Appliances aren't the only household items that fail because of lack of grease and oil. Other home equipment that requires lubrication are hand and power tools, ventilation fans, furnace blower motors, sump pumps, lawn and garden tools, door locks, sliding-door closet channels, drawers, sliding and hinged doors of cabinets and furniture, water faucets, shower heads, and pulleys and rollers of overhead garage doors.

In fact, almost everything around a home that moves will operate more smoothly and silently and will provide longer service if it is lubricated on a regular basis (Fig. 2).

One purpose of this discussion is to provide specific service information. Another purpose is to suggest items of equipment which require lubrication. As you will notice, not all are hardware items—that is, appliances and mechanical objects that one would normally consider for lubrication (Fig. 3).

Figure 3. Heavy equipment like bicycles should be lubricated semiannually with proper oil.

Figure 4. Keep aware that even wood-to-wood sliding surfaces work better with lubrication.

Figure 5. Metal or wooden window channels will move freely if treated with silicone spray.

For example, there are several objects in a nonhardware oriented room, such as the living room, that require lubrication. A spray of silicone grease will keep sliding cabinet doors from binding (Fig. 4). In addition, silicone grease applied to double-sash window channels in the living room and other rooms of the house allows windows to open and close with ease (Fig. 5).

A drop of white grease on window latches will keep them operating freely. If windows are of the casement or jalousie type, a drop of lightweight household oil on cranking mechanisms will allow them to give life-long service. Applying a thin film of white grease to casement and jalousie window channels will permit the windows to move freely.

Other objects in the living room (and other nonhardware oriented rooms) that will work more efficiently with lubrication include drapery slide rods, rolling furniture such as serving carts, and zippers on seat covers which will open and close easily for many years if they get a periodic coating of silicone lubricant.

Because there are so many objects around a home that require lubrication, you should devise a plan. This plan, or lubrication chart, should include those objects that need to be lubricated, how often to lubricate them, and what lubricants to use.

Before outlining this plan, however, there are several important rules concerning home lubrication that should be stressed. They are as follows:

1. Never over-lubricate objects, especially machinery. Excess grease or oil will damage a piece of equipment. If the equipment requires a liquid lubricant, such as oil, one to three drops is sufficient (Fig. 6). If the equipment requires a paste-type lu-

Figure 6. Don't overlubricate. Only a couple of drops are required when servicing a unit.

Figure 7. To lubricate hinges, apply a drop of grease and then work the hinge pin up and down.

bricant, such as grease, a thin, light film is required (Fig. 7).

2. When possible, follow the instructions provided by the manufacturer of the equipment. Appliances, power tools, some hand tools, lawn and garden equipment, and household machinery (furnace blower motors and exhaust fans, for example) are generally accompanied by instructions that explain frequency and method of lubricating (Fig. 8). If these instructions have been lost, write to the manufacturer and ask for them. His name and address are usually attached to the equipment.

3. Always use the correct lubricant for the job. The chart provided in this section will help you to determine which lubricants to use where.

4. Lubricate before damage is done. Practice preventive maintenance. Lubrication will prevent squeaks, rattles, binding, and failure of the equipment (Fig. 9). By practicing prevention, equipment (and money) can be saved.

Figure 8. Most home machinery is accompanied by instructions that provide lubrication data.

Figure 9. A drop or two of oil in storm door snubbers will assure that cups remain flexible.

Figure 10. Lubricate hand tools and small machinery with good quality light lubricating oil.

Figure 11. Large home equipment requires lubrication with oil that has a heavier viscosity.

5. If possible, clean a surface before applying lubricant. Alcohol, kerosene, and household detergent in water are good cleaning agents. Make sure the surface of the equipment is dry before lubricant is applied.

There are five types of lubricants that the homeowner has the most need for. They are as follows and can be purchased in a hardware store in the form of a handy-to-use dispenser, such as a spray can or tube:

Lightweight household oil. This is used to lubricate tools and light machinery, particularly small electric motors of ⅛ horsepower or less that operate such equipment as small electric fans, blenders, some power drills and saws, and automatic can openers (Fig. 10).

Heavy household oil. This is the lubricant to use on machinery which is equipped with a motor that is larger than ⅛ horsepower, such as those used to operate sump pumps, large ventilation fans, oil burners, hot air furnace blowers, and clothes washers (Fig. 11).

Silicone white grease. This product is available in stick and spray form. It is used to lubricate metal and wooden sliding surfaces.

General purpose white lubricant. This lubricant is recommended for use on metal-to-metal parts, such as hinges, latches, gears, and sliding surfaces (Fig. 12).

Figure 12. Use a small dab of general-purpose white grease on metal-to-metal slide surfaces.

Figure 13. Lubricate with liquid graphite where resistance to cold weather is necessary.

Figure 14. Try not to overlook items that require lubrication, such as garage door flip locks.

Liquified graphite. This is a mixture of powdered graphite and oil. It is a weather-resisting lubricant that is used to protect locks and equipment which are used out-of-doors, such as lawn tools (Fig. 13).

The lubrication chart below lists some household equipment that requires lubrication. It can serve as the basis for your lubrication plan. However, keep in mind that there is probably equipment in your home which is not included in the chart but should be included in your plan. In other words, the chart below should serve as a guide.

To make a complete lubrication plan, go from room to room in search of items that require lubrication. In bedrooms, for example, don't overlook drawers, doors, and windows. In the kitchen, don't overlook appliances and cabinets. However, in each room, ask yourself if there is anything else that needs lubricating besides the obvious items. As you find additional equipment, add them to your lubrication plan (Figs. 14, 15, and 16).

Figure 15. Aluminum combination doors offer several areas that require oil, such as latches.

Figure 16. Don't overlook overhead garage door pulleys. They work better with lubrication.

Basic Household Lubrication Plan

Item	Lubricant	Where to Lubricate	Amount	How Often
Light machinery (& light appliances)	Lightweight household oil	As per manufacturer's instructions	As per manufacturer, but usually 1–3 drops	Twice each year
Heavy machinery (& heavy appliances)	Heavy household oil	As per manufacturer's instructions	As per manufacturer, but usually 1–3 drops	Twice each year
Locks	Graphite-oil	Open latch, apply lubricant through keyhole	2 drops. Work into crevices by inserting key several times	Twice each year
Hand tools	Lightweight household oil or general-purpose white lubricant	At metal-to-metal points	1 drop. Work tool to spread lubricant	Twice each year
Power tools	Lightweight household oil	As per manufacturer's instructions	As per manufacturer, but usually 2–3 drops	Twice each year
Drawers & sliding furniture doors	Silicone	On sliding surface	Light, but covering coat. Work back and forth to spread lubricant	Twice each year
Sliding closet doors	Silicone	In channels	Light, but covering-coat. Work door back and forth to spread lubricant	Twice each year

Basic Household Lubrication Plan (Continued)

Item	Lubricant	Where to Lubricate	Amount	How Often
Hinges	Lightweight household oil or general-purpose white lubricant	On hinge pin	1 drop. Remove pin, clean, apply lubricant, work pin back and forth in hinge	Twice each year
Double-hung windows; combination storms and screens	Silicone	Along channels	Light, but covering coat. Work window after application	Twice each year
Window latches	Lightweight household oil or general-purpose white lubricant	At joint	1 drop	Twice each year
Casement & jalousie cranking mechanism	Lightweight household oil	At handle spindle	1 drop	Twice each year
Casement & jalousie channels	General-purpose white lubricant	Along channels	Light, but covering coat. Work window to spread lubricant	Twice each year
Power lawn mowers	Heavy household oil	Control mechanisms & bearings. See manufacturer's lubrication chart	As per manufacturer's instructions	Twice during the season

Basic Household Lubrication Plan (Continued)

Item	Lubricant	Where to Lubricate	Amount	How Often
Outdoor tools	Graphite-oil	On all exposed metal	Thin but covering film	After use
Sliding & overhead garage doors	Graphite-oil	Along tracks, at pulleys, at locks	1–3 drops. Work parts after application	Twice each year
Storm door snubber	General-purpose white lubricant & lightweight household oil	On sliding surface & in snubber	1 drop of grease on sliding surface; 2 drops of oil in snubber	Twice each year
Furnace blower motors	Heavy household oil	In cups (Some have no cups. They need no lube.)	As per manufacturer but usually 2–3 drops	Twice during the season
Plumbing fixtures	Graphite-oil	At moving surface	1 drop	Twice each year
Sliding shower & medicine cabinet doors	General-purpose white lubricant	In channels	1–2 drops. Work door to spread lubricant	Twice each year

METAL

The number of metal fixtures on the outside of your home may surprise you. It may include railings and posts, lawn furniture, casement window sash, shutters, light fixtures, and mailboxes. All are subjected to conditions which can cause them to rust.

The purpose of this discussion is twofold. It explains how to restore rusted metal, and it also discusses how to treat metal to prevent rust. There is much about these two areas which are the same.

The first point that should be stressed concerns the coating which is used to protect metal; specifically, rust-inhibiting paint. When speaking of rust-inhibiting paint, we mean a primer and not a top (finish) coat (Fig. 1). It is important that you get this distinction clearly in mind.

Rust-inhibiting primer contains rust-inhibiting chemicals. A finish coat does not. Thus, in most cases, you will use two separate products when painting metal.

There is an exception, however. Some paints, such as Derusto, have primer and finish coat combined into one product. These are advantageous if one coat of paint will suffice. If one coat will not adequately cover a surface, though, it is immaterial whether you apply two coats of a single all-purpose paint or one coat of rust-inhibiting primer and one coat of finish.

In selecting a paint for metal, do not be misled by label displays or advertising. The labels of some paint cans state boldly that the paint will "stop rust." However, instructions on the label, which are printed in much smaller type, point out that the paint will resist corrosion only if a primer is used. In other words, if the paint is used without benefit of a rust-inhibiting primer, the paint will not stop rust.

Be cautious of advice that you should not employ conventional house paint on metal. Actually, good results can be expected if you use a high quality solvent base or latex base exterior house paint when the metal surface is first treated with a rust-inhibiting primer.

A rust-inhibiting paint (primer) contains a chemical that prevents the oxidation of metal by absorbing moisture. Zinc chromate is the rust-inhibiting chemical in widest use, but lead compounds, such as lead-silico-chromate and zinc dust, are also employed.

Figure 1. Rust-inhibiting paint is a primer which serves as a base for regular finish paint.

Figure 2. Proper preparation of the surface to receive primer must be done with thoroughness.

Red lead is one of the oldest of the rust-inhibiting chemicals and is still widely used for protecting structural steel. However, it is not suitable for household metal, because it is too soft and dries too slowly.

Most primers for household ferrous metal surfaces, which are surfaces of iron and steel, are either red, mustardy, or gray in color, although all may contain the same rust inhibitor. The color depends on the tint that is added to the primer by the manufacturer.

A red primer, for instance, has iron oxide mixed into it and is recommended if a dark-colored finish coat, such as black, dark gray, green, red, blue, or brown is going to be applied. Mustard color and gray primers are suggested as base coats if lighter colored finish coats, such as white, yellow, light gray, and ivory, are going to be applied.

In buying a primer you will discover that there is a difference of as much as $8 per gallon among products. The more expensive paints contain more rust inhibitor and will generally protect metal for a longer period of time.

Unfortunately, you cannot usually learn what you are buying since many manufacturers do not print formulas on paint cans and others use generalized terms to describe the contents of their products. However, there is one way of determining whether the primer you wish to buy will meet some standard. Write to the manufacturer (his name and address will be printed on the can) and ask him if his product meets or exceeds Federal Specification TT - P - 636C.

This standard, which manufacturers of rust-inhibiting paint must meet in order to sell their products to the government, stipulates that a paint must provide good protection for metal when two coats are exposed for 18 months in the vicinity of Washington, D.C.

The best primer in the world will fail prematurely if it is applied to a rusty or dirty surface. Paint failure on metal is most often caused by the inability of the primer to adhere firmly to the metal, because it is blocked by oil, grease, dirt, or rust,

Therefore, start by washing the surface with a strong household detergent solution and a scrub brush. Remove peeling, scaling paint, and rust with a wire brush or sandpaper (Fig. 2). If grease spots and rust remain, use mineral spirits, turpentine, or a phosphoric acid solution to eliminate them (Fig. 3).

If you encounter old paint on a flat surface that has chipped, leaving an uneven surface, use a coarse emery cloth followed by sanding with a medium-grit aluminum oxide sandpaper to reduce unevenness (Fig. 4). A power sander can be employed

Figure 3. Washing the surface with a solvent will get rid of rust, grease, and other matter.

Figure 4. A smooth surface must be present if you expect a smooth finish. Be thorough.

Figure 5. If you are finishing a large surface, sanding of the surface may be done with power.

Figure 6. Welding flux which is on the metal should be removed for proper adhesion of paint.

if chipping is wide spread (Fig. 5).

Examine the metal of railing in particular for weld flux. If this alkaline material is not removed before paint is applied, it will cause the primer's vehicle to breakdown, resulting in loss of adhesion. Flux should be filed off (Fig. 6).

Apply the primer, but be sure to read instructions on the can's label first for best results (Fig. 7). Instructions vary somewhat from product to product. Some primers, for example, require frequent stirring to prevent the paint's ingredients from settling to the bottom of the can.

Figure 7. In applying primer, lay down a smooth coating that will cover the entire surface.

Figure 8. Paint can be applied to larger surfaces with a flat sash paint brush of proper size.

Figure 9. The right paint brush to use on metal railings is a 1 or 1½ in. round sash brush.

Figure 10. You should not use a flat sash brush on railings. The bristles will be damaged.

Also be sure to select the right paint applicator for the task (Fig. 8). For instance, if you are painting railings, use a 1 or 1½ inch round sash brush (Fig. 9). The shape of this brush prevents bristles from fishtailing as would happen if a flat sash brush were used (Fig. 10). Fishtailing will damage a brush.

Pipes and other cylindrical metal surfaces can be easily painted with a pipe painter, which is a unique roller that wraps itself around the surface (Fig. 11). To paint in back of the pipe or at any other angle, loosen the handle from the roller frame, obtain the desired angle, and tighten the handle.

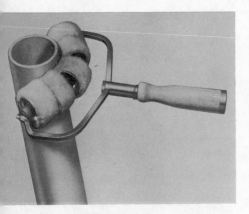

Figure 11. The pipe painter is a series of roller pads which wrap around cylindrical items.

Figure 12. Mask off metal fixtures with newspaper and tape before painting them by spray.

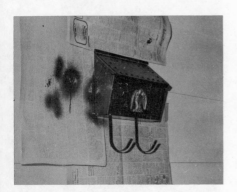

Figure 13. The purpose of masking, of course, is to prevent overspray from marring an area.

Figure 14. During the spraying operation, keep the spray can moving to avoid paint sagging.

If the old coating is badly worn or bare metal is exposed, apply at least two coats of primer. Allow the primer to dry for at least 24 hours if the temperature is 65° or above before applying a second coat of primer or the finish coat. Allow a drying period of three or four days if the temperature is 50° to 60°. Do not paint if the temperature is below 50°.

Rust-inhibiting primer is available in aerosol spray cans. Although satisfactory, the spray paint simply does not provide the same results as you get when applying paint by brush. In order for the paint to perform properly when it is sprayed through a nozzle, the paint's formula has to be adjusted. In other words, the paint must be thinner. This affects its application. Naturally, when paint is applied with brush a much heavier film can be laid down.

However, if you decide to use paint from a spray can, mask the area around the object to be painted so that overspray doesn't get on surrounding surfaces (Figs. 12 and 13). Keep the spray moving as paint is being applied so that sags aren't created (Fig. 14). Sags are caused when too much paint is applied to a spot.

Do not confuse rust-inhibiting paint with paint that is designed for galvanized metal, aluminum, tin, and other nonferrous metals. Galvanized primer contains no rust inhibitor, because nonferrous metal objects, such as gutters, downspouts, fence posts, and galvanized out-buildings, do not rust.

Galvanized primer allows you to apply an attractive finish coat to an object without first having to etch the metal. Make sure, however, that dirt, grease, and oil are first removed by washing the surface with a sudsy household detergent solution.

MILDEW

Mildew is fungus mold. Under warm and humid weather conditions, it can gain a foothold on the outside of your home. Mildew strikes most often on the shady side of a house where the sun seldom shines.

The homeowner who mistakenly thinks that mildew is dirt and paints over it will soon have his new paint job ruined. The mold will continue to grow beneath the paint surface, will extend itself upward and outward, and will soon break through the surface.

Mildew is not easy to recognize without a test. As mentioned above, it often looks like dirt. However, it may also have a green, red, purple, gray, or white cast.

The best way to determine if a mildew problem exists is to perform the bleach test. Simply wash the affected area with an ordinary household bleach. If the blotches on the house begin to lighten in color in about two minutes, the condition is mildew. Dirt will not be affected by bleach.

Figure 1. Mildew on a house can be destroyed by mixing together these ordinary household items.

Figure 2. Use a scrub brush to scrub the fungus-affected area with mildew-fighting solution.

Figure 3. Rinse away the mildew solution and, with it, the mildew. Use a good deal of water.

To get rid of mildew, mix together 3 ounces of a cleaner that contains trisodium phosphate, such as Soilax, Oakite, or Spic & Span; 1 ounce of a powder detergent; 1 quart of household bleach; and 3 quarts of warm water (Fig. 1). This will provide you with 1 gallon of mildew fighting solution.

Now, scrub the affected area thoroughly with a bristle brush (Fig. 2). Make sure that the solution is applied to every crack and crevice. Be thorough.

Follow this scrubbing with a thorough rinsing with clear water (Fig. 3). Repeated scrubbings and rinsings may be necessary if the mildew condition is particularly heavy.

Be sure to cover shrubbery with drop clothes to protect it from the solution.

This treatment will kill the existing fungus, but it will not prevent new fungus from appearing. The best way to do this is to use a mildew-resistant paint the next time you paint the house (Fig. 4).

If the mildew condition is unusually heavy and/or you re-

Figure 4. If mildew is a problem around your house, mildew-resistant paint should be used.

Figure 5. Paint dealers stock mildewcide additives that will fortify paint against fungus.

side in an area of the country that is normally warm and humid, fortify the paint with a mildewcide additive, which is available in paint stores. Simply mix the additive into the paint (Fig. 5).

If your paint dealer doesn't have a mildew-resistant paint of the color you desire, you can add the mildewcide to any kind of paint. It will make nonmildew-resistant paint mildew-proof.

MOTOR BIKES

The information in this section deals primarily with motor bikes, often referred to as minibikes. However, the information is also applicable to lightweight motorcycles.

The emphasis of this discussion concerns itself as much with the detection of trouble as with the repair of damage. The reason for this should be obvious. Since motor bikes are generally driven by youngsters, safety should be of primary concern. A safe bike is a bike that is in good mechanical condition.

Keep in mind that the small physical characteristic of a minibike is deceiving. These machines are capable of negotiating 50 degree slopes, of hitting 50 miles per hour on a straightaway, and of traversing rugged cross country terrain. They are not toys.

The inspection outlined in this section should be conducted once every six months.

Start with tires (Fig. 1). Are they cut? Is side tread worn? If either of these conditions exist, replace the tire.

Although center tread may be like new, a tire should be replaced if the side tread is worn. Safe cornering of the bike requires that side tread be in sound condition.

A motor bike tire normally wears in a V-pattern, with the tread on the outside wearing away faster than the tread in the center. If wear is not in this manner, the bike may have a bent wheel rim. Inspect for this and replace the wheel if the rim is damaged.

Wheels must be true. If the bike is equipped with solid, so-called mag-type wheels, they should not be dented. If the bike

Figure 1. Safe tires are of utmost importance. Make sure that they are neither cut nor worn.

Figure 2. Fork legs are necessary for control. Inspect them for damage that may affect safety.

Figure 3. If the sprocket shows damage, the motor bike has not been used carefully.

has spoke wheels, there should be no broken spokes.

Be certain that spokes are tight. Strike each with a wrench. They should "ping." A loose spoke is revealed if it makes a dull sound. A spoke tightening wrench may be purchased from a minibike or motorcycle dealer.

Have someone lift the front wheel of the bike into the air and spin the wheel. Listen for scraping or ticking sounds which will reveal a bad wheel bearing. Do not drive the bike until the condition is corrected by a professional repairman. A bike that has a bad wheel bearing could lose the wheel.

With the front end in the air, grasp the bottom of the fork legs and shake them back and forth (Fig. 2). If there is any play in the legs or if drops of oil appear, new fork leg bushings and seals are needed. This should be done as soon as possible, since control of the bike is maintained by the fork legs.

Put the bike on a level floor. Sight down the fork legs and examine the entire frame to make sure that everything is straight, especially if the bike has experienced a spill. If the fork legs or frame are bent, do not drive the bike. It will be difficult to maintain safe control. Consult a professional repairman.

Sit on the seat and bounce your weight up and down. The suspension should be firm, with good recovery. If the bike bottoms as you bounce on it, new shock absorbers are probably needed. Again, have this repair made before using the bike. Shock absorbers assist in controlling the machine.

Inspect the chain and sprocket. The chain should be clean, with no rust. If it isn't, clean it off with kerosene. Now, apply a good application of bike chain lubricant, which you can get in a bike or motorcycle repair shop.

Try to pull the chain off the rear of the sprocket. If you can do this, the chain has stretched. In time, this will happen. It needs to be adjusted. If the adjusted chain is still too loose, have a link removed.

Examine the sprocket (Fig. 3). Teeth must not be sharpened to a point, hooked, chipped, or missing. They should be smoothly round. If a sprocket is in bad condition, it will cause the chain to skip, and you may loose the chain on a drive. This is hazardous, so have a new sprocket put on.

Incidentally, the only reason why a sprocket goes bad is hard use by the driver. Don't spin your wheels.

Check the brake control. You should not have to activate the control more than ½ inch for the brake to engage. If you do, adjust the rear brake control cable to take up the slack. However, if the end of the cable projects through the brake control lever by ½ inch or more, it means that brake linings are worn (Fig. 4). Have them replaced.

Be sure the lights work. Give the bike a general overall inspection to make sure that such things as wires and cables are in good shape. They shouldn't be kinked, frayed, or broken.

Now comes time to test the motor. The best way to do this is to start it up. The small engine used in a minibike can usually be started in two ways: electrically and manually. Do it both ways.

When starting the engine manually, look for prompt combustion. Also notice the amount of effort that is needed to pull the starter rope (Fig. 5). It should give resistance and snap back strongly from its fully extended position. If manual starting meets little or no resistance, it indicates that engine compression is bad and that the bike will soon need an engine overhaul.

Figure 4. If the brake control cable extends through this lever by ½ inch, overhaul brakes.

Figure 5. Test engine compression by activating the starter.

*Figure 6. You can hear whether the en-
gine is knocking by drowning out the
noisy combustion sound.*

*Figure 7. Signs of oil in the exhaust pipe
usually signify that piston rings are
damaged.*

When starting the engine electrically, look for prompt starting. If the engine is sluggish, the battery is weak or the ignition
system has a malfunction. Consult the section in this book on
Engines, Repair and Maintenance, for information on how to
handle problems with minibike engines. Minibike engines are of
the same type as are dealt with in that section.

As the engine is idling, stuff a rag in the exhaust pipe for a
few seconds to drown out normal combustion noise (Fig. 6). If
the engine knocks, it will need an overhaul. Also check the exhaust pipe for traces of oil, which indicate that the engine's
rings or valve guides have gone bad (Fig. 7).

If you have a two-cycle engine in your bike, however, keep
in mind that oil and gasoline are mixed and burned together
and that the exhaust pipe will generally show an oily residue.
Traces of oil in the exhaust pipe are something to be concerned
about if the engine is four-cycle.

Carefully examine outside engine covers for signs of oil (Fig
8). This will indicate that a crankcase oil seal has ruptured and
should be repaired.

Finally, drive the bike to test its performance. If it has a
clutch, the clutch lever should have a ¼ to ½ inch of play before
the clutch engages. If the minibike possesses an automatic
transmission, shifting should be smooth.

*Figure 8. Traces of oil on an engine
cover indicate that a crankcase oil seal
is ruptured.*

NAILS

The nail is one of the items most frequently used by the homeowner for making repairs. However, it is important to note that there are hundreds of different types of nails available at a hardware store or lumber yard, and that one size and shape is best to use for the job you are doing.

Nails are classified as either general purpose or special purpose.

General purpose nails are used for general carpentry and construction. There are four kinds: common, box, casing, and finishing.

Common and box nails have flat heads and diamond points, but the heads of box nails are somewhat larger than those of common nails. However, the major difference between the two is their diameter. Although common and box nails of a particular size have the same length, their diameters are different.

For instance, a 10-penny (10d) common nail, which is 3 inches long, has a 9-gauge diameter (0.1483 inch), while a 10-penny box nail, which is also 3 inches long, has a 10½-gauge diameter (0.1277 inch). Thus, if you are using a common nail that is apparently causing the wood to split, switch to a box nail of an identical penny size. It will probably eliminate the trouble.

As you can see by the chart on the next page (Fig. 1), the same difference in diameter distinguishes casing and finishing nails. A finishing nail of one size has a smaller diameter than a casing nail of the same size. Furthermore, finishing nails have brad heads which are not suitable for countersinking, while casing nails have heads that can be countersunk.

Common, box, casing, and finishing nails of the same penny size are all of the same length. You can order common nails either by penny size or by length. Use Fig. 1 as a guide. Penny size is the more common way to order. In general, you will receive the following number of common nails per pound in penny size:

2d – 847	8d – 101	20d – 30
3d – 543	10d – 66	30d – 23
4d – 296	12d – 66	40d – 17
6d – 167	16d – 47	60d – 11

Special purpose nails, as the name implies, are for specific uses. However, what may confuse you is that some special purpose nails are available in a number of different points to compensate for the hardness of various woods.

TYPES OF POINTS

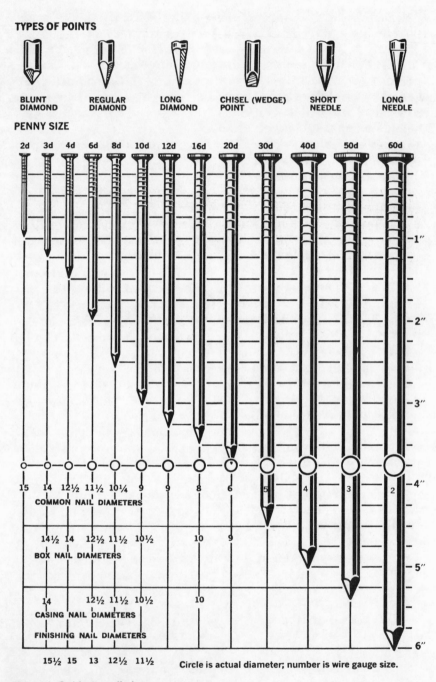

BLUNT DIAMOND   REGULAR DIAMOND   LONG DIAMOND   CHISEL (WEDGE) POINT   SHORT NEEDLE   LONG NEEDLE

PENNY SIZE

2d 3d 4d 6d 8d 10d 12d 16d 20d 30d 40d 50d 60d

COMMON NAIL DIAMETERS
15 14 12½ 11½ 10¼ 9 9 8 6 5 4 3 2

BOX NAIL DIAMETERS
14½ 14 12½ 11½ 10½ 10 9

CASING NAIL DIAMETERS
14 12½ 11½ 10½ 10

FINISHING NAIL DIAMETERS
15½ 15 13 12½ 11½

Circle is actual diameter; number is wire gauge size.

1" 2" 3" 4" 5" 6"

Figure 1. Guide to nail sizes.

For example, standard flooring nails that are used in soft-wood flooring are made in 8d (2½ inch) length and are designed for flooring made of such woods as pine and fir. They have regular diamond points and are made of 10-gauge steel.

If standard flooring nails are driven into *hardwood* flooring, they will either split the wood or bend. For this reason, a special hardwood flooring nail is made. It too is 8d, but it has a blunt diamond point that shears through hardwood fibers without bending. Furthermore, it is made of thinner 11½-gauge steel, which will not split the wood.

The chart below sums up the uses of the more popular types of special purpose nails and depicts the types of points and heads they have (Fig. 2). Where nails have long diamond points, such as drywall nails, they are used for penetrating easily without causing material such as drywall to crumble. Gutter spikes use another type of point, called a chisel point. It allows deep penetration for firm anchoring of heavy objects, such as gutters.

As Fig. 2 illustrates, nails also differ in the size and shape of their heads. With dual-headed nails, for example, you can easily construct sturdy forms to accept fresh concrete. The nail's lower head anchors in wood, while the upper head is left protruding to remove nails easily when dismantling the form. In this way, the form will not be damaged and can be reused.

Roofing nails have a broad flat head to keep water from seeping beneath the head and through the roof. One variation is the umbrella head, which also prevents leaks.

Nails also vary as to the materials from which they are made. Common materials include steel, aluminum, copper, and brass. Nails made of metals other than ordinary steel are designed for fastening objects of the same metal. This matching greatly reduces the corrosive action that occurs when different metals are placed in contact with one another. Aluminum nails, for instance, should be used to secure aluminum gutters to aluminum siding.

Many nails, especially those for outdoor use, are often given a metal coating, such as zinc or brass, to help prevent rust and corrosion. Zinc-coated asbestos siding nails, for example, help to offset the normal deterioration of the nail.

While the shanks of most nails are smooth, there are nails with helical, barbed, and annular shanks. They should be used if extra holding power is needed.

These grooved nails cost about twice as much as regular nails, but they provide up to ten times the holding power. You should keep them in mind if you have a problem such as nails popping out of drywall. Grooved drywall nails have better re-

NAIL	PURPOSE	TYPE OF POINT	TYPE OF HEAD	SPECIAL FEATURES	*STANDARD SIZES
BOX 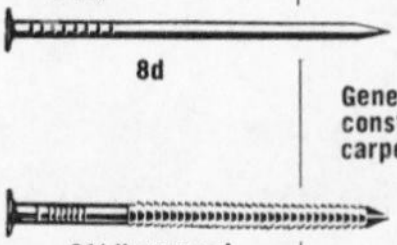 8d / 2½″ grooved	General construction, carpentry	Diamond	Large flat	Available with grooved shank	3d (14½), 4d & 5d (14), 6d & 7d (12½), 8d (11½), 10d (10½), 16d (10), 20d (9)
BRICK SIDING ¾″	Installation of brick siding	Diamond	Checkered flat	Galvanized and painted to match siding. Available in red, black, buff	¾″ (13), ⅞″ (13), 1″ (13), 1¼″ (13), 1½″ (13), 1¾″ (13), 2″ (12½), 2½″ (11½)
CASING  8d	Fine finish work	Diamond	Deep countersunk		4d (14), 6d (12½), 8d (11½), 10d (10½), 16d (10)
COMMON 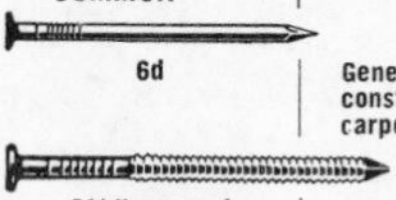 6d / 2½″ grooved	General construction, carpentry	Diamond	Flat	Available with grooved shank	2d (15), 3d (14), 4d & 5d (12½), 6d & 7d (11½), 8d & 9d (10¼), 10d & 12d (9), 16d (8), 20d (16), 30d (5), 40d (4), 50d (3), 60d (2)
CONCRETE AND MASONRY 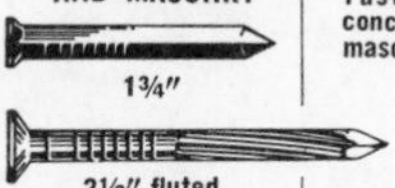 1¾″ / 2½″ fluted	Fastening into concrete, masonry	Diamond	Flat or square	Some with fluted shanks	Available in fractional lengths of ½″ to 3″ and in various gauge sizes
FLOORING 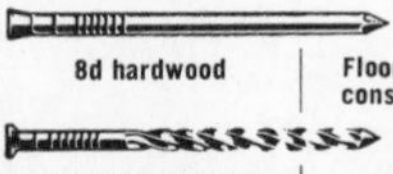 8d hardwood / 2½″ hardwood, grooved	Floor construction	Diamond or blunt	Deep countersunk	Available in grooved shank to eliminate squeaks. These have flat countersunk heads and blunt points. Sizes: 6d, 7d, 8d—all 11½ ga.	Standard flooring nail: 8d (10). Hardwood flooring nail: 8d (11½)
WALLBOARD 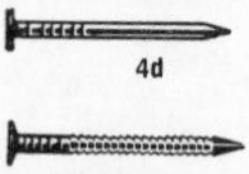 4d / 1½″ grooved	Installing gypsum wallboard	Diamond	Flat	Smooth or grooved shank. Available also with coating for extra holding power	Smooth shank: 4d (14), 5d (13½), 6d (13). Grooved shank: 1¼″, 1⅜″, 1½″—all 12½ ga.
DUAL-HEAD  6d	Temporary lumber construction	Diamond	Dual		6d (11½), 8d (10¼), 10d (9), 16d (8), 20d (6)
FINISHING  8d	General construction, carpentry	Diamond	Brad		3d (15½), 4d (15), 6d (13), 8d (12½), 10d (11½)
INSULATION BUILDING BOARD  1¾″	Installing insulation board	Needle	Flat	Available in barbed shank with diamond point	1¼″ and 1¾″ (17), 2″ (11)
ROOFING  1″ Smooth 1″ Barbed	Roofing installation	Diamond	Large flat or umbrella	Available with grooved or barbed shanks and coated	Fractionally from ⅞″ to 2″, usually in 11 ga.
FIBERBOARD  1⅛″	Fast nailing of soft materials	Needle	Flat	Available bright, galvanized or cadmium-plated	1″, 1⅛″, 1¼″, 1⅜″, 1½″, 1⅝″, 1¾″—all 17 ga.

NAIL	PURPOSE	TYPE OF POINT	TYPE OF HEAD	SPECIAL FEATURES	*STANDARD SIZES
UNDERLAY 1¼″	Installing floor underlayment	Diamond	Flat	Available with grooved shank	1¼″ (14)
WOOD SHINGLE 3½d	Installing shingles	Diamond	Flat	Available with grooved or barbed shank	3d (13), 3½d (12½), 4d (12)

*Figures in parentheses are gauge numbers

Figure 2. Guide to nail uses.

sistance to conditions that cause regular drywall nails to pop.

Also consider using grooved nails when nailing shingle or shake siding to a house. They will hold the siding firmly against heavy winds and storms.

OUTBOARD MOTOR, MAINTENANCE

An outboard motor can provide many years of trouble-free service if it is properly maintained. The compilation of maintenance tips outlined below was gathered from professional outboard motor repairmen. If you follow them, it is almost certain that your outboard motor will be going strong long after the other fellow's is on the scrap heap.

1. Keep your motor clean, especially if it is operated in salt water. Wash it down after each use. Ordinary household detergent mixed in water may be employed as a cleaning agent. Apply it with a sponge and follow with a thorough rinsing of water from a hose. However, be sure to first wrap a piece of household plastic wrap around the carburetor to keep water out.

If the engine becomes oily, clean off grime with an engine degreaser, such as that made by Tempo (Fig. 1). The products mentioned in this section may be purchased from a dealer of outboard motor supplies.

Be sure to keep the motor cover waxed to prevent weather from fading the paint. Touch up chipped and cracked paint as soon as possible to stop corrosion.

Figure 1. Use engine degreaser to remove grime from a motor.

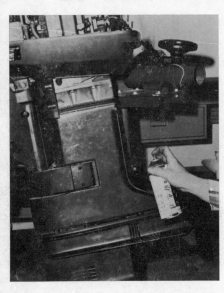

Figure 2. Corrosion inhibitor protects the lower unit.

Figure 3. To determine whether water has gotten into the lower gear case, remove the bottom plug.

Spray an anticorrosion inhibitor, such as CRC, over the lower unit (Fig. 2). This compound, which withstands water that rushes around the lower unit as the unit plows through the water, protects the outside of the gear case.

2. Once every month, check to make sure that no water has gotten into the lower unit. Remove the bottom plug (Fig. 3).If there is water in the lower unit, it will have settled in the bottom and will start to run out of the drain plug hole. Water in the lower unit means that a seal has ruptured. Have this repaired as soon as possible. Otherwise, gears and bearings will rust. When this happens, you might as well get rid of the outboard motor.

3. Lubricate the motor. Your owner's manual advises you to do this once or twice each boating season. However, professionals lubricate once every other week, especially if the motor is operated in salt water (Fig. 4). The more often you lubricate an outboard motor, the less chance there will be that the motor will develop a problem.

Figure 4. Thorough lubrication is the most important service to provide for outboard motor.

Figure 5. A rubberized coating protects electrical connections and terminals from corrosion.

Figure 6. A dielectric compound is recommended since it keeps wires in good condition.

Consult the lubrication chart in your owner's manual for what to lubricate and for what lubricants to use. If you have lost this manual, write the manufacturer for a new one. Be sure to tell him which model motor you possess.

4. Check the steering cables for cracks in the plastic covering and check pulleys for correct alignment once each week. Make sure that the plastic covering hasn't been chafed. This would cause the bare cable to jam against the pulley. A chafed cable will also corrode and may snap while you are steering the boat. This could lead to a serious accident.

5. Apply a rubberized coating, such as that made by Tempo or Gaco, directly to all electrical terminals to keep them from corroding (Fig. 5).

6. Periodically examine fuel system hoses. They are subject to heat and vibration which will cause them to crack. A cracked hose should be replaced as soon as possible to prevent major damage. Gasoline that drips from a bad hose presents a fire hazard.

7. Because they are flexible, ignition high tension wires may chafe. To prevent this, coat wires with a dielectric compound, such as Dow Corning's DC-4 (Fig. 6). This compound allows the cables to maintain their electrical qualities while protecting them against chafing.

8. Always tilt the motor up out of the water when you dock

 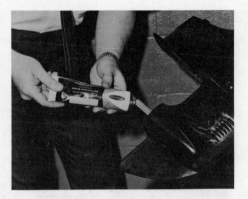

Figure 7. Remove the propeller by blocking it with a piece of 2 × 4 as you remove the prop nut.

Figure 8. Clean off the propeller shaft and spread on a thin coat of anticorrosion grease.

to prevent a build up of algae, grass, and barnacles. Foreign matter on the lower unit will create cavitation and corrosion. About midway through the boating season, pull the boat from the water and clean off the bottom.

If you keep a cover over the motor when the boat is tied up at the dock, keep it loose to allow ventilation around the motor. Condensation will build up on internal engine parts and cause rust if good ventilation isn't maintained.

9. Check the condition of the propeller often. Do not allow minor nicks to go untreated. They will get worse and result in a prop that is too badly damaged to repair.

When minor nicks are spotted, remove the propeller and dress down this damage by lightly filing it with an ordinary mill file (Fig. 7). Before returning the prop to the prop shaft, clean off the shaft and coat it with a light film of lubricant (Fig. 8).

If the propeller is bent or distorted, replace it with a new one, because if you don't, the damaged prop will create a great deal of vibration that could damage the engine. Make sure that you use the right size prop for your motor. A propeller that is not of the correct size will cause the motor to lug, which will lead to overheating, high fuel consumption, preignition, rapid spark plug wear, and ignition failure.

10. About midway through the boating season, inject engine cleaner into your motor by removing the spark plugs and inserting the cleaner in through the spark plug holes (Fig. 9). This compound will clean out carbon and varnish and will free piston rings. Apply the same treatment at the end of the boating season. Consult directions on the can concerning how to use engine cleaner.

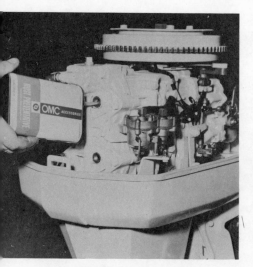

Figure 9. Engine cleaner purges the motor of foreign material.

Figure 10. A dirty fuel filter causes rough engine operation.

11. Remove and clean the fuel filter every couple of weeks to keep the fuel system clean and the engine running smoothly (Fig. 10). Consult the owner's manual to determine the location of the filter in your motor.

12. If the motor begins to idle rough and you have been operating in cold water for several hours, check the tips of spark plugs for wet fouling, which is a concentration of moisture on the electrodes. If you wish to continue boating in cold water, switch to a spark plug that is one degree hotter in the heat range to allow you to avoid wet fouling.

13. If you buy another gasoline tank, make sure it has the proper size pickup to accommodate your motor. A tank that is too small will not deliver the correct amount of fuel. Although the motor will run, an inadequate supply of fuel can cause pistons to score. A fuel tank made for your engine by the manufacturer of that engine is always the best one to use.

14. Heavy silt and abrasive material in some bodies of water can damage the motor's cooling system, causing early water pump failure. The Mississippi River, for example, consists of 90 percent silt. Operation in this kind of water should be tried only if the motor is equipped with a heavy duty water pump, which is designed to withstand corrosion and abrasion. You can get one for your motor at a dealer that sells your make.

For additional maintenance information, see the section on Outboard Motor, Winter Storage.

OUTBOARD MOTOR, TROUBLESHOOTING

Unless you take a logical, systematic approach when attempting to locate a malfunction in your outboard motor, you can waste a good deal of time and money. This systematic approach to troubleshooting, which is used by professional outboard motor mechanics, is done in five steps, as follows:

1. Write down all the facts concerning the problem.
2. Use past experience to suggest a quick and easy solution.
3. If no solution is forthcoming to this point, isolate the trouble to one of the three major engine areas: the fuel system, the ignition system, or compression.
4. Consult the troubleshooting charts in the service manual to guide you in tracking down the specific cause of the trouble.
5. Fix the trouble if you have the tools and are able.

Let us examine each of these steps in greater detail.

Step 1: Write down all facts relating to the problem. When did it start? How did it start? What are the symptoms? Have you taken any corrective action and, if so, what?

Quite often, a simple remedy to a problem may be suggested by seeing all the facts on paper.

Step 2: Does past experience suggest a solution? Suppose, for example, your outboard motor once developed an intermittent starting problem and finally wouldn't start at all. At that time, a mechanic found that the trouble was being caused by a clogged fuel filter. If the same condition arises again, the fuel filter is the first thing you should check.

Step 3: If past experience doesn't suggest a solution, isolate the trouble to one of the three major systems of the motor. Keep in mind that three things must be present for combustion to take place in your engine: fuel, ignition, and compression (Fig. 1).

Figure 1. The three major areas of an outboard motor are the fuel system, ignition system, and compression.

Figure 2. Examine the tip of a plug. If it's dry, fuel is not getting to combustion chambers.

Figure 3. If there is no spark as you crank the engine, there is a breakdown in the ignition.

Turn the flywheel slowly by pulling the starter cord. If you feel resistance, compression is probably sufficient. If there is no resistance and the flywheel feels sloppy, low compression is causing the trouble. The engine probably needs to be over-hauled.

Check for fuel and ignition by first cranking the engine several times. Now, remove a spark plug. If the tip of the plug is dry, which means that fuel is not getting into the combustion chamber, the trouble is in the fuel system (Fig. 2).

Place the spark plug on the powerhead and crank the engine by pulling the starter rope. Be sure the high tension cable is firmly attached to the spark plug. If you don't see a spark jumping across the spark plug electrode gap, the cause of the trouble is in the ignition system.

Steps 4 and 5: Consult the proper troubleshooting chart in the service manual. Each chart is headed by a symptom, such as "engine won't start." Note that troubleshooting charts specify many causes and suggested remedies. Take a logical approach to remedial procedures, proceeding from the easy to the hard.

For example, suppose your engine doesn't start and the problem has been isolated to the fuel system. The chart suggests actions that range from checking for fuel to tearing down of the carburetor. Why overhaul a carburetor when all that is needed to cure the difficulty is to fill the fuel tank?

If you don't have a service manual for your motor, you may order one from the manufacturer. Be sure to give him full information about your engine when ordering, including year, horsepower, and model number.

OUTBOARD MOTOR, WINTER STORAGE

When it comes time to store an outboard motor for the winter, the task must be done properly to avert the chance of costly damage. More outboard motors are lost to the scrap heap because of improper winter storage than for any other reason.

Winterizing service is provided by most local marine dealers for a nominal fee. This service includes inspection, cleaning, lubrication, and storage. If you do not have a good place to store your motor, it is suggested that you avail yourself of this service. However, if you decide to service and store the motor yourself, thereby saving between $20 and $50, depending upon the size of the motor, the following describes what should be done.

With your boat still in the water, warm up the engine and remove the cowl or wraparound. Disconnect the fuel line and, while the engine is idling, inject storage seal into the carburetor air intake. Storage seal and other materials mentioned in this section may be purchased from a dealer of marine supplies.

As the carburetor (or carburetors) starts to run dry, apply an extra liberal dose of storage seal. This procedure will effectively distribute this protective compound throughout the crankcase to prevent internal corrosion and will also use up fuel in the carburetor to prevent varnish and gum formation.

Remove the motor from the transom, but keep it upright and resting on its skeg for several minutes until all water has drained from the driveshaft housing. Now, place the motor on a

Figure 1. A test stand to hold a motor while working on it and for storage is a valuable tool.

Figure 2. To clean silt, sand, and deposits from the engine, flush it out with fresh water.

Figure 3. It is convenient to use a thin piece of wire to clean out drain holes.

Figure 4. Storage seal provides rings and cylinders with protection against harmful rust.

test stand, which you can buy for a nominal price, or on a firm wooden stanchion, such as a sawhorse (Fig. 1). You can keep the motor on the stand over the winter.

Flush the cooling system with fresh water to clear out silt, sand, and mineral deposits (Fig. 2). Instructions on how to do this are contained in your owner's operating manual. If you have lost this publication, write the manufacturer of your motor for another.

Operate the manual starter until the water pump has forced all water from the cooling system. Make sure that all water drain holes in the housing are open and free (Fig. 3). Also be sure that the flushing plug is removed so that all water will drain out. This is vital! Trapped water may freeze and expand, thus cracking the gear housing or water pump housing.

Remove the spark plugs and inject a small quantity of storage seal into each spark plug hole (Fig. 4). Reinstall the plugs and operate the manual starter to distribute the storage seal throughout the combustion chamber. This extra dose will assure full protection of the piston rings and cylinder walls.

Lubricate swivel pin steering tube, throttle linkage, and all other points as directed in your owner's maintenance guide.

Remove the air vent screw and grease filler plug with their accompanying washers from the lower unit. Insert a tube of the proper lubricant for your outboard's gear case into the grease filler hole and inject new grease until old grease starts to flow out of the air vent hole, indicating that the housing is filled (Fig. 5). Next, replace the vent screw, filler screw, and washers.

Wash or wipe the entire motor, especially if there is an accumulation of grime and salt incrustation. Spray the powerhead

Figure 5. Lubricant inside the gear case must be replenished.

Figure 6. Chipped, cracked, and worn paint on covers should be sanded to metal and repainted.

with a coating of corrosion preventive to protect the finish of all parts inside the cowl. The exterior of the motor can either be sprayed with corrosion preventive or coated with a thin film of clean, fresh engine oil.

If paint on the cowl and lower unit is chipped or cracked, sand the spot and retouch with aerosol spray paint that you can buy for the purpose at a dealer of outboard motor supplies (Fig. 6).

Remove the propeller and clean the shaft with steel wool (Fig. 7). Apply anticorrosion grease or silicone grease to the shaft and reinstall the propeller.

Take the battery out of the boat and clean the top surface thoroughly of grease, dirt, and corrosion deposits (Fig. 8). Apply exterior corrosion and rust preventive, such as anticorrosion grease or petroleum jelly, to battery posts. Check electrolyte and add distilled water to bring the level to the full mark.

Charge the battery until the specific gravity of the electrolyte reaches 1.260. The recharge rate should not exceed 6 amperes. Every 45 to 60 days during the storage period recheck the

Figure 7. Inspect the propeller for damage, and clean and lubricate the propeller shaft.

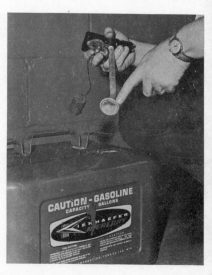

Figure 8. The battery should be cleaned
and stored separately.

Figure 9. The fuel tank filter should be
cleaned in kerosene.

electrolyte and take a specific gravity reading. Apply a booster charge if the hydrometer reading drops below 1.230. This is particularly important if the battery is stored in a cold location, since the battery is apt to freeze if the specific gravity reading falls too low. The battery should be stored in a cool, dry place in a dry carton or box. Keep it off a concrete floor.

For more information on battery care, see the section on Automotive, Battery.

Fuel remaining in the fuel tank should not be stored over the winter. Dump it. Stored fuel tends to break down and leave gum and varnish in the fuel system, which will cause carburetor problems.

After discarding fuel, pour a small amount of two-cycle oil into the fuel tank and slosh it around to distribute a thin film on the inner walls of the tank. Remove the fuel tank filter, clean it thoroughly with a brush and solvent, such as kerosene, and replace it (Fig. 9).

Store the motor in a clean, dry location. It should be covered, but there must be enough ventilation to prevent moisture buildup. The motor storage area can be either cold or warm, as long as the temperature remains constant; otherwise, condensation will occur, leading to corrosion.

PAINT

Paint is the most widely used product for keeping a home in good condition (Fig. 1). It is also one of the most misused. There

Figure 1. Paint is available in many types. For the best paint job, select the correct paint.

Figure 2. Gloss or semigloss paint should be used in rooms where walls have to be washed.

are many different varieties of paint, with each one designed for a specific purpose. It is easy for a homeowner to buy the wrong kind.

The purpose of this discussion is to acquaint you with the different kinds of paint, so that you can select exactly the one you need for the task you are doing. For organization purposes, the section is divided into two main topic areas: interior house paint and exterior house paint.

Interior house paint. Paints for use inside the house are of two basic types: gloss and semigloss (considered as one) and flat (or nongloss). Semigloss is also called eggshell.

1. *Gloss and semigloss* paints are used in kitchens and bathrooms where spattering of wall surfaces with grease, soap scum, and other dirt is likely (Fig. 2). These paints can be washed and will withstand scrubbing.

There are three different types of gloss and semigloss interior house paint. They are called wall paint, enamel, and latex. Use these names in asking for the one you want. Differences between the three are as follows:

Wall paint is the oldest and is being replaced by the other two. It has an oleoresinuous vehicle, consisting of natural resins and oil. Although wall paint is easy to apply, it doesn't retain its gloss for long, it yellows, and it can't withstand washings with modern alkaline household cleaners.

Enamel contains an alkyd vehicle, which is a combination synthetic alkyd resin and oil. It retains gloss very well, it doesn't yellow, and it can be cleaned repeatedly with an alkaline cleaner (Fig. 3).

Latex paint consists of a polymer dispersed in water. Unlike

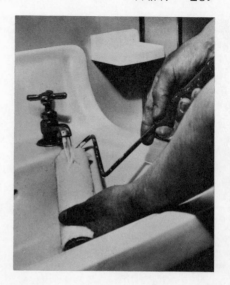

Figure 3. Enamel interior gloss house paint has a solvent base.

Figure 4. Latex interior gloss house paint, which has a water base, washes away with water.

wall paint and enamel, it offers the advantage of easy cleanup. Brush or roller and spatter marks can be washed off with water (Fig. 4). Cleanup of wall paint and enamel requires the use of turpentine or mineral spirits. Latex paint cannot be applied over an old glossy enamel or wall paint finish without first sanding the surface to assure good adhesion. New surfaces, such as raw gypsum wallboard, must be primed before latex can be applied.

2. *Flat* (nongloss) paints are designed for use in bedrooms, living rooms, and dining rooms where only superficial dirt on the surface is expected (Fig. 5). Although an occasional smudge may be washed away with a damp sponge, nongloss paint will fail if washed repeatedly.

Usually, you can use the same flat paint for walls and ceilings. It provides a smooth finish. There are two basic types of interior flat paint: alkyd and latex.

Figure 5. Flat, nongloss paint will not withstand the rigors of one washing after another.

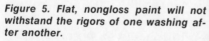

Figure 6. Alkyd flat wall paint can be used for painting doors as well as walls and ceilings.

Figure 7. In painting with latex flat, be certain that the surface is thoroughly covered.

Alkyd flat wall paint is superior to latex in covering power. If the wall surface is very dirty, you can often avoid having to give it two coats by using alkyd (Fig. 6).

Latex flat wall paint is free of odor. Paint tools and spatter can be washed with water. Alkyd requires cleanup with turpentine or mineral spirits. Don't spread latex paint too thin since the paint's ability to cover the surface will be adversely affected (Fig. 7). Never apply latex directly to a porous surface, such as unfinished gypsum wallboard. Use a primer first.

Special types of flat interior wall paint that you will want to be familiar with are ceiling paint, textured paint, and sand-finish paint.

Ceiling paint is a special paint designed only for ceilings. It contains more pigment than regular alkyd or latex flat to hide dirt better. Badly soiled ceilings can often be covered by one coat instead of the two that would probably be needed if regular flat was being used. Since ceiling paint dries to a much flatter finish than regular flat paint, it should not be used on walls.

Textured flat wall paint is a heavy-bodied substance which, when applied with a roller, produces a heavy stipple effect. When applied with a brush, a striated appearance can be created by brushing in straight lines. You can also produce a swirl effect by twisting the brush handle back and forth as the surface is painted. Textured paint hides surfaces that are rough and badly marred.

Figure 8. Exterior house paint is the best and least expensive product for home conditioning.

Figure 9. Latex exterior house paint can be applied to a damp substrate; oil-base paint cannot.

Sand-finish flat wall paint also is used to cover rough surfaces and badly marred walls. It dries to a sand finish that resembles concrete. The paint contains granules of perlite or a similar gritty substance. If you apply the paint with a roller, work quickly to avoid leaving lap marks. If you use a brush, apply the paint liberally. Be careful not to brush it out too thin. This will leave an uneven finish.

Exterior house paint. Paints for the outside of the house are of three basic types: oil-base, latex, and alkyd enamel. Oil-base and latex are designed for use on the body of the house (Fig. 8). Alkyd enamel is used for painting trim.

Oil-base house paint offers the following advantages:

• The finish of white oil-base paint has a "controlled" chalking capability; that is, the surface has the ability to clean itself. As rain washes off chalk, it also washes away dirt. Thus, a white oil-base house paint holds its color better than a white latex house paint.

• Oil-base house paint covers more area than an equal amount of latex paint and lays down a heavier film that provides better covering power. You can often get by with one coat of an oil-base paint where two coats of latex may be needed.

• Oil-base house paint can be used to paint aluminum and plastic siding. Latex house paint doesn't adhere well to these surfaces.

Latex house paint offers the following advantages:

• Colored latex paint provides better color permanence than colored oil-base house paint.

• Latex dries in hours. Oil-base paint takes two or three days. The danger of bugs and dirt drying on a latex surface, therefore, is less.

I. Interior House Paint Usage Guide

	Latex Flat	Alkyd Flat	Gloss Enamel (alkyd)	Gloss Latex	Varnish
Gypsum board walls & ceilings (kitchen and bathroom)			X	X	
Gypsum board walls & ceilings (bedrooms, living room, dining room)	X	X			
Plaster walls & ceilings (kitchen and bathroom)			X	X	
Plaster walls & ceilings (bedroom, living room, dining room)	X	X			
Basement wall, masonry	X				
Doors & windows, wood	X	X	X	X	X
Doors & windows, metal		X	X		
Baseboards & woodwork	X	X	X	X	X
Wood paneling	X	X			X
Kitchen cabinets			X	X	X
Furniture & built-ins			X	X	X
Metal pipes & radiators		X			

• You can apply latex to a damp surface (Fig. 9). The substrate must be dry before oil-base paint can be applied.

• Latex resists blistering and peeling, because it provides a semipermeable film that allows water vapor to escape (Fig. 10).

• Latex can be used on masonry (Fig. 11). Oil-base house paint, which isn't alkali resistant and will tend to chalk, shouldn't be used on masonry.

• Latex is easier to clean up.

Alkyd trim enamel is made of long-oil resins that have a high proportion of fatty acids. It brushes on easily and retains its gloss and color extremely well. This is especially true of silicone-alkyd trim enamel.

II. Exterior House Paint Usage Guide

	Oil-base Paint	Latex Paint	Alkyd Enamel
Wood siding, clapboard – vertical	X	X	
Wood siding, horizontal	X	X	
Wood shingles & shakes		X	
Asbestos shingles		X	
Aluminum siding	X		
Plastic siding	X		
Stucco, brick, cement		X	
Wood windows & doors, screens & storms	X		X
Trim, cornice, fascia			X
Metal Windows & doors	X		X
Wood gutters	X	X	X
Metal gutters	X		X
Downspouts	X		X

The charts on this page and page 270 outline on which surfaces to use various types of interior and exterior paints.

Figure 10. Latex paint can be used on several different kinds of surfaces, including shakes.

Figure 11. Latex paint may be applied confidently to masonry.

PAINT BRUSHES

When neglect has caused a paint brush to harden, there are a number of ways to restore the tool to usable condition (Fig. 1). The quickest method is to pour hot vinegar into a can and permit the brush to soak. When bristles become pliable, comb them out with a brush comb, which can be purchased in a hardware store or paint supply store (Fig. 2).

If this method fails, identify the brush bristles as either natural or nylon. If bristles are natural, soak them in lacquer thinner or in a commercial brush cleaner, which is available in hardware or paint stores. Allow the brush to remain in the solvent for a day. Then, rinse bristles in mineral spirits or turpentine to remove paint particles. Comb the bristles.

Brushes which have nylon bristles are treated differently. If the brush had been used in paint or varnish, soak it in a 15 percent solution of boiling trisodium phosphate. Then, wash the brush in a warm detergent solution. Rinse thoroughly in water and hang the brush up to dry. Trisodium phosphate may be purchased in a hardware store.

If a nylon brush was used in lacquer, soak it in methylketone cleaner, which you can buy in a paint store. When bristles become soft and pliable, wash the brush in warm detergent solution. Rinse in clean water and hang the brush up to dry.

A nylon brush that was used in shellac should be soaked in alcohol and washed in warm detergent solution. Rinse and hang up to dry.

Naturally, the best time to clean a paint brush is immediately after painting. A good quality brush will give many years of service if cleaned properly.

Figure 1. Paint brushes may be reused time and time again for many years, if they are kept clean.

Figure 2. After a paint brush has been cleaned, use a brush comb to make bristles straight.

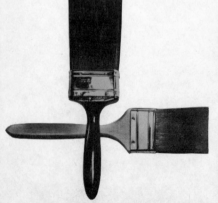

Figure 3. Brushes used in oil-base paint are cleaned in solvent agent, such as turpentine.

Figure 4. Clear away paint by kneading the bristles from the heel of the brush to the tip.

When cleaning a brush right after you paint, be sure to use a cleaning agent that contains the same solvent as that used in the paint. Specifically, if you painted with an oil-base paint, enamel, or varnish, clean the brush in turpentine or mineral spirits (Fig. 3).

If you painted with a water emulsion paint (latex), clean the brush with soap and water. Incidentally, never use a natural bristle brush for applying latex paint. Water will cause bristles to swell. Use nylon.

If you applied shellac with the brush, clean it in denatured alcohol. After using a brush in lacquer, use a lacquer thinner for cleaning.

Allow a brush to soak in its respective cleaning agent for several minutes. Then, squeeze bristles from the heel of the brush toward the tip to work out the paint (Fig. 4). Repeat this procedure, using fresh cleaning solvent, until the brush is clean. Then, comb the bristles.

The objection that most people have to cleaning a paint brush is that it is a messy job. A plastic bag will make the task easier.

Pour the correct cleaning solvent into the bag, put the brush in, tie the bag closed, and knead the brush through the bag.

If you aren't going to use the brush again soon, wrap the bristles in heavy paper. Hang the brush up so that bristles are suspended or lay the brush flat so that the tips of the bristles have no pressure on them.

PAINT DAMAGE

The way that paint on the outside of a home fails will indicate what must be done to prevent a new paint job from failing too. Exterior paint will fail if conditions, such as excessive moisture, exist or if the paint was applied improperly.

The most common paint failure is blistering and peeling of the paint film (Fig. 1). In most cases, this will occur when moisture is trapped beneath the film and pushes upward to produce blisters that eventually burst and peel back. Moisture can originate inside the house or seep behind the paint film through cracks in the outside of the structure.

Blistering and peeling will also occur if the paint is applied to a substrate that is too dirty, chalk covered, or glossy. A dark-colored paint is susceptible to blistering if it is applied in direct sunlight on a hot day. The surface of the paint film may dry before solvents in the paint have time to evaporate. The solvents are trapped beneath the film and cause it to blister.

To determine if blistering or peeling is a result of moisture, rent or borrow a moisture meter from a paint store. Insert the prods of the meter into the home's siding and read the scale.

If the reading is 12 or less, moisture is not causing the problem. Consider some of the other reasons that have just been mentioned.

If the reading is from 13 to 19, moisture is present but can be controlled by repainting the home with a water-thinned (latex) house paint rather than an oil-base house paint. Latex house paint allows a certain amount of trapped moisture to escape through the film. Oil-base house paint doesn't.

Figure 1. Blisters will develop when moisture becomes trapped beneath the paint film surface.

Figure 2. Structural cracks in the home's exterior should be caulked to prevent blistering.

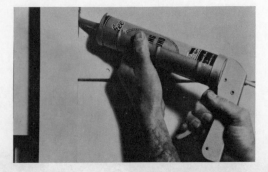

Figure 3. It is necessary to scrape off blisters or peeling surfaces before fresh paint is applied.

Figure 4. If bare wood is present after peeling paint is removed, prime before painting.

If the moisture meter shows a reading of 20 or above, do not repaint the house until the moisture condition has been brought under control. Information on how to treat a moisture problem is given in the sections on Condensation (Moisture) and Caulking. Caulking should be done whenever a home is repainted whether or not a moisture problem exists (Fig. 2). It will help to avert trouble.

Before a blistered or peeling surface is repainted, scrape off old blistered and loose paint (Figs. 3 and 4). If the condition is widespread over the entire house, you may have to remove old paint to bare wood. This can be done with scraping tools and a propane or blow torch, which is used to loosen paint. Naturally, use care when employing the torch. You may also remove old paint with an electric power sander (Fig. 5).

Another common paint problem is excessive chalking. A certain amount of chalking, which is a gradual wearing away of a paint surface, is normal. The paint surface slowly gives off a powder that is washed away with rain. This is desirable, because when chalk is washed off a house, dirt that has settled on the paint is also washed off.

Figure 5. If it becomes necessary to remove old paint, the task can be done with a sander.

However, excessive chalking is something else again. It is rapid deterioration of the paint film. One of the main reasons for the problem is improper application of the paint. If paint is spread too thin, or if it is applied in rain, fog, or dew, excessive chalking will occur.

Another reason for excessive chalking is application of paint on a surface that is too porous. A porous surface will rapidly absorb the paint binder and upset the chemical balance of the paint, thus retarding its ability to chalk properly. Be certain that the substrate on which paint is to be applied isn't worn away to a point where bare wood shows. An old paint surface forms an undercoat for new paint. If it is worn away to bare wood, you should prime the surface before applying a new coat of paint.

Poor quality paints chalk rapidly. To assure that paint provides the longest possible life, use a well-known, good quality product.

To determine if a paint surface is chalking excessively, rub a piece of coarse cloth over the surface. If the pores of the cloth become filled with chalk, chalking is excessive. This must be removed before new paint is applied to keep the new coating from failing prematurely. If chalking isn't excessive, all that is required before you paint is that the house be washed down with water from a hose.

Excessive chalk can be removed from a surface with a scrub brush and a solution made of 1 quart of household bleach, 1 ounce of laundry detergent, 3 ounces of paint cleaner, and enough water to make 10 quarts. After scrubbing the surface, hose it down with water and allow it to dry before painting.

Apply two coats of paint to a surface that has shown excessive chalking. You should also apply two coats of paint if you are putting a colored paint over an old white paint surface since white paint is purposely made to chalk freer than other colors.

Be aware that the type of paint you use has a bearing on how coats should be applied. Specifically, if you are repainting with an oil-base house paint and two coats are required, you can employ the house paint for both. However, if you are repainting with latex paint, the first coat should be a latex primer that will absorb the chalk. When the primer has dried, apply the latex finish paint.

If an old paint surface is too glossy, the paint will not adhere and will start to peel. This will frequently happen in areas that are protected from weather. To prepare a surface such as this for repainting, scrub it down with the cleaning solution used in preparing an excessively chalky surface.

Figure 6. If an old paint surface is checkered, sand smooth before fresh paint is applied.

Figure 7. To make sure that new paint won't crack, mix it well.

Checking is a common paint problem that is characterized by tiny cracks over the paint surface. It is caused primarily by using poor quality paint or by not allowing sufficient drying time between two coats of paint. Checkered paint should be sanded away before new paint is applied (Fig. 6).

Paint will develop long, thin deep cracks and peel back at the edges if there is excessive moisture on the surface when paint is applied, if the paint isn't brushed out thoroughly when applied, or if the paint isn't mixed thoroughly (Fig. 7).

Other paint damages include wrinkling and mildew. Wrinkled paint has a rough texture and is usually caused by applying a coat of paint that is too thick. The paint surface dries faster than the underbody, which leaves soft paint beneath the film that eventually contracts. Wrinkling will also occur if paint is applied to a cold surface. Wrinkled paint must be removed and the substrate made smooth before new paint can be applied.

Mildew is discussed in a separate section in this book.

ROOF

If you are nervous about walking on a roof, do not attempt repairs yourself. Hire a professional.

When roof shingles are damaged, water can leak into the home. However, damage can often be found and corrected before a leak actually develops by making periodic inspections of the roof.

This section explains what to look for and how to repair what you may find. It is divided into three separate areas: composition roofing, wood shingle roofing, and built-up roofing.

Figure 1. To repair a shingle that has lifted, apply roof cement and press down into place.

Figure 2. Hexagon tab shingle.

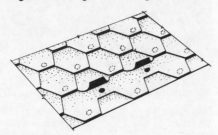

Composition roofing. Composition (asphalt) shingle is the most widely used roofing material. The following are the types of damage to look for and the corrective actions to take:

Small Breaks. Repair a small break in an otherwise sound composition shingle roof by applying black plastic roof cement in and over the break with a pointing trowel. This will bind and seal the damage.

Use only black plastic roof cement for repairing composition roofing. It is a composition asphalt and asbestos material that expands and contracts in relation to temperature variations and will not dry out or crack.

Lifted Shingles. A shingle that has lifted may indicate a serious problem. Carefully raise the shingle that is *above* the damaged shingle and determine if nailheads have ripped through the shingle. If they have, reattach the shingle with aluminum or galvanized roofing nails, which are the only types of nails that should be used on a roof. They will not rust. Cover each of the enlarged nailhead holes with black plastic roof cement.

Now, apply roof cement beneath the edges of the lifted shingle and press it down (Fig. 1). If a lifted shingle is badly torn or won't stay flat, replace it.

Badly Damaged Shingles. In order to replace a badly damaged (or missing) shingle, first become familiar with the type of shingle you are dealing with. This will help you determine how many

Figure 3. Dutch lap shingle.

Figure 4. 3-tab hexagon shingle.

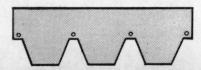

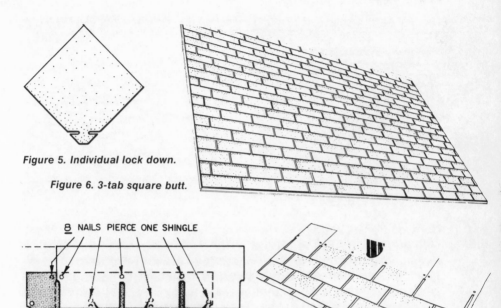

Figure 5. Individual lock down.

Figure 6. 3-tab square butt.

8 NAILS PIERCE ONE SHINGLE

THREE HIDDEN

Figure 7. Removal of a shingle requires removal of all nails.

Figure 8. Shingles are held by nails that are nailed into the shingle above.

nails are holding it. Diagrams on this page and page 278 show various types of composition shingles (Figs. 2, 3, 4 and 5).

The 3-tab square butt shingle is the most common of all. When viewed from the ground, the roof appears to consist of separate shingles (Fig. 6). However, the 3-tab square butt shingle is actually one unit that is held by eight nails (Fig. 7). Four nails are hammered directly into the shingle. The others are hammered into the shingle above, but they pass through the shingle that you are working on (Fig. 8). All nails must be removed before a damaged shingle can be replaced.

To remove a damaged shingle, pull all nails with a nail puller or claw (Fig. 9). Slide the damaged shingle from place (Fig. 10).

Figure 9. Pull all nails with a nail puller or claw to prevent ripping of sheathing.

Figure 10. When nails have been removed, slide the shingle out.

Figure 11. Be sure that the new shingle is placed so it butts tightly against the one above.

Figure 12. Hip and ridge.

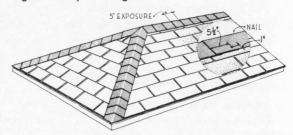

If it binds, do not tug on it. You may rip the roofing paper beneath the shingle, which will present a major problem. Instead, look for undetected nails. When the damaged shingle has been removed, slide a new one firmly into place (Fig. 11).

Hammer nails into the new shingle by first lifting the shingle above and hammering four nails directly into the new shingle. Put them at the very top. Now, lift the shingle above that (the one that is two courses above the new shingle) and hammer in four more nails. Use Figure 7 as a guide. Nailheads should be hidden.

Damaged hip and ridge shingles. Small breaks in shingles that cover hips and ridges can be repaired by covering the damage with black plastic roof cement. A missing hip or ridge shingle or one that is badly damaged should be replaced.

Hip and ridge shingles are held by four nails, two to each hidden corner, spaced 1 inch apart (Fig. 12). After pulling nails and removing the damaged shingle, spread a layer of black plastic roof cement over the area. Then, install a new shingle, pressing it into the cement. Nail down the top corners, but make sure that 5 inches of the shingle is left as exposure.

Wood shingle roof. The following describes damages that affect wood shingle roofing most often:

Loose Shingles. Reattach loose shingles by nailing them back into place.

Warped Shingle. Split the shingle down the center of the warped area with a chisel and slip a piece of roofing paper beneath the split so that it extends about 2 inches to each side of the split. Nail down the split edges with roofing nails. If the outer edges of the shingle have curled, nail them down, too.

Badly Damaged Shingles. Remove nails with a nail puller. There are normally two per shingle. Insert and nail a new shingle of the same width. Try to purchase new shingles that are weathered so that they blend in color with the older shingles on the roof.

Dried-Out Shingles. Wood shingles would probably not split or warp if they were kept from drying out. Prevention requires an annual coating of shingles with a mixture of one part of linseed oil to one part of turpentine. This will replenish the wood's natural oils. Apply the mixture with a paint brush.

Dry Rot. Linseed oil will keep shingles from developing dry rot. Once a shingle falls victim to dry rot, it must be replaced at once and the entire roof must be treated with linseed oil to keep the fungus from spreading.

Never paint wood shingles. Paint will close the pores of the wood, which will prevent moisture that has seeped beneath the shingle from escaping. Moisture will hasten the onset of dry rot. Use only linseed oil or a commercially manufactured wood shingle stain.

Built-Up Roofing. Common damage to built-up (flat) roofs include breaks in the top layer of material and curling back of the material at edges.

If the roofing material develops a break, cut back the break with a sharp knife and remove loose ends. Spread a liberal amount of black plastic roof cement over the area, extending it out about 2 inches on each side of the damage. Cut a piece of asbestos saturated felt, which you can buy in a roofing supply store and lay it on top of the area. Press it into the cement, but make sure that the felt extends out about 2 inches beyond the edges of the area (Fig. 13).

When the felt has been put into place, nail around its perimeter with roofing nails. Then, apply another layer of cement around the edges and spread gravel or dry sand over the repair to protect it from the elements.

Built-up roofing has a tendency to break away at edges, such as where the material butts against a vertical section of a building. Water can seep into the structure through this break. To make repairs, spread black plastic roof cement beneath the curled edges and press it back into place. Hammer in several roofing nails and then spread cement over the edge.

Figure 13. Breaks in built-up roofing are covered with an asbestos saturated felt material.

SCREWS

There are two types of screws with which you will be concerned: wood screws and sheet metal screws. Wood screws are used to fasten pieces of wood to each other and to anchor objects to a wood surface. Sheet metal screws, which are also called tapping screws and self-threading screws, are used for fastening pieces of metal together and for attaching objects to a metal surface.

You should not use wood screws to do a job best left to sheet metal screws and vice versa. The two screws can be distinguished by examining their threads. Sheet metal screws are threaded all the way from the point to the head. Wood screws, however, have threads extending only two-thirds of the way up from the point. A smooth shank extends the rest of the way to the head.

When should screws be used in preference to nails? If the task you are doing falls into one of the following categories, use screws:

• If the pull of the load is directed along the length of the fastening device, requiring that maximum holding power be utilized as, for example, when hanging a door.

• If there is a chance that you may want to take the work apart in the future. It is far easier to remove screws than to pull nails. Furthermore, there is less chance of damaging the work.

• If there is a possibility that you will damage the piece of work while applying the fastener. For example, there is less chance of a screwdriver slipping and damaging a fine finish than of a hammer slipping.

• If you plan to leave the fastener exposed. Screws are somewhat more decorative than nails.

If the task you are doing does not fall into one of these categories, it is best to employ nails. They are less expensive than screws and require less time and effort to install.

In selecting screws, there are four things to consider: (1) the type of head, (2) the metal that the screw is made of, (3) length, and (4) diameter.

In selecting the type of head to use, take into consideration both the style and the shape. Style refers to the notch in the head. It can be a straight-slot or a Phillips (cross) slot. Wood and sheet metal screws are available in both styles.

A Phillips head permits you to apply maximum driving pressure when installing the screw, because a Phillips screwdriver makes a close fit with the cross-shaped slots. This allows pres-

Figure 1. Flathead screws.

Figure 2. Roundhead screws.

Figure 3. Ovalhead screws.

Figure 4. Trusshead screws.

Figure 5. Panhead screws.

sure to be applied on four sides rather than on only two as with a straight-slot head. There is less chance of a screwdriver slipping out of a Phillips head and marring the work.

There are five major head shapes from which to select: flathead, roundhead, ovalhead, trusshead, and panhead. Each has different characteristics.

Flathead screws do not protrude above the work surface (Fig. 1). They can be driven flush with the surface or can be countersunk and concealed with wood putty or small wooden plugs.

Roundhead screws protrude above the surface more than any other type, but they afford good slot depth and are designed for universal application were the protruding head is of no consequence (Fig. 2).

Ovalhead screws are, in essence, a combination of roundhead and flathead screws (Fig. 3). The bottom of the head is countersunk into the surface, while the rounded top increases the depth of the slot. Ovalhead screws are quite decorative.

Trusshead screws have a wide, low-profile configuration and are often referred to as ovenhead screws. They are useful for covering large diameter holes in sheet metal (Fig. 4).

Panhead screws resemble trusshead screws in that they are low with a large diameter. However, they have thicker outer edges to allow for maximum driving power where needed (Fig. 5).

Screws are most commonly made of steel and brass. Use brass screws for lightweight work; steel screws where work is heavy. If there is a chance that corrosion will be a factor, as there would be if screws will be subjected to weather, use screws made of aluminum or those that have a protective plating, such as galvanized steel, zinc chromate, or plated cadmium.

In considering what length screw to select, simply keep in

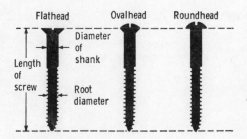

Figure 6. Measuring length.

mind that you should pick the longest possible screw that will not pass entirely through the wood. Maximum holding power is achieved when as much screw body as possible is in the wood. Length is measured differently, according to the shape of the head (Fig. 6).

You may obtain screws as long as 6 inches by placing a special order. However, sizes generally available range from ¼ inch to 4 inches in length. Screws of less than 1 inch in length increase by ⅛-inch increments. Screws of 1 inch to 3 inches in length increase by ¼-inch increments. Screws longer than 3 inches increase in size by ½-inch increments.

The diameter of screws is expressed by an arbitrary numbering system which represents relative differences in the thickness rather than the actual measurement (Fig. 7). Wood screws range in diameter from No. 0 (0.060 inch) to No. 24 (0.372 inch). Hardware stores generally carry sizes from No. 2 (0.086 inch) to No. 18 (0.294 inch).

You must know the screw's diameter in order to select the correct drill size for making lead (pilot) holes. The chart accompanying this section will assist you in selecting the correct drill for a lead hole once the diameter of the screw has been determined (Fig. 8).

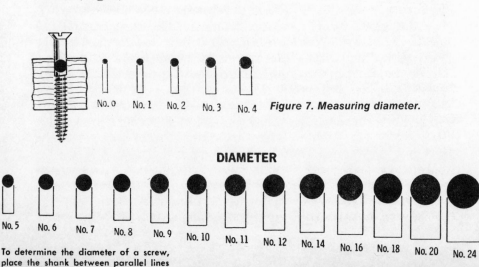

Figure 7. Measuring diameter.

DIAMETER

To determine the diameter of a screw, place the shank between parallel lines

Screw Size (No. and diameter)	Drill Size (No. and diameter)	
	Hardwoods	Softwoods
0 (.060″)	70 (1/32″)	
1 (.073″)	66 (1/32″)	71 (1/32″)
2 (.086″)	56 (3/64″)	65 (1/32″)
3 (.099″)	54 (1/16″)	58 (3/64″)
4 (.112″)	52 (1/16″)	55 (3/64″)
5 (.125″)	49 (5/64″)	53 (1/16″)
6 (.138″)	47 (5/64″)	52 (1/16″)
7 (.151″)	44 (3/32″)	51 (1/16″)
8 (.164″)	40 (3/32″)	48 (5/64″)
9 (.177″)	37 (7/64″)	45 (5/64″)
10 (.190″)	33 (7/64″)	43 (3/32″)
12 (.216″)	30 (1/8″)	38 (7/64″)
14 (.242″)	25 (9/64″)	32 (7/64″)
16 (.268″)	18 (5/32″)	29 (9/64″)
18 (.294″)	13 (3/16″)	26 (9/64″)
20 (.320″)	4 (13/64″)	19 (11/64″)
24 (.372″)	1 (7/32″)	15 (3/16″)

NOTE: Lead holes aren't usually required for Nos. 0 and 1 screws. For sizes smaller than No. 6, lead holes can be eliminated in softwoods, except near the edges and ends of boards.

Figure 8. Drilling lead holes.

In drilling lead holes into softwood, such as pine and spruce, make them only half as long as the threaded portion of the screw. If you are working with hardwood, such as oak, maple, or birch, drill lead holes as deep as the screw itself.

How much of a load can you put on different size screws? This depends on the wood that you are using. The chart entitled "Safe Load Per Inch of Threads" will provide you with a guide which you can use in making this determination (Fig. 9).

WOOD	Safe Load per Inch of Threads				
	SCREW NUMBER				
	4	8	12	16	20
In Oak	80 lbs.	100 lbs.	130 lbs.	150 lbs.	170 lbs.
In Yellow Pine	70 lbs.	90 lbs.	120 lbs.	140 lbs.	150 lbs.
In White Pine	50 lbs.	70 lbs.	90 lbs.	100 lbs.	120 lbs.

NOTE: Keep in mind that the threads of a wood screw represent two thirds of the length of the screw. Also, setting a screw into end grain reduces the holding power by 40 percent. For example, a No. 20 screw set with threads 1 in. into the cross grain of white pine will hold 120 lbs. Set into the end grain, however, it will hold only 72 lbs. If threads penetrate only ½ in. into end grain, the holding power drops to 36 lbs.

Figure 9. Determining safe load.

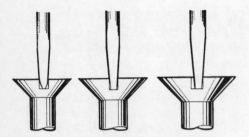

Figure 10. The illustration in the center shows the way that a screwdriver should fit a slot.

Figure 11. Type A.

Figure 12. Type B.

Figure 13. Type C.

Figure 14. Type F.

Figure 15. Type U.

Figure 16. Type 21.

The selection of a screwdriver is very important (Fig. 10). The blade should be as near the length of the slot as possible and should be thick enough to fill the slot, but thin enough to reach the bottom. A blade that is worn or doesn't fit properly will damage the slot.

To make it easier to drive screws into wood, coat threads with paraffin or graphite. Do not use soap, which will eventually turn to a form of glue that will cement the screw into the hole. Soap may also cause corrosion.

There are six common types of sheet metal screws: A, B, C, F, U, and 21. They have different characteristics, as follows:

• *Type A* has coarse threads and is used for joining pieces of sheet metal that have a gauge which ranges from 0.015 to 0.050 inch (Fig. 11). These sheet metal screws are available in diameters of No. 4 through No. 14 and in lengths of from ¼ to 2 inches. They are available in either straight-slot or Phillips head.

• *Type B* sheet metal screws can be used for the same jobs as Type A. However, they are recommended also for joining of sheet metal which has a gauge that ranges from 0.050 to 0.200 inch (Fig. 12). These screws come in the same diameter and length as Type A and in both straight-slot and Phillips heads.

• *Type C* has standard threads rather than coarse threads (Fig. 13). Type C sheet metal screws are used for joining sheet metal that has a gauge which ranges from 0.030 to 0.100 inch. These screws are available in diameters of ³/₁₆ to 1¼ inch.

• *Type F* sheet metal screws should be used to join metal that ranges in thickness from 0.050 to 0.5 inch (Fig. 14). These screws come in diameters from No. 2 to ¼ inch and in lengths from ⅛ inch to ¾ inch. You can get them in either straight-slot or Phillips head.

• *Type U* sheet metal screws are installed with a hammer rather than a screwdriver (Fig. 15). They are used to join heavy gauge metals of from 0.050 inch to 0.5 inch and come in lengths of from ⅛ inch through ¾ inch.

• *Type 21* sheet metal screws are often used to fasten other materials, such as fabric, cardboard, and leather to metal (Fig. 16). These, too, are installed with a hammer. They are available in three lengths: ¹¹/₃₂ inch, ⁷/₁₆ inch, and ½ inch.

SEPTIC SYSTEM

Septic system repair is a job for a professional. However, the homeowner can do a great deal to avoid this extremely expensive proposition by learning the true facts about septic tanks and leaching fields. Unfortunately, these facts have been clouded by rumors and untruths.

For example, it is not true that treatment with chemicals will help dissolve solids which build up in a septic tank. Neither is it true that soaps and detergents will harm a septic system.

The Public Health Service of the U.S.Department of Health, Education, and Welfare says the following:

"There are no known chemicals, yeasts, bacteria, enzymes, or other substances capable of eliminating or reducing the solids and scum in a septic tank so that periodic cleaning is unnecessary.

"The purpose of a septic tank," the Public Health Service states, "is to treat household wastes, including soapy water from the laundry and the bath, discarded food scraps, and body wastes. The normal use of bleaches, detergents, soaps, and drain cleaners does not harm nor interfere with the operation of the system."

The organization adds that a garbage disposer unit can be employed in a home that is equipped with a septic system. This is contrary to what you may have heard.

However, the Public Health Service points out that "a septic system will serve a home satisfactorily only if it is properly lo-

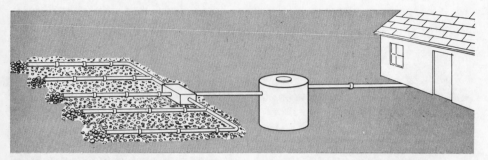

Figure 1. A septic system consists of a septic tank, distribution box, and leaching field.

cated, designed, constructed, and adequately maintained.... To obtain satisfactory service, the homeowner must know something about the design, operation, and maintenance of his own septic tank system."

A septic system consists of two main sections (Fig. 1). One is the septic tank; the other is the drainfield (or leaching area).

Wastes coming from the house pass into the septic tank through a pipe. The tank is a watertight structure in which organic solids are decomposed by natural bacterial process. As sewage enters the tank, the flow slows to allow solids and liquid to separate.

Finer particles remain in liquid suspension and pass out of the tank to a distribution box. From here, liquid and small particles enter lines which lead to the drainfield.

Meanwhile, in the tank, bacteria which thrive in the absence of oxygen decompose solid waste. The decomposed material is called septic. The volume of solids is reduced by the bacteria, but residue remains and is stored. Eventually, this residue must be cleaned out or the system will clog.

A problem in the septic system makes itself known in one of several ways, as follows:

• Home drains will back up, and sewage won't flow into the system. This indicates that the septic tank is filled, or that the drainfield has been flooded by heavy rain. If the latter, the condition will eventually abate.

• Low-lying drain vents boil over with sewage. This is a sign that the septic tank is filled.

• The ground above the drainfield suddenly erupts with gas. Check with community officials, especially the town engineer. Ordinances governing installation of a septic system are strict, and this condition suggests that the system was not adequate to begin with. The contractor could be held responsible.

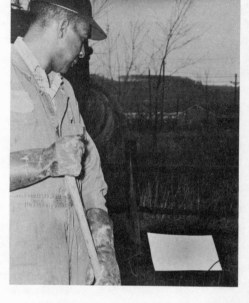

Figure 2. Pumping equipment is required to clean out a septic tank. Do this job frequently.

Figure 3. A diagram of the system will facilitate the work.

• Grass takes on a dark hue and grows more vigorously above the drainfield than elsewhere. Untreated sewage is leaving the drainfield and acting as a fertilizer.

Many septic system problems occur because of inadequate maintenance on the part of the homeowner. Keep in mind that inadequate maintenance is a much more expensive proposition than conscientious maintenance because of the repair problems which are caused by lack of care.

When a septic tank overflows, solids flow into the leaching pipe system and block the flow of liquid. This must be repaired by uncovering, cleaning, and possibly relocating the entire leaching system. However, if the septic tank is cleaned out before overflowing occurs, this very expensive repair can be avoided.

You should allow a professional serviceman to clean out the septic tank once every two or three years. If your home is equipped with a garbage disposer unit, the tank should be cleaned once a year.

A serviceman uses a special pumping truck to remove sludge from the tank (Fig. 2). However, make certain that he does not completely drain the tank, and you should never insist that this be done. An empty tank will impede fermentation action which decomposes waste. Draining a septic tank completely will cause wastes to build up at a more rapid rate.

To facilitate cleaning and to prevent damage to the system,

Figure 4. Being careful to cut out sod in chunks, the serviceman uncovers the septic tank.

Figure 5. The hose is inserted into the tank to pump out sludge.

you should have a diagram of your septic system that shows the location of the tank and the leaching system (Fig. 3). This should have been given to you by the contractor. If you have no such diagram, consult with your town's engineering department, which often keeps such documents on file.

A diagram allows a serviceman to go directly to the tank. In addition, it insures that he won't drive his heavy truck over the leaching field, which could cause serious damage.

Aided by the diagram, the serviceman should uncover the tank. A careful professional will cut out the sod in chunks so that it can be replaced later (Fig. 4).

The hose of the pumping equipment is inserted into the tank and sludge is pumped out (Fig. 5). When the job has been completed, the tank is covered (Fig. 6). If the job is done properly, you should hardly be able to see where the soil has been tampered with (Fig. 7).

There are two questions that often bother homeowners about septic systems. They are:

Figure 6. Be sure that a shallow layer of sludge is left in the tank to aid fermentation.

Figure 7. When the job is completed, sod is laid in place.

1. Will grease harm a septic system? Grease will not cause any more harm to a septic system than it causes to a regular sewer system. It will not damage a septic tank since grease will decompose as other wastes do. However, a considerable amount of grease poured into a drain will clog drain pipes, so limit the quantity you discard down the drain.

2. Is it necessary to bypass the septic tank with a drain line from a washing machine to prevent detergents from entering the tank? No! In fact, feeding a drain line directly into the leaching area will cause damage to that area. Detergents can clog the leaching field. Conversely, detergent scum that enters the septic tank can be cleaned out when the tank is cleaned.

STORM DOORS

An aluminum storm door needs to be repaired when the door's bottom scrapes against the threshold. To detect the misalignment condition before it reaches this point, inspect the top of the door every so often. The space between the door and frame should be even over the full length. If it isn't, the screws holding the door to the house have loosened, hinge screws have loosened, or the house has settled, all of which cause the door to shift.

Tighten all hinge and frame screws. Recheck the space along the top of the door. If it is now even, the repair has been made. However, if not, the door must be readjusted.

The degree of adjustment can be determined by placing a square on the top or bottom edge of the door (Fig. 1).The space between the square and the door indicates the degree of misalignment and, thus, how much adjustment is necessary.

Aluminum storm doors are held at each corner by an internal bracket. They are also held across the middle by an internal reinforcing piece that extends from one side to the other. In total, there are 18 or 20 screws that attach the door pieces to the

Figure 1. To determine how much adjustment is necessary, align a square to the door's bottom.

Figure 2. Make sure all screws are loosened. If they aren't, the door cannot be readjusted.

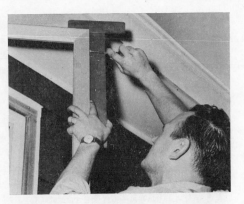

Figure 3. With the door square, tighten screws in that corner first; then tighten all others.

internal reinforcing pieces; that is, some doors have 18 screws, others have 20.

Four screws are located in each corner and one on each side of the sash in the middle. In addition to these 18, those doors with 20 screws have two additional screws in the middle to support a wider reinforcing piece.

To adjust an aluminum storm door, loosen *all* screws (Fig. 2). Place the square at the top or bottom of the door, and shift the door by hand until the door lines up with the square.

When the adjustment has been made, hold the door firmly and tighten the screws at the corner in which you are working (Fig. 3). Once these screws are tight, the door will hold firmly until you can tighten all other screws. As long as one corner of the door is square, all other corners will fall into place.

Most aluminum storm doors are equipped with a pneumatic or hydraulic cushion control (or snubber) that controls the speed

Figure 4. To adjust the rate at which an aluminum door closes, manipulate the cylinder screw.

Figure 5. A couple of drops of oil every 12 months will keep piston cups from deteriorating.

at which the door closes. To adjust the rate of closure, turn the screw on the end of the cylinder (Fig. 4). However, adjust it only a small amount at a time, between tests of the closing rate. Turning the screw "in" decreases speed; turning it "out" increases speed.

Most snubbers have leather piston cups that can dry out and crack if they aren't lubricated regularly. When this happens, the control loses its snubbing action and has to be replaced.

To avoid this, remove the adjustment screw at the end of the cylinder every 12 months and squirt in two drops of lightweight household oil (Fig. 5). Reinstall the screw and slowly open and close the door several times to distribute oil. Then, adjust snubbing action.

STORM WINDOWS

Let's discuss aluminum storm windows first. The most common problem is cracked or broken glass. Replacing it is easily accomplished without the need for special tools.

Glass in aluminum storm windows is held in place by strips of vinyl that set into channels around the perimeter of the sash. These strips must be removed before glass can be replaced.

Slip a putty knife beneath the corner of a strip, lift up a small section, grasp it with your fingers, and slowly pull it from the channel (Fig. 1). When each strip of vinyl has been removed in this manner, lift the broken glass out, but be careful not to cut yourself.

Now, measure the length and width of the opening from channel to channel. Go to a glazier and have him cut a pane of glass to this size. Place the glass into the frame.

To facilitate reinsertion of vinyl strips, brush soapy water

Figure 1. Carefully pull vinyl strips from aluminum channels so as not to tear them in half.

Figure 2. To make it easier to reinsert vinyl strips, use plenty of soapy water on channels and strips.

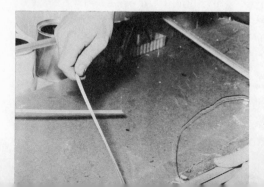

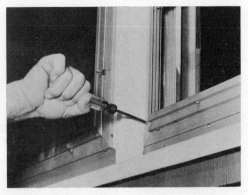

Figure 3. Reseat the strip with your fingers. Use a putty knife at corners to prevent cracking.

Figure 4. To assure that aluminum storms are draftproof, tighten screws once each year.

on the channels and on each strip (Fig. 2). Now, carefully seat the vinyl into the channel with your fingertips (Fig. 3).

If the strip binds, do not force it. Instead, coat the spot with more soapy water and use the edge of a putty knife to push the strip into place.

The most critical areas to watch are the corners. These are the weakest points. When you get to them, make sure channel and vinyl are well coated with soapy water and use a putty knife to seat the strip.

Aluminum storm windows present other problems. Screws that hold storm sash to the house can loosen, allowing cold air to leak into the house. In the fall, tighten all screws and replace any that are missing (Fig. 4). When buying screws, be sure to specify that you want aluminum screws for aluminum storm sash.

Aluminum windows may become difficult to slide up and down. This is corrected by spraying channels with silicone lubricant or by rubbing paraffin into the channel. Only a thin coating is needed.

Open and close the window several times to distribute lubricant over the entire channel. Latch locks that bind should be treated with a drop of lightweight household oil.

Examine the inside bottom aluminum sash for small holes. There should be two—one at each end. These are weep holes to prevent condensation. If your aluminum sash doesn't have them, insert them with an electric drill and a 5/32-inch bit (Fig. 5).

Wooden storm windows present problems that are different from problems of aluminum windows. Replacing a broken pane of glass is done the same as replacing a pane of glass of a regu-

Figure 5. If the aluminum sash doesn't have weep holes, drill them in to stop condensation.

Figure 6. You may reinforce corners of wooden storm sash with metal corner braces.

lar window. The way to do this is discussed in the section on Window Glass.

Hangers should be examined each year. If they have rusted, replace them with new ones. Hangers sold today are corrosion resistant. If hangers are in good condition, make sure that the screws holding them are tight.

Sash joints that have separated may be reinforced with metal corner braces. Carefully tap the joint back together with a mallet and screw the corner brace into place so that it holds the corner securely (Fig. 6).

Naturally, wooden storm windows should be painted when necessary to protect the wood from the elements.

SWIMMING POOLS

The majority of residential swimming pools has plastic liners. If proper maintenance procedures are followed, as discussed here, damage will be held to a minimum.

Water can be left in pools with plastic liners throughout the year. However, when the pool is closed for a period of time (because of cold weather, for example), it should be covered. Upon reopening the pool, use a vacuum to syphon off water that has accumulated on the cover. Leaves should be allowed to dry so that they are easy to brush away, thus minimizing damage to the cover. When the cover is free of water and debris, remove and store it in a protected area, such as a shed or basement.

To get the filter ready for service, remove the cover of the multiport valve assembly and inspect the gasket for damage

Figure 1. A damaged multiport valve gasket leads to ineffective filtration of pool water.

Figure 2. Be sure that the hair and lint trap is unobstructed. It must be completely clear of debris.

(Fig. 1). Consult the manual which accompanied the filter when it was purchased to identify the location of parts. Replace the gasket if it is cut, cracked, or dried out.

Apply a thin film of water-seal lubricant to all sliding surfaces of the multiport valve assembly. Materials may be purchased at a dealer of swimming pool supplies.

Remove the hair and lint trap and make sure that it is clear of debris (Fig. 2). Apply a drop or two of heavy lubricating oil to the filter motor (Fig. 3).

Now, fill the pump strainer with water and start the filter, but be sure to follow the filter manufacturer's instructions on how to do this. Methods vary from filter to filter. If the filter makes noise, shut it off at once and call a repairman. The motor may have a bad bearing that should be replaced. Running the motor with this condition will result in complete motor failure.

If the pool was covered during the time that it was closed, run the filter for two hours. During the last five minutes, switch the filter to "backwash" position. Now, add chlorine to the water

Figure 3. Apply a drop or two of heavy lubricating oil to the oil cups you find on the motor.

Figure 4. Only a normal amount of chlorine is necessary if the pool was protected by a cover.

Figure 5. An ordinary household cleanser can be used to clean off the ring around the liner.

(Fig. 4). Since the pool was covered, there will be no dirt, debris, mud, or algae in the water, and the amount of chlorine normally recommended for your size pool can be used. You can now begin to swim.

To treat a plastic-lined pool that was not covered during the shutdown period, follow instructions regarding filters as outlined above. Run the filter continuously for two straight days. At the end of this period, give the water a heavy dose of chlorine to kill algae and bacteria. If you use 2 pounds of chlorine, allow 24 hours before you start to swim. If you use 5 pounds of chlorine, you can cut the time to 12 hours.

The sides and floor of a plastic liner pool should be scrubbed often with a pool brush. Remove scum that forms on the bottom by hooking up a swimming pool vacuum and sweeping the pool on or close to the bottom with the filter in the "waste" setting. The scum ring that forms on the sides of the liner at water level can be cleaned off with household cleanser or whitewall tire cleaner (Figs. 5 and 6).

Figure 6. Use a vigorous scrubbing action to eliminate dirt.

Figure 7. One type of plastic liner patch kit includes a few patches and a tube of adhesive.

Figure 8. Another type of patch kit contains patches that have self-adhering hold-fast backs.

A tear in the plastic liner is the most serious damage you can face. Fortunately, most tears are small and can be repaired with a vinyl patch kit (Fig. 7). This kit contains patches and adhesive. Another type of patch kit contains patches that have contact self-adhering backs (Fig. 8). Either type of patch may be used.

Successful patching depends on a perfectly clean surface so that the patch will adhere properly. To obtain a clean surface, use a so-called fusion patch. Apply a patch to the damaged area and then rip it off. This will remove a layer of vinyl and, with it, surface dirt. The finish patch can now be applied.

Vinyl patches can be applied underwater. If the liner is torn where the damage can't be reached from poolside, you will have to dive and stay submerged for a few seconds while you adhere the patch in place. If the damage is on the bottom of the pool, stand on the patch for about 30 seconds after it has been applied to assure good adhesion.

Tears larger than six inches present a major problem. To try to salvage the liner, drain the pool below the damage and work a patch beneath the tear. Then, apply another patch on top of the tear. If this doesn't prove successful and the pool leaks, the liner will have to be replaced.

Part of pool maintenance should be a periodic application of paint to wood decks. Make sure that the paint is recommended for such purpose. It should, for example, be resistant to water and sun (Fig. 9).

Concrete swimming pools form the second largest block of residential installations. They should be painted when the old paint is almost worn down to concrete. However, this does not

Figure 9. Wooden decks and adjacent areas should be painted.

necessarily have to be done every year. In fact, if an epoxy paint is used, paint will last for as long as five years. Epoxy paint, however, is more difficult to apply than regular rubber-base pool paint.

Whichever paint you use, be sure that it is compatible with the paint that is now covering the surface. If the new coating is different from the old coating, the new coat will alligator and strip off.

If you are not sure what type of paint is on the surface, apply a 6-inch swath of new paint and let it dry. Then, give it a twist with your thumb. If the patch slides off, the paints are not compatible.

Before painting, examine concrete for cracks. Use a chisel to widen hairline cracks to about ⅜ inch so that filler material will have a good base on which to take hold. Clean particles and dust from the crack with a wire brush and use an underwater elasticemeric or epoxy sealer to fill the crack.

If a crack is larger than ¾ inch, fill it with dry oakum and lead before applying the elasticemeric or epoxy sealer. If concrete is in very bad condition and water is leaking through cracks, have a plaster coating applied and a plastic liner installed. Be sure that the contractor who does the job fits the liner precisely, so that no folds or laps are left.

If old paint is in good condition, scrub the surface with a nonsoapy detergent and rinse with water before repainting. Mildew can be eliminated by scrubbing with a cleaner that contains sodium hypochlorite or trisodium phosphate.

An old paint surface that is in bad shape (peeling, blistering, etc.) should be removed before new paint is applied. The fastest way to do this is by sandblasting. If you have time and patience, however, you can use a power sander.

After paint is removed, fill cracks and etch the surface. Etching involves washing the surface with a 10 percent solution of muriatic acid, rinsing with water, washing the surface with a trisodium phosphate cleaner, rinsing again, and letting the surface dry before painting. Wear rubber gloves, boots, and goggles when etching.

The following are important procedures to observe when painting a concrete pool:

- Make sure all pits and crevices are covered by paint.
- Never apply paint to a damp surface.
- Paint when the temperature is above 50°F and in the shade, if possible.
- Allow sufficient time for the paint to dry before filling the pool. A minimum of one week is required if the weather is warm and dry. Longer if it is not.
- To avoid lines, start and end in a corner. Paint from the top down and from left to right to keep from dripping on a freshly painted surface.

TOILET TANK

Before repairing a toilet tank, analyze the problem. This is easily done when you understand how the flushing mechanism functions.

When the trip lever is activated, a flush valve stopper ball is raised off its seat by linkage that connects the lever to the ball. Water stored in the tank flows into the toilet bowl.

As the water level in the tank drops, a float pulls a ballcock valve from its seat in the water supply line and the flush valve stopper ball reseats itself. No more water can enter the toilet bowl, and fresh water flows into the toilet tank from the water supply pipe. As the water level rises, it raises the float which, at a predetermined level, reseats the ballcock valve to close off the water supply.

Figure 1. If the sound of water is heard, purchase a new float.

Figure 2. A slight bend in the float rod could stop the leak.

Figure 3. If the ballcock valve washer is worn, there will be a persistent leak. Get a new valve.

Figure 4. Lubricant keeps the trip lever in good condition.

From this description, you can see that two problems can occur: (1) water can keep running out of the tank into the bowl; (2) water can drip into the tank. Both conditions create noise.

If you hear the sound of water, but cannot see water flowing into the toilet bowl, remove the toilet tank cover, unscrew the float from its rod, and shake it near your ear (Fig. 1). If you hear water sloshing around inside, the float is damaged and must be replaced.

If there is no water in the float, bend the float rod slightly at its present bend so that the float level will be lowered (Fig. 2). This should cause the ballcock valve to seat itself more firmly.

Flush the toilet to check results. If water still continues to run, turn off the main water valve to the toilet and flush the toilet so that the tank empties. Unscrew the ballcock valve from the top of the water supply pipe (Fig. 3). The washer is probably worn. To obtain the right size washer, take the valve to a hardware store.

Now, if the annoying sound of running water is accompanied by a flow of water into the bowl, jiggle the trip lever. If the flow stops, the mechanism is sticking, which is preventing the flush valve stopper ball from dropping into place. Apply a thin coating of waterproof white grease to the surface of the trip lever on the toilet tank side (Fig. 4).

If the trip lever is working properly, water running into the toilet bowl signifies that there is a leak past the stopper ball. Turn off the main water valve and operate the trip lever. Watch the stopper ball. When it drops back into place, it should completely cover the flush valve hole. If it doesn't, adjust the guide

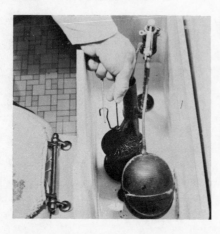

Figure 5. If the stopper ball doesn't fully cover the outlet valve, a leaky toilet results.

arm that is attached to the overflow pipe. To do this, loosen the screws that hold the guide arm. Move the arm to realign the stopper ball (Fig. 5).

If the leak persists, install a new stopper ball and linkage, but first clean dirt and corrosion from the valve seat with a piece of steel wool.

Another problem that often affects a toilet tank is condensation which forms on the outside of the tank and drips on the floor. This is caused by water in the tank being much colder than the temperature of the surrounding air.

The best way to fix this is to have a plumber install an anti-sweat valve, which replaces the present main water valve. It will keep the water which enters the tank at 65°F.

UPHOLSTERING

Upholstering furniture is a challenge that involves both mechanical and artistic skills. Each step, whether it is application of padding which will be hidden from view or installation of the top covering which will be visible, has an important bearing on the final result. Thus, be extremely careful that each step is done to perfection.

The tools and materials that you will need may be obtained from a professional upholstery shop. They are mentioned throughout this section, but let us put emphasis upon the upholsterer's magnetic hammer, which you will not be able to do without.

The smaller end of a magnetic hammer is magnetized to hold upholstery tacks as they are started into furniture. The larger end of the hammer is shaped to conform to the heads of

Figure 1. *Use a mallet and ripping chisel to strip the piece.*

Figure 2. *Discard all fabric so that the wood frame is exposed.*

upholstery tacks to minimize slipping of the hammer and marring of furniture. The hammer seen in the pictures accompanying this section is the upholsterer's magnetic hammer.

If someone in the family is handy with a sewing machine, let him make the finish covering. Otherwise, allow a professional tailor to do the job. Ask him for advice on how to measure the furniture so that the exact amount of material needed may be ascertained.

Begin by stripping the furniture to the frame with a mallet and ripping chisel, which is an upholsterer's tool that removes old upholstery without damaging the wood frame (Fig. 1). Discard old material, including cambric, covering, webbing, topping, batting, burlap, and foam rubber or polyester (Fig. 2). Inspect coil springs and the Marshall spring unit, if there is one. The Marshall unit is a spring unit that is used in construction which doesn't employ polyester or rubber padding.

Cut away old twine holding coils. If a coil has come loose, reattach it to the frame with upholstery staples. If any section of the Marshall unit is broken, replace the entire unit. Marshall units cannot be repaired.

Work on the bottom side of the furniture first. Tie coil springs together with Italian imported spring twine to hold them firm. Knot one end of the twine around a No. 14 upholstery tack that is hammered into the frame, tie twine around coils, and knot the other end around a No. 14 tack on the opposite frame (Fig. 3). Coil springs should be firmly tied when you have finished (Fig. 4).

Use jute sagless on the underside of the furniture instead of old-fashioned webbing to support coils. Sagless is more durable. In measuring for the amount that you need, allow 2 inches extra on each side for stretching.

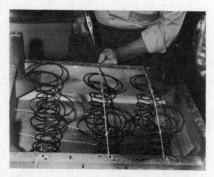

Figure 3. Attach twine to frame pieces using upholstery tacks.

Figure 4. This is the proper method for tying springs firmly together.

Figure 5. The stretching tool is used to pull sagless taut.

Figure 6. Trim excess sagless with a pair of shears.

Figure 7. When nailing sagless to the wooden frame, fold over edges to strengthen the hold.

Figure 8. Cover the Marshall spring unit with burlap. Tack the burlap to the wood frame.

Attach one end of the sagless to the frame with No. 14 tacks. Fold over the ends being tacked to allow tacks to hold firmly without ripping the material.

Now, stretch the sagless taut with a stretching tool (Fig. 5). When purchasing this tool, be sure to specify that you want a stretching tool for sagless. Other types are made for webbing.

Trim excess sagless with shears (Fig. 6). Now, complete tacking of the sagless to the frame, making certain that it is tight and that the ends through which nails are installed are folded (Fig. 7).

Turn the piece of furniture over and attach 10-ounce burlap to the frame with No. 4 tacks (Fig. 8). If the furniture doesn't have a Marshall unit, foam rubber or polyester padding is applied, followed by a muslin covering and, finally, the finish covering.

The operation is a bit more intricate if a Marshall unit is employed. After tacking burlap to the frame, lay a knitted hair or cotton top over the burlap, making sure that it overlaps about 2 inches on each side. This top protects the springs of the Marshall unit and also adds softness to the furniture.

Stitch the top to the burlap. Ordinarily, this is done with No. 252 stitching twine and a 3-inch curved needle (Fig. 9).

Now, spray the topping with Scotch Brand Grip Spray Adhesive No. 44 (for foam and fabric). Cut a layer of 1-inch polyester to size and spray that, too. Lay the polyester on top of the hair or cotton top (Fig. 10). The polyester acts as a further covering and contributes to the padding of the furniture.

It is now time to install the finish covering, which in the installation seen here consists of two pieces: a main covering and an apron. The method you will use in installing your finish covering will be the same or similar.

Tack the main covering to the frame with No. 3 tacks. Since an apron will be used, the main covering can be tacked directly to the frame without the need for blind tacking. Blind tacking is explained below.

In attaching the covering, make certain that the fabric is

Figure 9. Place a knitted hair cover over burlap to protect Marshall spring unit.

Figure 10. Install the finish cover. Note the polyester pad.

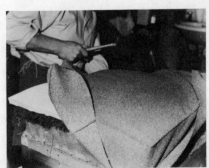

Figure 11. To tack the apron to the frame, place tacking tape on the apron to receive nails.

Figure 12. When the job is completed, the upholstery should be lying straight and smooth.

straight and taut. If any "hitches" develop, they will mar the finished appearance. Take your time and be critical. Before tacking the covering to the frame, stuff cotton or hair around the entire perimeter to provide firmness.

Before installing the apron, draw a straight guideline around the main covering with chalk, using the bottom of the frame as a reference point for the ruler. The purpose of the guideline is to assure that the apron will be straight.

Blind tack the apron to the frame with No. 3 tacks. Blind tacking keeps tacks from showing. To do this, flip the apron up and lay down a length of tacking tape. Tack through the tape (Fig. 11).

The last step in upholstering a piece of furniture is to join the two ends of the apron together with needle and thread (Fig. 12).

WINDOW GLASS

All broken glass must be removed. Wear a pair of work gloves to keep from cutting yourself (Fig. 1). Work glass out of the putty by moving it back and forth.

Figure 1. To protect your hands from cuts, wear gloves as you remove broken glass from sash.

Figure 2. Make certain that the channel is clear of particles.

Figure 3. Measurements must be exact so that glass will fit.

Old putty must be removed. Do this by scraping it out of the channel with a putty knife, but take care not to dig into the wood. At the same time, remove old glazier's points. These small metal triangles, which keep glass wedged in place, can be discarded. New ones should be used to secure the new pane.

The channel should be cleaned thoroughly. Use an old paint brush to brush away dust and dirt (Fig. 2). Dampen a cloth with turpentine or mineral spirits and wipe the channel down to dissolve foreign particles.

With the channel clean and ready to receive new glass, measure the window opening precisely (Fig. 3). When buying a new piece of glass, bear in mind that it should be $1/16$ inch shorter all around than the measurement to allow for shrinkage of the sash as weather changes.

Place the glass into the channel and secure it on each side with glazier's points. These can be purchased in a hardware store and are usually accompanied by a driving tool which is used to drive points into the sash. Place the tool on the point and tap it down with a hammer until it is secure. If you don't have this tool, use your putty knife to drive points home, but do it carefully so as not to crack the glass (Fig. 4).

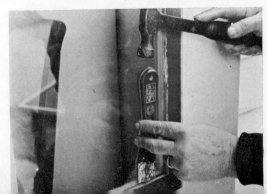

Figure 4. Tap glazier's points into position with gentle taps.

Figure 5. To assure a tight installation, apply putty firmly.

If the pane of glass is 12 to 16 inches, use two points per side. For larger panes, drive in a point every 8 inches. Be sure that the glass is secured by points on all four sides.

After setting points, apply a coat of paint or linseed oil to the sash channel. This protects the wood against moisture and prevents putty from drying out prematurely.

Apply putty or glazing compound into the channel a little at a time, press it firmly into place, and shape it with the putty knife so it forms a slight slope from the glass to the end of the wood (Fig. 5).

If you wish to paint putty, first allow it to set for several days. Then, apply a primer followed by a finish coat. If you paint too soon, the putty may bleed, causing paint discoloration.

WINDOW SCREENS

The most common damage to window screens is the development of small holes. These can be closed with a drop of airplane glue, household cement, or nail polish (Fig. 1). If strands of wire have been pushed out of line, which will allow insects to get through the screen, use a nail or awl to straighten out the strands (Fig. 2).

Figure 1. Small holes in screens can often be closed with a drop of nail polish or household cement.

Figure 2. Use a nail or an awl to straighten misaligned strands to keep insects from getting through the screen.

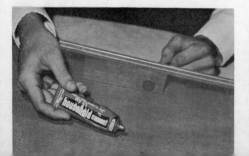

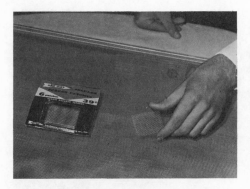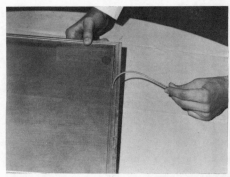

Figure 3. Large holes in screens can be repaired with screen patches.

Figure 4. To replace screening in aluminum frames, first remove the splines.

The best way to repair large holes is with a screen patch that you can buy in a hardware store. Press the patch over the hole. Edges of the patch have hooked wires that are bent over the strands of the screen to keep the patch in place (Fig. 3).

If screening that is in a wood frame is badly ripped and cannot be patched, carefully pry off the moulding strips that hold it in the frame with a putty knife. Now, remove the tack or staples which hold the screening in place and remove the torn screen.

Examine the joints of the frame to be sure that they are tight. Loose joints may be tightened by tapping them together with a mallet. Now, reinforce corners with corrugated metal fasteners or angle brace. Paint the frame, if it needs it. Wood frames must be kept well painted to protect them from weather.

Attach new screening with a staple gun. Try to buy the screening to the exact width and length required. If this is not possible, cut the screen to the desired dimensions with tin snips, but leave just enough overlap so that the screen can be fastened to the frame with ease.

Position the edges of the screen in the grooves around the frame and fasten the screen to the frame by inserting a staple every 2 inches. Trim off excess screening and reattach the molding strips.

To replace badly damaged screening in aluminum frames, pry up and pull out the stringlike material, which is called the spline. This holds the screening in grooves around the frame.

Use a screwdriver to pick up the spline at one corner. Now, carefully pull it out of the groove by hand (Fig. 4).

Center the new screening in the frame and press the spline back into place with a screwdriver or other blunt-edged tool

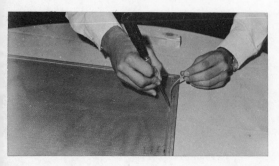

Figure 5. After screening has been re-placed, press splines back into grooves.

(Fig. 5). Pull the screen taut. The last step is to trim off excess screening that may protrude from around the spline.

WINDOWS

Problems with windows, such as sticking, slipping, and binding, can usually be corrected by making minor adjustments. The trouble lies most often with the opening-closing mechanism. The mechanism that the windows in your home employ depends on the type of window.

There are seven types of windows now in use: double-hung, horizontal-sliding, casement, awning, jalousie, top-hinged, and bottom-hinged (Fig. 1). However, there are only two kinds of opening-closing mechanisms.

Modern double-hung and horizontal-sliding windows employ a channel mechanism; that is, the ease of opening and closing the window depends upon the ability of the aluminum channels on each side to exert the right amount of pressure on the sash. Channel mechanisms can be adjusted to increase or decrease this pressure.

Casement, awning, and jalousie windows employ rotor gear mechanisms that are cranked by hand to open and close the window.

Top-hinged and bottom-hinged windows have no opening-closing mechanism. They are simply hinged at the top or the bottom and are opened and closed by hand. These windows are used primarily in basements.

Modern *double-hung* windows are of two types: those that can be removed from the frame and those that can't be. *Horizontal-sliding* windows are simply double-hung windows that are turned sideways. They have aluminum channels, can usually be removed from the frame, and are treated in the same manner as double-hung windows.

When a modern double-hung or horizontal-sliding window

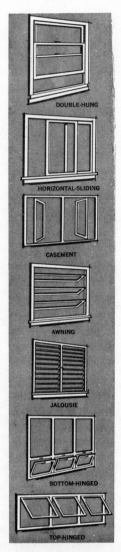

Figure 1. These sketches portray the seven different types of windows.

Figure 2. Get rid of dirt in channels that may be causing the window to bind.

Figure 3. Maintain good window operation by lubricating channels periodically.

becomes difficult to slide in its channel, lack of lubrication and a buildup of dirt in the channels are the most common problems. The first thing to do, therefore, is to clean dirt from channels with an old paint brush and apply a light coating of paste wax, paraffin, or all-purpose silicone spray lubricant (Figs. 2 and 3). Be sure to clean and lubricate both tracks. Slide the window up and down in the channels a couple of times after lubricating to spread lubricant.

Figure 4. To remove corrosion from aluminum channels, clean them with No. 00 steel wool.

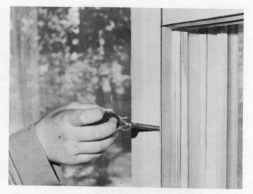

Figure 5. Some double-hung windows are adjusted by crimping the flexible aluminum lips.

In areas where salt water is present, as in homes along the ocean, oxidation may become a problem even if aluminum channels are anodized. As soon as you notice traces of oxidation (whitish pit marks) in the tracks, clean them with No. 00 steel wool (Fig. 4).

If cleaning and lubrication fail to make the window operate without trouble, channels probably need to be adjusted. Windows that can be removed from the frame have adjustment screws. Windows that cannot be removed from the frame do not have adjustment screws, but can still be adjusted.

In the case of windows with adjustment screws, turning the screws clockwise releases pressure on the window, while turning screws counterclockwise increases pressure. Screws will be found in one channel only. The channel opposite the one that has screws contains a spring mechanism. It does not have to be adjusted.

When making an adjustment, keep in mind that the top and bottom screws of double-hung window channels and the far left and far right screws of horizontal-sliding window channels are turned in more than the center screw to produce a slight bow in the channel, which is necessary to hold the window firmly in position.

Turn screws a little at a time and test the movement of the window. You will know that a window is properly adjusted by the ease with which it slides and, in the case of double-hung windows, if it maintains its position without creeping. Horizontal-sliding windows can be tested by exerting upward pressure on the unit. A properly adjusted window will have no play (looseness).

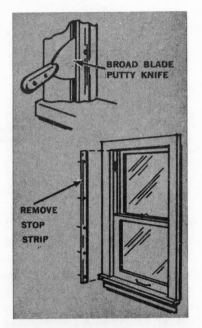

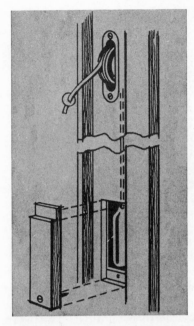

Figure 6. To repair an old-fashion double-hung window, pry off the stop strip.

Figure 7. Remove the pocket cover, pull the sash weight from place, and untie the broken cord.

In the case of nonremovable double-hung windows that don't operate properly and have no adjustment screws, adjustment is made by simply crimping the flexible aluminum lip along the length of the channel with a screwdriver (Fig. 5). Bend the lip a little at a time along the entire length and test.

Older double-hung windows are controlled by sash weights and cords. The one big problem that can exist with these windows is that a sash cord may break. To repair one, pry off the stop strip with a broad-bladed putty knife (Fig. 6). This allows you to remove the window from the channel. Pull the broken piece of sash cord from the channel and disconnect it from the window.

At the bottom of the window channel you will find a pocket cover which is either nailed or screwed into place. Remove it. You can now reach in and pull the sash weight and the remainder of the broken cord from place (Fig. 7).

New sash cord (or chain) can be purchased in a hardware store. To install it, first tie a nail to a length of strong, thin string. Insert the string, nail end first, over the sash pulley and drop it down the channel. Feed it out until it drops to the open pocket. Tie the new sash cord to the end of the string and pull

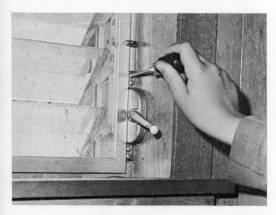

Figure 8. Damaged gear boxes should be removed and replaced. They cannot be repaired.

the sash cord into position by pulling the string out of the pocket.

Tie one end of the sash cord to the sash weight. Put the weight back into place. Tie the other end of the sash cord to the window and put the window back into place.

Raise and lower the window to assure that the new cord is the correct length. The sash weight should not hit the pulley when the window is closed, and it should not rest on the bottom of the pocket when the window is raised.

Remove the window from the frame once again, make necessary adjustments to the sash cord, replace the pocket cover, and reinstall the window.

The major cause of damage to a rotor-geared window is misuse of the gear box. When a window is locked shut, someone may accidentally turn the crank without unlocking the window. The force can break a gear tooth. Also, many people have a habit of cranking the window beyond the closing point. This puts undue strain on the gear mechanism.

To replace a damaged gear box, remove all screws holding the box to the window (Fig. 8). Some boxes are also held to the frame by a retaining screw. Remove this, too.

Now, go outside and unscrew the activating arm of the gear box from the lever that is attached to the window. You will notice that the screw which joins the arm and lever may be fitted with a small cotter clamp. Be sure that you don't lose this.

Casement windows are somewhat different. The activating arm fits directly into a slide mechanism. Thus, once a gear box is unscrewed from the window, it is simply pulled from place.

To replace the damaged box, just slip the new one into place and reattach it. The gear box and activating arm are sold as a unit. You can buy it in a hardware store or where windows are sold.

CHARACTERISTICS OF WOOD

	Easy to work	Resists shrinking, warping, swelling	Un-usually strong	resists decay
SOFTWOODS:				
Cedar	X	X		X
Cypress	X	X		X
Douglas fir	X		X	
Redwood	X	X		X
Spruce	X	X		
Western larch			X	
White pine	X	X	X	
Yellow pine	X		X	
HARDWOODS:				
Ash			X	X
Basswood	X			
Birch			X	
Cherry		X	X	
Gumwood	X			
Mahogany		X	X	X
Maple		X	X	X
Oak		X	X	X
Poplar	X			
Walnut		X		X

NAIL SIZES

Penny number	Length in Inches	Number per pound — Common	Box	Finishing
2	1	876	1010	1351
3	1-1/4	568	635	807
4	1-1/2	316	437	548
5	1-3/4	271	406	500
6	2	181	236	309
8	2-1/2	106	145	189
10	3	69	94	121
12	3-1/4	64	87	113
16	3-1/2	49	71	90
20	4	31	52	62
30	4-1/2	20		

GRADES OF SANDPAPER

Grit designation	Alternate designation	General designation
600	—	
500	—	SUPER-FINE
400	10/0	
360	—	
320	9/0	
280	8/0	VERY FINE
240	7/0	
220	6/0	
180	5/0	FINE
150	4/0	
120	3/0	
100	2/0	MEDIUM
80	1/0	
60	1/2	
50	1	COARSE
40	1-1/2	
36	2	VERY COARSE
30	2-1/2	
24	3	

Sandpaper can be ordered by either the grit designation or the alternate designation. If you order by the general designation, you would generally receive 6/0 for "very fine," 4/0 for "fine," 2/0 for "medium," and 1/2 for "coarse."

WOOD SCREW SIZES

Number*	Actual length	Gauge (shank size) Number
2	1/4 inch	0, 1, 2, 3
3	3/8 inch	2, 3, 4, 5, 6, 7
4	1/2 inch	2, 3, 4, 5, 6, 7, 8
5	5/8 inch	3, 4, 5, 6, 7, 8, 9, 10
6	3/4 inch	4, 5, 6, 7, 8, 9, 10, 11
7	7/8 inch	6, 7, 8, 9, 10, 11, 12
8	1 inch	6, 7, 8, 9, 10, 11, 12, 14
9	1-1/4 inch	7, 8, 9, 10, 11, 12, 14, 16
10	1-1/2 inch	6, 7, 8, 9, 10, 11, 12, 14, 16, 18
11	1-3/4 inch	8, 9, 10, 11, 12, 14, 16, 18, 20
12	2 inch	8, 9, 10, 11, 12, 14, 16, 18, 20
14	2-1/4 inch	9, 10, 11, 12, 14, 16, 18, 20
16	2-1/2 inch	12, 14, 16, 18, 20

*The numbering system of screws is an arbitrary system and doesn't represent real measurement. Refer to "actual length".